# BUMPY ROAD

# BUMPY ROAD

### The Making, Flop, and Revival of
## *Two-Lane Blacktop*
### SYLVIA TOWNSEND

University Press of Mississippi / Jackson

The University Press of Mississippi is the scholarly publishing agency of
the Mississippi Institutions of Higher Learning: Alcorn State University,
Delta State University, Jackson State University, Mississippi State University,
Mississippi University for Women, Mississippi Valley State University,
University of Mississippi, and University of Southern Mississippi.

www.upress.state.ms.us

The University Press of Mississippi is a member of
the Association of University Presses.

Copyright © 2019 by University Press of Mississippi
All rights reserved

First printing 2019
∞

Library of Congress Cataloging-in-Publication Data

Names: Townsend, Sylvia, author.
Title: Bumpy road : the making, flop, and revival of Two-lane blacktop / Sylvia Townsend.
Description: Jackson : University Press of Mississippi, [2019] | Includes bibliographical references and index. |
Identifiers: LCCN 2018029672 (print) | LCCN 2018034556 (ebook) | ISBN 9781496820860 (epub single) | ISBN 9781496820877 (epub institutional) | ISBN 9781496820884 (pdf single) | ISBN 9781496820891 (pdf institutional) | ISBN 9781496804143 (cloth) | ISBN 9781496820952 (pbk.).
Subjects: LCSH: Two-lane blacktop (Motion picture) | Motion pictures, American—History and criticism. | Cult films—History and criticism.
Classification: LCC PN1997.T652 (ebook) | LCC PN1997.T652 T69 2019 (print) | DDC 791.43/72—dc23
LC record available at https://lccn.loc.gov/2018029672

British Library Cataloging-in-Publication Data available

*For Geoffrey Martin and Tiger*

# Contents

Acknowledgments . . . . . . . . . . . . . . . . . . . . . . . . . . . . . . . . . . . . . ix

1 Starting Line . . . . . . . . . . . . . . . . . . . . . . . . . . . . . . . . . . . . . . 3
2 Stalled . . . . . . . . . . . . . . . . . . . . . . . . . . . . . . . . . . . . . . . . . 28
3 A Jump Start . . . . . . . . . . . . . . . . . . . . . . . . . . . . . . . . . . . . . 44
4 On the Road . . . . . . . . . . . . . . . . . . . . . . . . . . . . . . . . . . . . . 62
5 The Fast Lane: Sex, Drugs, and Rock 'n' Roll Stars . . . . . . . . . . . . . . 84
6 Potholes . . . . . . . . . . . . . . . . . . . . . . . . . . . . . . . . . . . . . . . . 96
7 The Wreck . . . . . . . . . . . . . . . . . . . . . . . . . . . . . . . . . . . . . . 105
8 A Restoration . . . . . . . . . . . . . . . . . . . . . . . . . . . . . . . . . . . . 122
9 Picking up Speed . . . . . . . . . . . . . . . . . . . . . . . . . . . . . . . . . . 142
10 The Finish Line: The Film Catches Fire . . . . . . . . . . . . . . . . . . . . . 157

Appendix: *Two-Lane Blacktop* Location Personnel List . . . . . . . . . . . . 171
Notes . . . . . . . . . . . . . . . . . . . . . . . . . . . . . . . . . . . . . . . . . . 173
Index . . . . . . . . . . . . . . . . . . . . . . . . . . . . . . . . . . . . . . . . . . 185

# Acknowledgments

Thanks to Gary Kurtz for giving me hours of his time, letting me use his photos, and gathering up heaps of paper nobody else cared about and giving them to USC, in case somebody like me came along one day. Thanks to Bonnie Prendergast Freeman for answering innumerable questions and letting me use her photos. And I'm grateful to Monte Hellman for talking to me and letting me use his lovely photo.

People who graciously let me pester them with seemingly endless questions include Beverly Walker, Michael Laughlin, Dennis Bartok, and Jay Douglas. Others who were particularly helpful include Danny Selznick, Jim Thornsberry, Buck Wheatley, Mark Steiner, John Bailey, Jim Rosenthal, Rebecca Soriano, Rudy Wurlitzer, and Walter Coblenz. Thanks also to Ned Comstock at the USC Cinema Arts Library for his considerable help and enthusiasm. Many thanks to Billy Kincheloe for digging up Will Corry's script. And, just for being cool, acknowledgments to Martin Landau, Kelly Reichardt, Will Oldham, Billy James, Floyd Mutrux, Bill Lustig, Craig Pinkard, Jim Aust, William Tyler, Harry Dean Stanton, and Reg Bisgrove.

Some quotes, identified as such, are from AFI's Harold Lloyd Master Seminar © 1971 courtesy of American Film Institute.

For reading the manuscript and correcting factual mistakes, thanks to Vincent LoBrutto and Oliver Wood. I undoubtedly put some mistakes back in after they had taken them out.

At the University Press of Mississippi, thanks to Leila Salisbury and Craig Gill. Peter Tonguette, a gifted film scholar and author in his own right, improved my manuscript with his copyediting.

Thanks to my excellent agent, Eric Myers. I am lucky to have him.

Thanks to James Taylor and Richard Linklater who, while being really famous, were nevertheless gracious and helpful and not condescending.

# BUMPY ROAD

# 1

# Starting Line

In early 1969, Michael Laughlin, a clever, debonair, thirty-two-year-old film producer and socialite, moved to Los Angeles with his wife, the glamorous Frenchwoman Leslie Caron. Laughlin, an American, and Caron, a ballerina-turned-movie-star known for *An American in Paris* (1951) and *Gigi* (1958), had been living in London. Laughlin, whose wanderlust eventually would lead to the end of the marriage, nevertheless would have been content to continue to live in London and produce films, but Caron's career had stalled. Although the thirty-eight-year-old Caron had appeared in some television series and small European films, she thought she would give Hollywood one last shot. Once they settled in Hollywood, Laughlin thought her fame and beauty would open doors into the world of promising young filmmakers he wanted to work with, but she says she felt that she was looked down upon as traditional because she hadn't appeared in any groundbreaking movies in these youth-oriented years: "The new people he would discover were not established any more than he was, and so I think they had confidence in somebody who was young and new and had ideas. And in regards to me, I think I had worked with some great people, but I think they tended to think I was of the old school rather than the new school." The couple courted old Hollywood and simultaneously sought out avant-garde filmmakers. Laughlin was independently wealthy, so he could pursue cutting-edge projects without having to worry about whether they would make much money.

Forward-thinking in the art of filmmaking, Laughlin nevertheless dressed like a traditional English gentleman, with oddball touches. Although he customarily dressed in a suit, he wore them for elegance, not conformity. In a Savile Row suit and tennis shoes, he was the antithesis of a "suit" in the sense of a square, white-collar businessman. In London, Laughlin had produced *Joanna* (1968), directed by Michael Sarne, about the mod scene in that city, and *The Whisperers* (1967), directed by Bryan Forbes; both films had received mixed reviews. In Hollywood, Laughlin and Caron rented a splendid house once owned by Orson Welles and Rita Hayworth in the flats of Beverly Hills, then later bought a mansion in Bel Air. In their elegant homes, they threw grand parties for famous people who included marquee young writers and directors such as Mike Nichols, Joan Didion, and John Gregory Dunne; an Old Hollywood crowd that included Gregory Peck and George Cukor; and elite, expatriate authors and filmmakers such as Christopher Isherwood and Jean Renoir.

Laughlin bought a couple of scripts by two men who'd never before written a screenplay. This was not particularly rash in those days because studios were scrambling to find fresh, innovative material to capture the imagination of younger audiences uninterested in the creaky, traditional movies that still made up most of Hollywood's fare. Laughlin bought one script by then-newcomer Floyd Mutrux called *The Christian Licorice Store*, about a tennis pro who gets caught up in life in the fast lane in Hollywood. He bought another by Will Corry, who had written and acted in some episodes of television shows. Titled *Two-Lane Blacktop*, the 136-page script was about a cross-country car race. Laughlin recalls that the son of the prolific, well-known producer of *Mildred Pierce* (1945), *Dark Passage* (1947), and *Key Largo* (1948) brought him the latter. "Robbie Wald, who was the son of Jerry Wald, the great producer at Fox, brought the script to me, and when I read it I knew then it was a masterpiece," Laughlin says, although it was later rewritten. Laughlin pitched the two projects to Cinema Center Films, an offshoot that the CBS television network had set up on its lot in Studio City not long before to branch into theatrical films.

Mack Sennett had established the first studio on this property in the San Fernando Valley in 1928 to make Keystone Kops films and other comedies. The surrounding area became known as Studio City. After filing for bankruptcy, Mack Sennett Studios left the lot, and Republic Pictures took over in 1935. In 1963, the television network took it over to produce shows, and named it CBS Studio Center.

Aiming to release a diverse slate of movies, Cinema Center Films was making Howard Hawks's Western *Rio Lobo* (1970), the racing picture *Le Mans* (1971), with Steve McQueen, and the Western/comedy/drama *Little Big Man* (1970), directed by Arthur Penn and starring Dustin Hoffman. Laughlin gave the two scripts to the production executive Jere Henshaw, who, he recalls, "gave them to their literary guy there, and their literary guy read both of them and called me up and liked both scripts enormously." The studio entered into a deal with Laughlin to make *The Christian Licorice Store*. For the director, studio executives wanted James Frawley, who had helmed episodes of several popular television shows, including *The Monkees*. Michael Laughlin Enterprises set up shop in a second-floor suite of offices at the studio.

Will Corry, who authored the original *Two-Lane Blacktop* screenplay, had written and acted in several episodes of the television series *Gunsmoke*, *Have Gun—Will Travel*, and *Kraft Suspense Theatre*. Laughlin remembers Corry as thin, small-boned, blond, of average height, and good-looking. "Poetic. Not long-haired. His own man. James Dean." Corry's script was about two hot-rodders in a 1955 Chevy, a white guy called the Driver and a black guy called Augustus, who challenge some rich kids in a brand-new GTO to a west-to-east, interstate race for pink slips, but never finish the race. Although the second screenwriter and the film's director later would dismiss Corry's script as unreadable, it is a lively, imaginative, well-written screenplay with humor and suspense. In one scene, a rapist has the heroine pinned down in a car and is about to attack her when a bounty hunter, who also is after her, shows up. As they fight over her, they conk each other over the head, allowing her to escape. Laughlin conjectures, "If that script had been made it would have been a masterpiece, too." He liked it so much, he says, that he paid the writer "real money." According to Laughlin, "I paid him $10,000 against $100,000, which was a lot of money in those days." (This means he gave Corry $10,000 up front and would pay him $90,000 when principal photography was completed or at some later date.)

To direct, Laughlin first considered William Friedkin, who had yet to become famous, but the producer wasn't convinced his visual style would be sufficiently fluid. (Laughlin emphasizes that of course this was *before* the 1971 release of *The French Connection*, so how was he to know?) For the director, he also considered Floyd Mutrux, whose vision of the script he admired. But Mutrux was involved in the story of some young drug addicts, who became the subjects of another film he wrote and directed, and Laughlin produced *Dusty and Sweets McGee* (1971).

Eventually, Laughlin approached Monte Hellman, then forty, whose Westerns *The Shooting* and *Ride in the Whirlwind*, both released in 1966, had been well-received in France but had not been shown in the United States. Hellman, who by then had attracted a small cult following, was born in New York and moved to Los Angeles when he was six. A graduate of Stanford University, where he studied speech and drama, Hellman did some graduate work in cinema at UCLA, then directed plays. He started his directing career in summer theater in northern California, where his girlfriend was the comedian

Carol Burnett. He also was an apprentice editor for films and television shows before he started a theater in Los Angeles in the late 1950s.

Around the time that Hellman was starting his theater in Los Angeles, Martin Landau was studying Method acting under the famed Lee Strasberg at the Actors Studio in New York. Strasberg was so impressed with the young actor's quick analyses of student performances and his astute advice on how to improve them that he suggested that Landau, then in his twenties, become a teacher. Landau started teaching in New York, and when he ended up in Los Angeles, for what he planned to be a temporary stay, he met Monte Hellman. Hellman was attracting talented actors to his theater to appear in plays he was directing, such as Eugene O'Neill's *The Great God Brown* and Samuel Beckett's *Waiting for Godot*. Landau recalls, "Monte asked me to talk to his actors at his theater, which I did. I talked about Delsarte. I talked about everybody, Stanislavksy, I talked about the Group Theatre, I talked about differences between Eleanora Duse and Sarah Bernhardt. I talked about methodology—all kinds of stuff. So much that Monte said, 'Hey, if you stay in California, will you teach a class to my people?' I said, 'Sure.'

"A year later, I was still here because people were hiring me like crazy, one job after another after another. *North by Northwest*, *Pork Chop Hill* with Gregory Peck, episodic television—*Maverick* and *Rawhide*—and God knows what." So Landau kept his promise and started teaching at Hellman's theater. Called, at various times in the late 1950s, the Dahl Theater and the Playgoers Company, it later became a revival movie house, the New Beverly Cinema, eventually run by Quentin Tarantino. Landau says, "I was a product of Strasberg's as well as others. So I brought New York Method to California in a way that had never been heard of or seen before." Word got out and his classes started to draw new students, including Jack Nicholson and the writer/director Robert Towne.

At the Hollywood Ranch Market on Vine Street, Landau met Jaclyn Ravell, who struck him as a sweet and attractive young woman. She told him she was an actress. Landau recalls, "I said, 'Well, that's great.' I said, 'You're very pretty, but I'm married,' which I was, so I said, 'I'm going to teach an acting class. Why don't you come to it?'" So Ravell started attending Landau's classes. There she met her future husband Hellman, who sat in on them. "He wasn't an actor. But he was directing these actors," Landau explained, and wanted to be a better director. "And a better writer. Better everything. Better filmmaker." In classes that Jaclyn attended, Landau spoke about sense memory and taught his students exercises to tap into it. She later imposed her own version of this technique on the novice actors in *Two-Lane Blacktop*, who unlike Landau's receptive pupils, rebelled.

Landau and Hellman became lifelong friends. The happiest time of Hellman's life, Landau says, was when he was attending UCLA and rooming with a friend, Frank Wolff. A free-spirited, larger-than-life actor, Wolff appeared in the soft-core art film *The Lickerish Quartet* (1970). Hellman gave Wolff a part as the bad guy in *Beast from Haunted Cave* (1959), but the actor's career didn't begin to flourish until he moved to Italy, where he appeared in *Once Upon a Time in the West* (1969) among other films. He committed suicide in Rome at age forty-three. Landau later wrote a script about Hellman and the actor, and Harvey Weinstein at Miramax was interested in making it into a feature. Landau asked Johnny Depp and John Cusack to play the lead roles, and they agreed, but Weinstein nixed them because they were not yet sufficiently famous. Landau suggested that Weinstein make the picture and put it on a shelf for two or three years, because by then, he predicted, the two actors would be stars. Weinstein didn't buy the idea and suggested two actors who were not acceptable to Landau, so the project died.

∞

When Monte Hellman's theater was disbanded, one of its investors, the quickie-movie impresario Roger Corman, hired him to direct (in twelve days) *Beast from Haunted Cave* and later to replace Francis Ford Coppola on *The Terror* (1963). Corman was known for hiring young, unproven, highly talented filmmakers to make low-budget movies for him.

Next, Hellman went to the Philippines to direct two pictures on the cheap with Jack Nicholson for Twentieth Century Fox, *Back Door to Hell* and *Flight to Fury*, both released in 1964. Gary Kurtz, the associate producer of *Two-Lane Blacktop*, worked with Hellman on his next films, *The Shooting* and *Ride in the Whirlwind*, again for Roger Corman. Kurtz recalls working "back-breaking" twelve- and fifteen-hour days for the producer of fast and cheap movies in the mid-1960s.

After *The Shooting* and *Ride in the Whirlwind* were released to acclaim in France, Hellman came to the attention of Laughlin, who was always interested in filmmakers who showed promise and attracted notice. His own brain brimming with fresh, unexpected and sometimes brilliant ideas, Laughlin, like Roger Corman, had an eye for nascent talent. Leslie Caron describes Laughlin, now her ex-husband, as "wonderfully innovative." She remembers that he came up with the idea of making a music video, and asked Randy Newman to write a song for one, in the 1970s, years before they became popular on MTV. After he read an article by then-recent Columbia graduate Bill Condon, Laughlin tracked down the young man, put him on salary, and gave him his start in the movie business. Condon's first screenplay was *Strange Behavior*, which Laughlin directed in 1981. Condon went on to direct *Dreamgirls* (2008), *Beauty and the Beast* (2017), and other high-profile movies, and he received an Oscar for writing *Gods and Monsters* (1998).

In 1969, Caron and Mutrux recall, the producer wanted Steven Spielberg to helm *The Christian Licorice Store* (1971) at a time when he was still working in series television and before he had directed the TV movie *Duel* or any feature films. In those days, Spielberg "was the most adorable person," Laughlin says. "He was very, very, very imaginative and fun. He came to dinner at the house a few times; he was always dating older women." Caron also thought Spielberg was extremely talented, but Cinema Center Films executives preferred James Frawley, who had directed twenty-eight episodes of *The Monkees* television show, as the director of *The Christian Licorice Store*. "I couldn't talk them into Steven. But I tried with Gordon Stulberg, the head of the studio, a lawyer kind of guy, a business guy," Laughlin recalls, "and I just couldn't quite pull it off."

"Michael was really very inventive and ahead of everybody else in Hollywood about music and in many ways, about filming," Caron recalls. Unfortunately, Laughlin often lacked follow-through. He would convince a potential collaborator that a book would make an excellent film, without having first secured the rights to the property. The "collaborator" would then nail down the rights for himself, leaving Laughlin out in the cold. Or, Laughlin would delegate the execution of an idea to someone who would then appropriate it. Caron says she witnessed this again and again. "He has a sort of lackadaisical manner, and would talk about his ideas to somebody who would say, 'Fine, thank you very much, goodbye.'" But despite her frustration at his lack of sense of urgency and caution, she praises his ability to predict trends and spot budding talent: "I do think the very best of Michael's power of seeing in advance what was going to be fashionable."

Although Laughlin and Hellman are both intelligent, well-read, and creative, their personalities differ radically. However, their relationship was amicable, and the sociable, urbane, party-giving producer asked the bookish, cerebral, hippie director of Roger Corman movies to helm Will Corry's script. For his part, Laughlin says he hired Hellman because the director was innovative—not because the two men shared similar tastes or sensibilities. A subscriber to the auteur theory, Laughlin would give Hellman free reign to make the movie his way, whether the producer liked it or not. "For Monte to bring his personality and his efforts to it, he needed to nudge it in a way that made sense to him, someone who had directed *Waiting for Godot*, and on what he believed to be his picture of the world. And now a lot of his picture of the world to me, arriving from London and married to Leslie, and hanging out with a different group of people who were talking about different things, I mean to me it was complete bullshit."

Hellman's two Westerns had been admired in France, which impressed Laughlin. Also, Hellman had been highly respected at the theater in Los Angeles, where he not only directed plays, he ran the operation. Landau comments, "He was a director. You're either a director, or you're not a director. You can either direct and stage plays and help actors, or not. Monte is a good director and an unusual thinker. You have to be if you're a good director. Otherwise, everything looks the same. The fact that *Two-Lane Blacktop* is a good movie, is a great movie, is because he's a good director." Although Laughlin didn't much like Hellman's movies, the director had a small following, and the producer figured he had promise. Laughlin had seen Hellman's two Westerns, and considered them sluggishly paced. "I just assumed that the script of *Two-Lane Blacktop* would override that," Laughlin says, "but it didn't."

Although the concept of a cross-country race appealed to Hellman, Corry's script did not. Hellman wanted the script rewritten and Laughlin agreed. Laughlin suggested Floyd Mutrux, a larger-than-life dynamo of a writer/director who was working at the producer's offices at CBS Studio Center on *Dusty and Sweets McGee*. "Floyd was very knowledgeable about cars and street racing," Laughlin notes, so he arranged for the two men to meet. Since Mutrux knew a lot about hot rods, Laughlin figured, he would be a good choice to rewrite a script about drag racers. Like Laughlin, Mutrux admired Corry's script. Corry, Mutrux says, "wrote it asshole to the rubber. He wrote it hard." The final screenwriter, "Rudy [Wurlitzer] wrote a really good script. So did Will Corry," Mutrux opines. "Nobody gives Will Corry credit," he adds, because Hellman and Rudy Wurlitzer both have mistakenly said many times in published interviews that they discarded nearly all of the original script and started basically from scratch. But the framework and some of the most celebrated features of the film originated in Corry's script, including the title, the premise of street-racer protagonists pitted against rich guy(s), the west-east route, the generic names for characters, their failure to finish the race, the '55 Chevy (which was the quintessential hot rod at the time), and pitting the Chevy against a GTO, the first "factory hot rod."

Laughlin asked Mutrux to come up with some suggestions before the producer set up a meeting with Hellman at his stately home in Beverly Hills, which had an added attraction: Leslie Caron lived there. Billy Kincheloe, who helped Wurlitzer with street-racing terminology and scenarios for *Two-Lane Blacktop*, remembers the impact, and the prestige conferred on Laughlin, of going to the house occasionally to see the producer and running into his movie-star wife: "She'd be home every now and then, and you'd go over to the house and go, 'My God! It's Leslie Caron.' And Leslie was just Leslie. She was just Michael's wife. And you're going, 'Holy Shit! It's Leslie Caron!' And what boy in the late sixties didn't have a crush on Leslie Caron?"

While Hellman and Laughlin got along despite their vast difference in style and disposition, the ebullient Mutrux, a car guy who moved at a whirlwind pace, and Hellman, the former theater director with a more low-key temperament, did not. After Mutrux came up with some ideas and rewrote a little of the script, he and Hellman met at Laughlin's house to discuss the project. "Monte and I did not click," Mutrux recalls. Not only did he find Hellman "difficult," Mutrux says, "He did not understand anything about cars." Laughlin agrees: "Floyd knew much more about cars," he notes, "and they didn't like each other." Although Mutrux is listed as an uncredited writer for the film on the Internet Movie Database and on the Turner Classic Movies website, the reason he didn't receive a credit is that his suggested revisions didn't make it into the final script.

Hellman suggested they hire Rudy Wurlitzer, who had written an avant-garde novel called *Nog* that the director admired. Wurlitzer, according to Mutrux, "was kind of a hip guy on the street in New York, you know, Max's Kansas City." Hellman went to New York to meet the writer, a descendant of the Rudolph Wurlitzer who manufactured organs, pianos, and jukeboxes. Wurlitzer recalls that he had just finished writing another novel, "and I really needed to get some work to pay for it all." He also liked Monte Hellman. "We got along, and it was very effortless, the whole process, it was outside of the studio realm. There was nobody else in the room but Monte and me, and he was very open and he was sort of coming to films from the Roger Corman school, so it was very much a kind of independent, low-road venture and I felt very relaxed with him and with the whole projection of what the film was."

Wurlitzer says he didn't like Corry's script any more than Hellman did. "I never really read the original script. I did read a few pages but it was nothing I could relate to, and Monte couldn't either, so I was given a lot of—total—freedom," Wurlitzer says. But, as noted previously, much of Corry's script survives in the final version and in the movie, and Corry receives sole story credit and shares the screenplay credit with Wurlitzer. Filmmakers submit their proposed screenplay credits to the Writers Guild of America for approval, and, Laughlin notes, "The Writers Guild protected Will, as they should have." Wurlitzer kept Corry's two main characters, a driver and a mechanic, and their car, a hot rod with a big-block engine. Corry's and Wurlitzer's scripts use identical words to describe it: a "'55 Chevy two-door. It is several shades of primer gray." Both scripts have the premise of two hot-rodders who challenge the well-heeled, well-dressed driver(s) of a new GTO to an interstate race, from west to east, for pink slips. In Corry's script, as in Wurlitzer's, they never finish the race. Both scripts call the driver "the Driver." Instead of calling the three guys in the GTO by their given names or surnames, Corry refers to them in generic terms as "the Freshman," "the Sophomore," and "the Junior." Wurlitzer follows suit by calling his character, who replaced them, "GTO" instead of his first or last name. The rewrite follows the original in having the Driver challenge his opponent(s) at a gas station, and uses similar dialogue in the scene.

Other scenarios in Corry's script that made it into the movie were the Chevy outrunning the cops, the Mechanic stealing a license plate, and the Driver and the Mechanic pulling over near cops who stopped the GTO to try to get their opponent in more hot water. Both scripts specify that a race with a fancy guy is set up, at night, with onlookers, at a root beer stand, in Santa Fe, New Mexico. Corry also describes the Driver acting out a race with his hands, a bit of business that made it into the movie (in a scene where GTO warns the Girl that the Mechanic and the Driver are interested in nothing but cars). In Corry's version and in the final film, they don't finish the race.

Some of the dialogue in the two scripts is extremely similar, particularly in the sequence at the root beer stand, the scene when the cops pull GTO over, and the one when they set up the race. In Corry's script at the root beer stand, Augustus the mechanic tells the Driver, "Call him a motherfucker," prompting the Driver to tell his opponent, "Make it $300 and you've got a race." In Wurlitzer's version, the Driver tells his opponent, "A yard and a half, motherfucker, and you got a deal." In Corry's script, when the Driver approaches the cops who have pulled over the GTO he asks, "Do you need some help, officer?" In Wurlitzer's version of the same scene, the Driver asks the cop, "You need me as a witness or anything?" In Corry's script, the mechanic says, "Stick to the country roads, the two-lane blacktops." In Wurlitzer's script, the Mechanic says, "Stick to the two-lane blacktop roads." Some of the dialogue in the two scripts is identical. For example, in Corry's version of the gas station scene, the Driver explains that the pink slips should be mailed to "General Delivery. First one there waits for his car." In Wurlitzer's version of the gas station scene, the Mechanic explains that the pink slips should be mailed to "General Delivery. First one there waits for his car."

Despite the key similarities, most of the scenarios and dialogue in the finished film are Wurlitzer's. The girl in Corry's script has a crush on the mechanic, drives her own Volkswagen, and follows them, but in Wurlitzer's version, she's a hitchhiker who rides with them. Also, in Corry's screenplay the mechanic is African American and in Wurlitzer's version he is a white guy. Although blacks usually didn't play leading roles in studio movies in these years, Michael Laughlin says this was Wurlitzer's decision, and there was "no studio pressure at all" to make the black guy white. On the contrary, Wurlitzer says he received uncommon leeway to write what he wished.

Not until later, Wurlitzer says, did he realize that his first experience as a Hollywood screenwriter was unique. "I was given total freedom, which was very unusual. There were no meetings with notes, or anything like that." Other writers had told him of being demeaned and undermined by executives bearing down on them with endless, inane notes and having their screenplays mangled, bowdlerized, and Hollywoodized. "It was a very good experience and one that I've always valued because it didn't happen much again. Then I could go back to my shack in Nova Scotia and write one of my weird novels." He recalls that he thought to himself, "'My god, I don't know why everybody's complaining about films. This is so much fun, and I can't wait to do another one.' I soon learned."

While Hellman was in New York meeting with Wurlitzer, he auditioned some actors. A friend recommended the teenaged Laurie Bird, a part-time model from Queens. Bird's mother died when she was very young and the girl didn't get along with her father, who was a strict Roman Catholic, or her older brother, so she had largely raised herself. The cinematographer John Bailey (*Groundhog Day* [1993], *As Good as It Gets* [1997]), who was an assistant cameraman on *Two-Lane*, remembers, "She was a street kid." A young beauty, she took the subway to Manhattan for jobs as a model and a movie extra. The unit publicist Eileen Peterson (*The Godfather: Part II* [1974], *Titanic* [1997]), who was then living in Manhattan, met Bird at this time. Peterson got to know Bird and saw her often, and recalls that the girl did not enjoy modeling. "Once she got into it, she hated it. She took her beauty very casually, so all this emphasis on beauty and makeup—she hated wigs and hated being told whether she was the right weight, or whatever." Bird had no acting experience, but Hellman was intrigued by her and chose her as the prototype for the Girl. She also became *his* girl. "Monte was from Day 1 falling in love with her," says Mutrux, who saw them frequently when he advised Laughlin about automotive matters during pre-production of *Two-Lane* and worked in the offices next door on *Dusty and Sweets McGee*. Besides her gorgeous looks, Bird had a sweetness and magnetism that drew many people to her, although others dismissed the troubled girl as a psychological mess.

According to Hellman, "She was almost the first person I found, and I met her before the script was written." Rudy Wurlitzer describes Bird as sweet and innocent, but also clueless about the process of filmmaking. "I think she was very excited and sort of romantic about what she was doing, but she had no idea what was really involved. And I think that was part of the character. Her being swept up in a journey that she had no idea what it was about. So she embodied her role in a way." Just as the Girl was a hitchhiker, Bird was a drifter. After Bird left home, she stayed with various men, some of them famous, bringing to mind a courtesan such as Pamela Digby Churchill Hayward Harriman, without the privileges. Despite similarities between Bird and the Girl, Wurlitzer says he didn't base the role entirely on her. "I don't think I was thinking initially of Laurie, but of course she was appropriate as the Girl."

Wurlitzer moved into the storied Chateau Marmont on Sunset Boulevard in West Hollywood to work on the script. He had been living in an apartment in a seedy Manhattan neighborhood where burglaries were so rampant that he hid his prized possession, his typewriter, in the kitchen oven. "I didn't have to do that at the Chateau Marmont," he observes. When he started writing, he says, he didn't know who would play all the roles. Although Hellman would not formally hire them for months to come, the director chose some of the actors before the script was finished, so Wurlitzer says he partially tailored the roles to them. Midway through writing the script, "I knew that Warren [Oates] was going to come in and who he was going to play and what chord that would strike and where the humor would lay in that," Wurlitzer says. "He was a great actor and a great guy, and very generous and really spontaneously funny. It was wonderful to write with him in mind."

In the final screenplay, and in the film, *Two-Lane Blacktop* is the story of two hot-rodders, the Driver and the Mechanic. Young, long-haired, and handsome, they make their living driving around the country and drag racing their '55 Chevy with a big-block engine in it. They pick up the Girl for an indefinite ride. Then they challenge GTO, a middle-aged man who wears a different colored cashmere pullover sweater every day and is named for his new car, to a cross-country race going west to east. The winner will get the pink slip of his opponent's car. GTO picks up a series of hitchhikers along the way, and tells each a different tall tale about himself, tailored to whatever he thinks will make him agreeable to the rider. He buys expensive sweaters and the latest model car to impress people; he is desperate for acceptance and love. The ultimate conformist, he sometimes copies what the Driver and the Mechanic do, such as steal a license plate, hoping to fit in. The race really isn't much of a race since they periodically switch cars and help one another out. The Driver and GTO both fall for the Girl, and she falls for the Driver. But the Driver and the Mechanic focus on their car and racing, to the exclusion of nearly everything else. The Driver neglects the Girl, and she takes off with a young motorcyclist. The race just peters out; they abandon it without a word and go their separate ways. The movie ends the way it begins, with the Driver taking off in a drag race. The last images are of the film catching fire, supposedly in the theater's projector.

The film hewed fairly closely to the screenplay. It deviated from the script by leaving out quite a few scenes so it would not be too long, and by including a fair amount of improvised dialogue. Also missing from the movie are several scenes of nudity and explicit sex, which Hellman didn't shoot because they did not fit his style. Like Corry's spirited original, the final script does not prefigure the film's leisurely pace. It is busier, jazzier, and talkier. For example, for the opening credits the screenplay describes a parking lot at a shopping center with thousands of cars, the most impressive ones parading, and "lots of chicks," as well as "hustling and sounding." Cops are atop the tallest building in the shopping center, and overhead a helicopter hovers, "casting an ominous pool of slowly moving light over the crowd." A huge man with a megaphone helps set up a race between the Mechanic and a Dodge driver, who insult one another before agreeing to a bet. Money changes hands, and as the credits end, a guy with a flashlight signals for the race to begin. The shopping center scene, with all its dramatic visual appeal, noise, and activity, didn't make it into the movie. In the film, the credits roll over footage of a yellow line in the middle of a street.

∞

Both Hellman and Wurlitzer admired Samuel Beckett's play *Waiting for Godot*, first performed in 1953. Wurlitzer's novel *Nog* (1968), *Two-Lane Blacktop*, and *Godot* have many similarities. All three works concern characters adrift without an anchor in a timeless, meaningless world as they vainly seek a purpose or identity. *Godot* appears to have influenced *Nog*, and Wurlitzer addressed some of the themes he'd taken up in his novel in *Two-Lane Blacktop*. In Beckett's play, the two main characters, Vladimir and Estragon, are adrift in a world ruled by chance and chaos. Life is meaningless, so time is meaningless; any change that it brings about doesn't change anything. As a consequence, their memories are poor. The two characters wait, by the side of a road, to be rescued from their helpless plight; they are isolated, alienated, and lonely in their meaningless world. They seek redemption in the form of meaning and purpose.

Vladimir and Estragon are stuck in a rut. They have no possessions, no apparent responsibilities, and nobody but each other. They can't understand or reach one another, yet they simultaneously need, and also resent, one another. They are nearly incapacitated, and have trouble taking any action or even moving from their place on the side of the road.

*Nog* chronicles the unsettling adventures of an unmoored young man who drifts from one place to another, wandering from rut to rut. He often has inertia, and for a while he is incapacitated and unable to move from a mattress in a hallway in a hippie crash pad. He is fearful, anxious, and desperate, and he tries to impose meaning or order on the world, at one point by alphabetizing cans of food. He has no possessions, no responsibilities, no anchor, no stability, no past. Time is unstable: events are jumbled and out of sequence. He consciously invents memories, and many sentences in the book abruptly change from the present to the past tense, or vice versa. Because he can't effectively communicate with others, he never has a meaningful conversation; after he briefly has a girlfriend, he sets her loose in a leaky lifeboat in the ocean.

Like the protagonists in *Nog* and *Godot*, the Driver and the Mechanic have no plans, no goals, no attachments, no anchor. They have no possessions except for their car, and although they go from place to place, nothing changes. Time has no meaning since they do the same old thing again and again, perpetually driving and street racing. They don't communicate about anything except automotive matters. They need one another, one to drive, one to maintain the car, but they sometimes resent one another; the Mechanic is irked about the Driver's attraction to the Girl and his sale of their tools. None of the characters in *Two-Lane* finds a fulfilling identity or a purpose to life. The Driver and the Mechanic drive and race, but that doesn't lead to anything except more driving and racing. The Girl finds another guy to give her a ride, becomes disenchanted and moves on to the next one; romance won't give her self-fulfillment. GTO craves acceptance and tries to get it through impressing others with his stories and possessions, but he is not finding what he seeks and he is becoming desperate.

Although the Driver and the Mechanic lack commitments, they are not free. Their universe is limited to driving, repairing, and racing their car to make their living, and they are blind to other possibilities. They are literally going nowhere fast: the end of the movie echoes the beginning, with the Driver, again behind the wheel, taking off in a drag race.

Samuel Beckett won the Nobel Prize for Literature. He captured a pervasive sense of post-World War II alienation. In the United States, people who had been through two world wars craved stability. In the 1950s, when Beckett wrote *Waiting for Godot*, conformity was highly valued. Whereas hippie culture, at least the speech and dress, was co-opted by mainstream society in the 1960s and early 1970s, beatniks and other nonconformists were marginalized in the 1950s. Freethinkers felt alienated from a society they considered closed-minded and repressive.

As artists working at the end of the 1960s, Wurlitzer and Hellman may have identified with the Driver and the Mechanic. Similar to the car guys, consumed with driving and auto maintenance, Wurlitzer and Hellman would become intensely focused on their projects. Like hot-rodders, artists inhabit the outskirts of mainstream society. The youth cult of the sixties considered anyone over thirty to be over the hill, and Wurlitzer was then thirty-three and Hellman, forty. Neither had yet received widespread acclaim, and they may have felt doors were closing. They were spinning their wheels, getting old on the road to nowhere (the title of Hellman's most recent film).

Even though the characters in *Two-Lane* are in a world of their own, they are obviously in the United States in the late 1960s or the early 1970s. The highways, the Coke signs, the billboards, the cars, the gas stations, the diners, and the characters' long hair and sideburns attest to that. In those years, disenchantment and opposition to the Vietnam War were growing in the US. Many young men, especially those who belonged to the counterculture, went to Canada or enrolled in college to escape the draft. In May of 1970, a few months before *Two-Lane* was filmed, the National Guard fired into a group of unarmed student war protestors at Kent State University in Ohio and killed four of them. Vietnam dominated the evening news on television and was at the forefront of the national consciousness. Yet *Two-Lane* depicts two draft-age young men with no apparent deferments, who show no concern or awareness of the war.

Wurlitzer explains: "*Two-Lane* represents a world and journey unto itself, a kind of genre road pilgrimage outside of politics, which is not to say that no one knew what was going on in the world—like a Western that never refers to the Civil War. And so on. *Two-Lane* exists in its own world, a pure existential experience." Yet the film does not entirely sidestep political and social issues of the day. Two of the hitchhikers are servicemen wearing military uniforms, and a menacing redneck confronts the Mechanic and the Driver at a diner in the South and wants to know if they are hippies. GTO picks up the servicemen, and it falls to him to deflect the redneck's anger. The Driver and the Mechanic are unaware or uninterested in almost everything outside of their Chevy and racing.

∞

Road movies have long been a staple of cinema, and they have been coupled with a number of other genres, such as comedies, dramas, outlaw pictures, and films noirs. They trace their roots back to Homer's *The Odyssey*. Road pictures are not usually solitary journeys; if the protagonist starts out alone, he often hooks up with others. Almost always, the road leads to some manner of change. The protagonist finds a better life, falls into a worse life, gains self-knowledge, becomes disillusioned, escapes from the law, gets caught by the law, dies, or is undone by fate or a woman. Like pioneers, many protagonists travel from east to west, in search of a better life and self-reinvention. Sometimes characters reflect segments of society, such as those in *Easy Rider* (1969) and *The Grapes of Wrath* (1940).

In Frank Capra's comedy *It Happened One Night* (1934), an heiress takes a bus-and-hitchhiking journey with a newspaperman and is transformed from a spoiled brat to a mature woman who learns she can find happiness in a simple life with a journalist. (This doesn't come off as far-fetched as it sounds since the newsman is played by Clark Gable.) In Edgar G. Ulmer's 1945 film noir *Detour*, an innocent man goes west to start a better life with his girlfriend, but fate intervenes and he is wrongfully suspected of murder. In John Ford's *The*

*Grapes of Wrath* (1940), Okies forced from their land during the Depression drive to California hoping for a better life, but are bitterly disappointed. The protagonists of Arthur Penn's *Bonnie and Clyde* (1967) want to transcend their mundane circumstances and become famous. They fall in love, turn into outlaws, achieve recognition, and then are gunned down by the law.

The eponymous hero of Preston Sturges's *Sullivan's Travels* (1941), who, like Sturges, is a director of comedy films, decides that his work is frivolous. Dressed as a hobo, he sets out on a road trip to learn about the dispossessed so he can make a socially conscious movie. Later, a real hobo mugs him and dumps him on a freight train. Sullivan wakes up disoriented and attacks a railroad bull who had roughed him up, then winds up on a chain gang with no prospect of escape. On movie night, the convicts see a Mickey Mouse cartoon and the director learns the joyous power of laughter to cheer even the most unfortunate. He manages to get released from prison, returns to Hollywood, abandons his planned film about the downtrodden and launches himself back into his career as a director of comedies, with a newfound respect for his specialty and its worth.

*Two-Lane Blacktop* dispenses with some road-movie conventions. Unlike virtually all other road movies, *Two-Lane Blacktop*'s characters and their circumstances don't evolve from beginning to end. Also, while characters in most road pictures pursue a goal—they are going somewhere, looking for someone or something, or escaping from someone or something—those in *Two-Lane* have no particular destination until they set up a race, and they abandon even that. Most road movies have a sense of resolution at the end, but *Two-Lane* doesn't conclude; it merely stops in the middle of a scene when the film supposedly catches fire in the projector. *Two-Lane* is unusual, but not unique, in going from west to east. And it resembles many road films in presenting protagonists who live on the outskirts of society and show little regard for the law.

For car guys, thumbing their nose at cops and straight people, plus making a lot of noise, are integral to the appeal of street racing, according to hot rod expert Jim Aust. Car guys appreciate *Bullitt* (1968), directed by Peter Yates, and *Vanishing Point* (1971), directed by Richard Sarafian, as well as *Two-Lane*, for their characters' believability and the movies' authenticity in general (except for *Vanishing Point*'s final crash, in which what had been a Challenger throughout the movie suddenly becomes a Camaro). First, the films portray their heroes as outlaws (even though Steve McQueen plays a cop in *Bullitt*, he is a maverick cop who insults bigwigs). According to Aust, "Every motorcycle guy or car guy to a degree wants to be a rebel, and make the pipes loud and squeal the tires, even if they're the most button-downed lawyer guy." Also, the three films were shot on the streets, rather than having the "driver" sit in a stationery car in a studio with rear projection showing the road supposedly passing by. Before *Bullitt*, Aust notes, "A lot of car movies looked very fake." Car guys also appreciate the three movies because so much screen time is given to the vehicles. Although the Dodge Challenger R/T 440 in *Vanishing Point* is a stock, factory-made car, the mustang in *Bullitt* is technically a hot rod, according to Aust. "You know that that guy has done something to it. The wheels aren't stock, some of the trim has been taken off, and it doesn't say that it's more powerful, but you can tell that it's been worked on by how it sounds and the way he drives it."

While they differ in tone, *Vanishing Point* has several similarities to *Two-Lane*. Both were shot on the road, in the Southwest, and both deal with a race across part of the country. Both conclude abruptly, with ambiguous endings. *Vanishing Point* is about a professional driver who is trying to deliver a car to San Francisco. When he refuses to pull over for some cops, he is relentlessly pursued by lawmen throughout the movie. At the end, police block his path by putting two huge bulldozers in the middle of the road in an effort to stop and capture him. Although he dies at the end, in a sense he wins the contest; he foils his enemies and evades capture by making the ultimate escape. He commits suicide using the equipment the cops had intended to snag him with.

With its indifference to the contest's outcome, *Two-Lane Blacktop* differs from other car-racing movies such as *Grand Prix* (1966), *Rush* (2016), *Days of Thunder* (1990), and *The Fast and the Furious* franchise films (the first of which was released in 2001), all of which emphasize struggles between competitors and the suspense of who will win. But *Two-Lane* is technically a hot rod movie, and a beloved one due to its realistic cars. However, it has little in common with the genre besides its emphasis on hot rods. *Two-Lane* came after the heyday of hot rod movies, the 1950s and early 1960s, when their heroes were cool and rebellious. Marketed to teenagers, these B movies often featured a buxom bad girl as the female lead and chronicled the exploits of teenage car theft rings, assorted crooks, juvenile delinquents, and other rebels who drove fast cars and were up to no good. Musical scores frequently featured rock 'n' roll. Titles, often provocative or exploitative, included *The Devil on Wheels* (1947), *Hot Car Girl* (1958), *Hot Rod Rumble* (1957), *Hell on Wheels* (1967), and *Dragstrip Riot* (1958).

Before Wurlitzer started writing *Two-Lane* he knew little about hot rods—that is, cars modified to go faster. The earliest hot-rodders raced in the dry lakes of the Mojave Desert east of Los Angeles in the 1920s. By the 1950s, hot-rodding and street racing had taken hold with many teenagers and young men in Southern California, particularly in the San Fernando Valley, north of Los Angeles. Some hot-rodders were skilled mechanics and designers who worked in the aerospace industry in Southern California. Many were teenagers who developed their own culture around hot-rodding. Kids didn't make their cars go faster with the intention of obeying the speed limit. Hot-rodding implied rebellion, nerve, adventurousness, and thrill-seeking. Street racers had their own set of rules. Hot-rodding was a subculture, not a hobby like golfing or gardening that was integrated into mainstream society.

For research, Wurlitzer hung out with hot-rodders in the Valley, which is on the other side of the Hollywood Hills from the Chateau Marmont. Wurlitzer recalls, "I explored this new, exotic world of cars which I didn't know much about, but I hung out with some car freaks in the San Fernando Valley, and I learned. It was like a new language." Michael Laughlin hired Billy Kincheloe, a hot-rodder and street racer who was also a painter working toward a master's degree in art at UCLA, to help Wurlitzer make the dialogue and the car-racing scenarios authentic. Kincheloe remembers that Wurlitzer wrote "a terrific script, but there were problems with the language, only because he didn't deal with that. Whatever he had done prior to that wasn't this sort of stuff. So he needed somebody to talk the talk." To make the movie more realistic, Kincheloe remembers, he suggested changes in some dialogue and scenarios where the Driver and the Mechanic dare other characters to race them.

In the scenes where the Driver challenges other street racers, he is rude and insulting; he belittles his opponents, their cars, and their mothers. There are two schools of thought on street racing etiquette. Some hot-rodders prefer to be courteous, and consider derision unnecessary when challenging a potential adversary, but others favor the hostile approach. According to Richard Ruth, who built the '55 Chevys for *Two-Lane*, the nasty attitude reflects "how male egos can get sometimes. And so it's always been, 'My dog is bigger than your dog, and my car is *faster* than your car,' see? And that's what that was, that whole attitude was, 'My car is the bad boy and yours isn't and we'll just have to see. We'll race each other and see who's the top dog.'"

Southern California, a sprawling area notoriously underserved by public transportation, was the hotbed of hot-rodding. Gary Kurtz, the associate producer of *Two-Lane*, grew up in Los Angeles in hot-rodding's heyday in the 1940s and '50s. "As soon as you got a driving license in Southern California you tried to get a car because there's no way to get around otherwise, and I did that too. I bought a car when I was sixteen—it was an old Plymouth—and rebuilt the engine."

Seeking to experience the exhilarating rush that comes from sudden and powerful acceleration, hot-rodders took engines out of big, mighty, expensive cars such as Chryslers, Buicks, Oldsmobiles, and Cadillacs. "You'd buy them from the wrecking yards and crashed cars," recalls Richard Ruth, the car builder. Then the hot-rodders put them inside Chevrolets or Fords or less expensive cars that were lighter so that they could go even faster than the big cars. Ruth explains, "You took an engine that was designed to move a heavy car and put it into a light car, now you had something. And then you hopped the engine up, and made it more powerful." The purpose, according to Ruth, was twofold: "It's all about being innovative and different. The custom car thing was a way to shine, to say 'My car's prettier than yours.' The male ego—that's what it's all about."

Many hot-rodders were street racers who would wait till the dead of night and race one another on designated roads, most notably in the suburban San Fernando Valley, or in the dry Los Angeles riverbed. Since street racing was illegal, they also sometimes had to outrun the cops. "Big Willie" Robinson, the head of the Los Angeles Street Racers Association, brought organization to drag racing in downtown Los Angeles to prevent racers, spectators, and innocent passersby from getting busted or killed. Billy Kincheloe remembers him: "He ran this organization very, very efficiently. I mean, it was an outlaw organization, *but* they had rules and regulations that you had to follow and they allowed people to bring their cars and race downtown." Big Willie later worked with the police to set up a drag racing track at Terminal Island near Long Beach. Ruth explains that Big Willie wanted drag racers to have "someplace to go where at least they had an ambulance around."

In the early 1960s, Detroit automakers cashed in on the hot-rodding craze and tried to co-opt it by manufacturing lightweight cars with powerful engines for laymen who wanted to go fast. Pat Ganahl, an award-winning author of books about hot rods, and former editor of *Street Rodder* and *Hot Rod* magazines, recalls, "That's what killed hot-rodding. In 1964 Detroit got hip to what the hot-rodders were doing and they said, 'Well, we can do this. We can put a 409 engine in a Chevy, and we can put a four-speed in it, we can put a positraction rear end in it from the factory and we can sell it for $4,000 instead of $2,000 for the 6-cylinder model.'" The Pontiac GTO, according to Ganahl, was the first "factory hot rod," making it the perfect foil for the genuine article, the '55 Chevy with a big engine in *Two-Lane Blacktop*.

But these factory hot rods, or muscle cars, which were phased out around 1971, also have devotees. Scott Tiemann was five years old in 1965 when his parents bought a brand-new GTO. (The GTO is named after the Ferrari 250 GTO and the initials stand for "Gran Turismo Omologato," which means the car is certified to participate in specified races.) After having grown up to become a GTO expert, he now has two of his own; Tiemann still has his parents' 1965 model, plus one that he races. For thirty years, he has owned a business in Portland, Minnesota, Supercar Specialties, that restores antique and classic automobiles, many of them muscle cars.

Before 1964, Tiemann explains, Ford and Chevrolet built some race cars that they sold to professionals. Then, with the US economy in good shape, the Big

Three automakers figured they could make money manufacturing specialized cars that went at high speeds. "There are lots of people with no mechanical ability, let's just say, but they want to drive a unique, special vehicle," Tiemann says. Ford put out the Mustang in 1964, "but they really didn't have big engines or anything in them," Tiemann notes. In fact, Mustangs were "little cars, they kind of call them 'pony cars.' But then in '64 Pontiac came out with the GTO, which had a way bigger V8 than the Mustang and a lot more options to make it a much, much, much faster car," Tiemann relates. "In general terms, most people in the car world consider the '64 GTO to be the first muscle car for the masses. Because there was no maintenance to the vehicle, you could hop in it just like any other car and drive it. You didn't have a lot of weird adjusting to do to the engine, like you would on some of the early race cars. It was a user-friendly automobile that had a lot more power than anything anyone had driven up to that point." The muscle cars caught on, especially with young people. Tiemann continues, "The GTO, and the Super Sport Chevelles, all those cars that had a lot more pizazz to them became desirable to young people because they were very affordable and they didn't look like your garden-variety Impala or Catalina—it was an image thing."

The Pontiac was always a cut above the Chevrolet, according to Tiemann. For example, higher quality fabric was used for the upholstery. "Just a little bit more effort was put into the design of the vehicle than a Chevrolet, and I'm sure Chevrolet guys will say that's a bunch of baloney, but that's just the way it was. I mean, it just is. So the dashboards in the Pontiacs were always way nicer than the Chevrolet. They had a lot sportier look to them with gauges and different things. If you bought a Super Sport Chevelle, it had the same dashboard as a normal Chevelle, it looked like your grandpa's car. But a GTO, they always put nicer gauges in them and just special things so you knew you were in a high-performance car, you weren't just in your grandpa's car."

∞

If Detroit struck a blow to hot-rodding, hippies delivered the coup de grace. Considered cool in the early sixties, hot-rodders, motorcyclists, and surfers were no longer in, and they gave way to hippies later in the decade. Hippies dismissed as crassly materialistic the flaunting of cars as status symbols, Detroit's planned obsolescence, and the social pressure to always drive a new model. They usually bought used, older cars, often Volkswagen vans or Bugs, that they used for transportation or, as their predecessors, as a place to listen to music, get ripped, and get laid. However, they'd sometimes decorate them with peace signs and flowers, and popular slogans such as "Make love, not war," and instead of drinking booze in their cars they'd smoke pot. They eschewed the car culture in favor of sex, drugs, rock 'n' roll, and protests against the Vietnam War. Songs about cars and surfing, many by the Beach Boys ("Little Deuce Coupe," "Surfin' Safari"), and puppy love gave way to hard rock and acid rock ("Strawberry Fields Forever," "White Rabbit"), a few of them by the Beach Boys ("Good Vibrations"). In the early sixties, songs about "speed" referred to driving fast; in the late sixties, songs about "speed" referred to getting wired on stimulants. For example, in 1964 Jan and Dean released "Drag City" and "Dead Man's Curve," and the Beach Boys put out "Fun Fun Fun," about a young female motorist who leaves race car drivers in the dust. Jump ahead a few years and find the Rolling Stones' "Mother's Little Helper" (1966) and Canned Heat's "Amphetamine Annie" (1968). Still, with diminished numbers, a strong subculture of hot-rodders survived, lured by the appeal of cars, tinkering, competition, and speed.

When the market for souped-up cars collapsed and put many people who made them out of business, some of them started making cars for Hollywood movies and TV shows. George Barris built the Batmobile, the jalopy the Beverly Hillbillies drove, and the Munster coach, which were much more lucrative than custom hot rods. Ganahl recounts, "Well, what they found out very quickly was in the movies the car only had to look good from twenty feet, and it only had to look good skin deep, and if they had a lawnmower motor in it, that's all they needed." Cutting corners became the norm, and customizers would build cars just good enough to make it through a show or movie before they broke down. Unlike serious hot-rodders, who have always spent virtually all of their free time working on their cars and taken great pride in them, customizers who made vehicles for movies often did as little as possible and just fabricated cars that looked authentic from a distance. "They became prop builders," says Ruth, "because the cars were just props." Car guys zoom in on vehicles in movies and pick them apart; for instance, they criticize automobiles in *American Graffiti* (1973) for using fake upholstery and note that the filmmakers substituted a car with different wheels for the one that supposedly rolls over at the end of the movie.

Richard Ruth was a street racer and car builder who grew up in Highland Park, in northeast Los Angeles, and was unaware that movie cars were fakes. Ruth was a friend of a friend of Billy Kincheloe, the hot-rodder Laughlin had hired as an automotive advisor to Wurlitzer. According to Ganahl, Ruth was the polar opposite of the high-priced, low-quality Hollywood car customizers: "He didn't know that movie cars didn't have to be realistic." Ruth recalls that the filmmakers had put the '55 Chevy out to bid. After he submitted a bid, and took the filmmakers out one night to experience the street racing scene, he got the contract. Ruth recalls, "They really didn't know what they wanted. They left it up to me, as far as how I was going to do it. Being that they were just studio people and not racers." Given free rein, he boasts, "I made the car of my dreams on the studio's money."

Gary Kurtz, who had worked with Hellman on *The Shooting* and *Ride in the Whirlwind*, came aboard as associate producer at this time during pre-production, after Wurlitzer had started to rewrite the script. They hired Kurtz partly because he, unlike Hellman and Laughlin, was familiar with hot rods. But the producer and director did make the effort to go to Van Nuys Boulevard and soak up some atmosphere. Michael Laughlin took along his elegant, but game, wife, Leslie Caron. She recalls. "I do remember going with Michael to see the street racing in the middle of the night. I only remember that it went very fast and the whole thing was wrapped up after a few minutes, before the police had time to get there." Kurtz remembers that Ruth gave him an "interesting" ride down Van Nuys Boulevard. Interesting, he says, "because it was very fast and not usually the way I drive down city streets."

Originally, Kurtz remembers, "We were going to try to get away with two [Chevys] and we decided after talking with several drag racers that we couldn't, we had to have one that was actually a proper racing car, so we'd have to have three." So Richard Ruth built three Chevy 210 sedans, which looked identical on the outside, at his shop in North Hollywood, Competition Engineering. One was built for interior shots. The doors and other portions were removable, to make it easier to put the camera inside or just outside the car. The second car was equipped for stunts and was used for long shots of the characters driving along a highway or pulling into a gas station. The final car was the real race car. The picture car for interiors had an LS6 engine, which, according to Ruth, "was a 454 with a little bit of horsepower." The second car had an LS5 engine, which, again according to Ruth, "was just a mediocre 454. I mean, like an Impala, or something like that." The race car had a brand-new 1969 L88 427, a high-performance engine that was generally used in the Corvette but could be special-ordered, and according to Ruth, was "GM's big race engine at the time."

The filmmakers told Ruth to put some ornamentation on the hood, so, he says, he copied a distinctive hood scoop the well-known drag racer Bill Jenkins recently had designed. To make the car lighter, Ruth gave it a fiberglass front, doors and trunk lid. He removed the window cranks and installed sliding plexiglass windows. And he stripped out the heater, the radio, the rear seat, and the door panels, which included armrests, to remove weight. "I built a real race car for the street," Ruth recalls with pride.

Billy Kincheloe remembers driving the race car, which got up to about 123 miles per hour: "The race car was just that. It didn't like to be driven anywhere in traffic, it didn't like to do anything except go like a bat out of hell and then stop. That's all it wanted to do. You wouldn't want to drive that car day to day or hour to hour, or get in it and drive around town. It would overheat, it would get nasty, it just would be a handful."

Striving for authenticity, Ruth worked meticulously on the car's exterior, because hot-rodders set great store by their cars' appearance. He did extensive prep work on the auto bodies, painted them powder blue with a few primered parts, and turned them in. Kurtz remembers that the filmmakers had many discussions about the cars' color. "Monte thought that powder blue was a terrible color because it seemed like it was what we call a 'pimpmobile' where it was trying to be a show-off car." The filmmakers, who, according to Ruth, "didn't understand the street scene," told him to add more primer. When he brought them back with additional primered parts, they told him they wanted the cars entirely primered. Ruth balked. Car guys spent much time and effort tending to their prize possessions' looks, unless they intentionally made them look ratty to fake out opponents. Although they would drive a primered car temporarily while they were still doing body work, they wouldn't leave it that way and go on the road. They would paint it.

When he asked why in the world they would want the Chevys entirely primered, Ruth recounts, Monte Hellman replied, "'Because drag racers are dirty.' And I was a drag racer, and I was a very hot-headed kind of guy at the time, so that kind of pushed them away from me a little bit. Quite a bit, actually." In fact, many drag racers are fastidious about constantly cleaning and polishing their cars. Serious car guys maintain their hot rods in pristine condition, and many literally do not have a speck of dust under the hood. Billy Kincheloe keeps a gleaming 1965 Cobra in his garage, and the engine truly looks clean enough to eat your dinner off of. Offended by Hellman's remark, Ruth remembers, "I just told him, 'I'm done. You guys are getting the cars like they are and you guys can do whatever you're going to do.'"

Primer is a foundation that is applied before paint and is not meant to last on its own; it rubs off, and it fades in the sun. Kurtz explains, "So we spent some time testing, spraying a lot of different colors, and said, 'How can we duplicate the gray-primer look but in a kind of finished, sealed paint that isn't going to flake off or look funny after three days in the sun?'" Finally, they came up with a solution. "They had a guy who was a painter that painted it so it looked like primer," Kincheloe explains. They went for a weathered, scruffy look. "If you leave a gray-primered automobile, or anything that's gray primered, outside for a while it gets streaks in it where dust settles on it and mist gets on it and it leaves a patina on it that looks like water has run down it and there are streaks and that kind of stuff," Kincheloe explains. To give the cars a permanent distressed look, Kincheloe continues, "these cars were built up near Simi Valley and there's a lot of dust up there and nastiness and that sort of stuff, and it gets on the paint and it just kind of runs, and then you leave it out on a misty night and voila! You have patina." The filmmakers, according to Ganahl, "took this beautiful car and made it look ugly."

Hellman is an intellectual filmmaker with a good heart and he simply wasn't familiar with the hot-rodding culture. Hippies generally did not understand hot-rodders, and they and many other laymen thought of them as guys who were continually under the hoods of their cars—grease monkeys and the image that label conjures up: dark and hairy, with oil-streaked face, arms, and coveralls, and black grime permanently embedded under the fingernails. For his part, Ruth found the filmmakers somewhat bizarre, pretentious, undiscriminating followers of fashion, and very Hollywood: "I'm a Levis and T-shirt kind of guy, and I wore bell-bottoms at the time, but they had weird-looking bell-bottoms." Ruth thought they were operating out of their league: "The culture was completely different between what they were trying to do and what they knew about," Ruth remembers. "I don't mean anything against Monte Hellman, but he just wasn't a car person, I mean, not even in any form, and he was trying to make a car movie."

From one perspective, the filmmakers' decision to use primer could be considered a wise one, and Will Corry called for a primered car in his script. Street racers often didn't have much money—that's why they were out racing in the street for bets. A hot-rodder with a fast car could make $100 or $200 on a race in the 1960s. When they had extra money, they would spend it on fixing their car up under the hood before they'd spend it on cosmetic enhancements. Also, one aspect of street racing was to fake the other guy out—you wanted your car to look ratty and junky so your opponent, thinking he would win, would up the bet. A hot-rodder with a bright, shiny car wouldn't find many takers. As Ganahl recalls, "You wanted to make it look like something that would barely get to the end of the track, but be really fast because it had all the good parts on the inside where they couldn't see them. And part of the deal was that you didn't open your hood." But Ruth belonged to the "male ego" school of thought on hot rods that held that you had to prove that your dick was bigger than the other guy's, and that appearance was all-important.

When the car was finished, Ruth recalls, he took the filmmakers for a final spin near Bob's Big Boy in Van Nuys. "We went drag racing with the thing too. It scared the hell out of Monte Hellman and Michael Laughlin." When Hellman realized Ruth intended to race, he wanted to get out. When it was Laughlin's turn, Ruth recounts, "I said, 'Put your shoulder harness on, and pull down on it, tighten it up a little bit,' and he said, 'Well, why do we have to do this?' I said, 'In case something happens, you know, we're liable to flip the car or something.' He said, '*What?*'"

The next film Gary Kurtz worked on, as co-producer this time, was *American Graffiti*. "For the car that the bad guy drives in *American Graffiti*, I thought the '55 looked just perfect, so I had it repainted, sprayed it black, and we used that for just a few days really. It didn't drive very well, and we didn't really want to spend a lot of money fixing it up because it was in the film for so little time, but it did look good."

∞

The filmmakers had much less trouble getting a muscle car; they just bought two brand-new 1970 Pontiac GTO The Judge models. The GTO was the famed engineer-and-auto-executive John DeLorean's baby. In 1969, when demand for the car started to falter as the newness wore off and competitors offered cheaper muscle cars, he decided to goose up the GTO to boost sales. At first, the division planned to bring out a cheaper version of the GTO to compete with the less expensive Plymouth Road Runner. DeLorean nixed that idea, and decided to make a more expensive option for the GTO. It is said that he liked to watch the popular television show *Rowan & Martin's Laugh-In*, which featured the catchphrase, "Here come da judge." So he decided to call the car "The Judge."

The Judges were more flamboyant than the standard GTOs: they were painted brighter colors, had stripes, and had a spoiler on the back. According to the GTO expert Scott Tiemann, the car had "a 366-horsepower Ram Air III engine, which you could get in a standard GTO if you wanted, but it was optional in a GTO and it was the standard engine in a Judge. So you're paying a few more bucks because you've got a little more powerful engine, and then you've got a bright color, you've got a wing, it was just a very flamboyant vehicle for 1969. And in 1970, in my mind, it got even a little bit more flamboyant, that car in the movie being a perfect example, because that color was called Orbit Orange, even though it was bright school-bus yellow." The jazzed-up GTO was a hit. "In 1969, that Judge model drew people into the showroom to see this weird new car with this bright color and these stripes," Tiemann says.

Pontiac stopped making The Judge after 1971, when its novelty had worn off and a gas crunch was starting. But the car still has committed fans, including the director Richard Linklater (*Slacker* [1991], *Boyhood* [2014]), who owns a 1968 GTO. Linklater explains the appeal: "That's what's so great about the muscle car era, the cars you could buy commercially were really powerful, wonderful cars. A short little era in car history, but a special one." The GTO, Linklater maintains, "is one of the great muscle cars of all time," and he featured his car in *Boyhood*. It belongs to the boy's father, played by Ethan Hawke, who drives it and promises he will give it to his son when he grows up, only to forget his pledge and sell it. Linklater continues, "The Judge ended up being one of the more famous GTOs that you would want to have. So I opened my film *Dazed and Confused* with one that wasn't actually a Judge. It was sort of what just happened a lot in the car world, you'd get a GTO for that year and you'd just put a sticker up on the exhaust up there and call it a Judge. But someone told me, 'Oh, that's kind of a fake Judge.' It looked the part, so I don't really know, but I liked the car."

∞

With a script written, and the cars assembled, the filmmakers proceeded to cast the movie and scout locations.

# 2

# Stalled

Floyd Mutrux was in Phoenix for the filming of the last scene of *The Christian Licorice Store*, which he had written and Michael Laughlin was producing. Even though he and Monte Hellman disliked one another and he didn't get the job rewriting *Two-Lane Blacktop*, Mutrux knew a lot about cars and drag racing, so he was advising Laughlin about automotive aspects of the film. Laughlin asked him to find someone to fill the crucial position of the mechanic who would go on the road with the *Two-Lane* film company and maintain the cars, particularly the finicky '55 Chevy race car, in working order. Instead of hiring a mechanic from Southern California, the home and hotbed of hot-rodding, near Phoenix Mutrux found a country boy from Cambridge, Maryland, for the job. The brothers Jay and Buck Wheatley raced as a team and ran a speed shop, where they sold and installed everything needed to make a car go faster, in their small town. Maryland, notes Buck Wheatley, "has got an ocean, and then it's got a bay, and we lived in the sticks in between." In 1969, the brothers were competing in the American Hot Rod Association Winternationals at the now-defunct Beeline Dragway in the desert near Mesa, Arizona. At their hotel in the evening after the Saturday race, they were working on their car, a Camaro, in the parking lot, and met Mutrux and the film crew of *The Christian Licorice Store*. The Wheatleys told the crew they were headed to race next in Pomona, California, near Los Angeles. Mutrux was impressed with their knowledge of racing, their dedication to cars, and their expertise in auto repair. Unlike the characters in the *Two-Lane Blacktop* script, Jay was a mechanic as well as a race car driver. Mutrux gave them a business card and asked them to stop by Cinema Center Films to talk about a forthcoming movie about car racing for Laughlin Enterprises.

The following week, the Wheatley brothers, driving a race truck, pulled up to the guard shack at CBS Studio Center and got directions to Michael Laughlin's offices. "We were country boys, we didn't know anything about this stuff," Buck recalls, but they expected to meet some staid, buttoned-down studio executives. When they arrived at Laughlin's offices, the receptionist told them to wait a moment before she admitted them. Once inside, Buck was mightily surprised to behold James Frawley, who was directing *The Christian Licorice Store*. "When you say 'executives,' you're used to people in suits and ties. This guy's wearing sandals and playing a pinball machine." Frawley, in fact, dressed like a hippie, according to Laughlin, and had worked for Bob Rafelson and Bert Schneider, who had produced the hit movie *Easy Rider* as well as *The Monkees* TV show, which is why Cinema Center Films executives wanted to hire him as a director. Frawley, Laughlin recalls, "was really playing the hippie role," but "wasn't a person that it fit. Like a lot of people's background and their upbringing didn't fit in that mode and so they always looked out of place trying, wearing the clothes and all that sort of thing." Laughlin, however, emphasizes that "*I* bent not one iota" to the whims of fashion.

The filmmakers interviewed the Wheatley brothers to determine their skills as mechanics. However, Buck recalls, "They didn't know anything about cars. They knew about movies." Buck remembers one question that they asked the brothers was: If the car's transmission was broken, how long it would take them to remove and replace it? "My brother and I looked at each other and said, 'Well, twenty minutes.' Well, they said, 'Wow!' That's the kind of stuff they wanted to hear." It was getting late, Buck recalls, and, "Of all things, they said, 'Well, we're going to go eat dinner.' And they said, 'You come on and eat dinner with us.'" Laughlin says that Mutrux was hooked up with bigwigs in the automotive world, and Chevrolet had supplied them with some new cars for product placement. Buck recalls they headed out to dinner in a small procession. "There were six or seven of us, and we went to eat dinner someplace and we took three brand-new Corvettes."

The Wheatleys had to return to Cambridge to take care of the speed shop they owned. But not long after they returned home, Buck says, "Lo and behold, they contacted us back and said, 'We want to hire you to do the movie.'" Buck stayed home to run their business, but the filmmakers hired Jay to maintain the Chevys and GTOs on the road and to do some stunt driving.

While pleased at his brother's good fortune, Buck was puzzled by the filmmakers' choice of a country boy from Maryland for a mechanic on a Hollywood film. "We were sitting in California, in the middle of the best hot-rodders in the world." Jay soon started work, traveling around Southern California to buy spare parts for the '55 Chevys that he would not be able to find in the small towns where *Two-Lane* would be filmed.

Monte Hellman thought that Gregory Sandor, who had shot his previous movies *The Shooting* and *Ride in the Whirlwind*, would do a good job filming the script and hired him. Sandor asked John Bailey, who had been working with him regularly and who had recently been admitted to IATSE (International Alliance of Theatrical Stage Employees), the union for cameramen for feature films, to be his assistant. (Bailey went on to become a prominent cinematographer, and in 2017 he was elected the thirty-sixth president of the Academy of Motion Picture Arts and Sciences, which awards the Oscars.) But this was Bailey's first studio film and his first job as first camera assistant. "I'd just gotten into the union, and legally I didn't have the seniority to be doing a major motion picture. I kind of skirted in under the radar," he remembers.

Like the acclaimed cinematographers Vilmos Zsigmond and Laszlo Kovacs, Sandor was from Hungary, but his more famous peers were more gregarious, self-promoting, ambitious, and assertive in furthering their careers. Bailey remembers that Zsigmond, Kovacs, and other cameramen struggled to get into IATSE: "These were people I knew and had worked with in NABET [National Association of Broadcast Employees and Technicians], and they slowly got into the union. Some of them had to sue to get in." Sandor, as well as Zsigmond and Kovacs, came from the classical school of Hungarian and Polish cinematography. For example, if an actor was sitting next to a window and facing away from it, they would typically direct the key light to the actor's face from the direction where he was looking so you could see it clearly. About this time, classical cinematography went out of vogue, while more realistic, source lighting became popular, so cinematographers started to bring the light through the window to shoot the same scene. "That's one reason why *Two-Lane Blacktop*, even though it's kind of a New Wave film, has such a classical look to it, because of the way Gregory worked," Bailey notes. Sandor mentored Bailey and taught him classical cinematography. "He taught me composition and lighting and camera movement," Bailey recalls fondly. "There was a tremendous amount of a sort of discipline and coherence and continuity to the way Gregory worked."

The two men started to collaborate after *Ride in the Whirlwind* and *The Shooting* were released in 1966. At that time, they both belonged to the Los Angeles local film unit of NABET, which was mostly a union for cinematographers who worked in television. As members of the film local, they worked on TV commercials and low-budget features. Sandor never married, lived with his mother in the San Fernando Valley until she died, and largely kept to himself. But he was friends with a group of Armenian Americans who owned gas stations and garages. They had a consortium in which each would invest $10,000 to make Armenian-language films, and Sandor and Bailey would shoot them. These were usually based on classic Armenian plays, sometimes farces, and they would hire Armenian-speaking actors and shoot interiors, because the movies were supposed to be taking place in Armenia in the 1940s and '50s. Sandor and Bailey shot them in black-and-white on short ends of film that they would buy from the camera departments at studios, which sold the last eighty or ninety feet of a 1,000-foot roll for greatly reduced prices to low-budget filmmakers. Bailey recalls, "So Greg and I did maybe half-a-dozen of these Armenian-language films that nobody's ever seen in this country, under the radar, they're not even on his resume."

Since *Two-Lane* was a studio picture, it was required to have a cameraman who belonged to IATSE, the union for cinematographers for feature films. The filmmakers had to hire a "standby" cameraman who was in the union, and pretend he was the director of photography. Sandor never was admitted to IATSE, but not because he lacked talent. The union was a closed shop at the time, Bailey says, "so once you were in, the union kind of protected you. And they would protect you to the extent of keeping good people, new people like Gregory Sandor out." Bailey (and many others) cites Sandor's work in the scene in *Two-Lane* where the race is set up at a gas station as outstanding, and evidence that he deserved to belong to IATSE: "It's very episodic, and one actor sort of concludes his episode and literally leaves the stage before another one comes on. That's part of that classical choreography of it. And that particular sequence I just find so beautifully designed and controlled, and it's really the setup for the whole movie." But, Bailey explains, not only was IATSE a closed shop, but Sandor was a loner: "He was not one of the guys." Monte Hellman agrees, and says he thinks Sandor was kept out of IATSE because "he wasn't a schmoozer." On location, Sandor would never eat dinner with the producer or director or anybody but his assistant, Bailey says. "He always ate with me. And I have the most wonderful memories of Gregory," who, at the end of a shoot, would always give away a new Panama hat he would wear during each of his films so his bald spot wouldn't get sunburned, more than once presenting one to Bailey.

Bailey's admiration, affection, and sadness are palpable when he speaks of his mentor: "Gregor never got into the IA so he always worked as an outsider." Bailey says that after he himself got into IATSE and started to work on studio feature films, he and Sandor grew apart. "I always thought it was a real loss for the American cinema that Greg was never absorbed into the mainstream the way that Laszlo and Vilmos and John Alonzo were." Jack Deerson, the standby cameraman, was credited as the director of photography on *Two-Lane Blacktop* but by all accounts did almost nothing on the film. Deerson, Gary Kurtz recalls, "didn't actually do anything except stand around."

Bailey remembers that before they left Southern California to go on the road, they asked Deerson "to do a handheld pass-by shot of a car driving by in the desert. And I gave him an Arriflex with a lens and one roll of film and asked him to go out and just shoot it handheld by himself. He dropped the camera and broke it. So the one thing that I know that we asked him to do he totally fucked up."

Hellman and Laughlin both wanted to use a widescreen format. Michael Laughlin says he insisted on it, and Hellman thought it had several advantages, one of them being that he could shoot three people in a car and keep them all in focus. They were on a tight budget, so they decided to shoot in Techniscope. Hellman says, "It saves money because the film goes twice as far. The main reason, however, is it utilizes spherical instead of anamorphic lenses, allowing greater depth of field." Sergio Leone used Techniscope for his Spaghetti Westerns, Bailey notes, which allowed everything in the frame to be in focus: "Somebody would have a cigarette in the foreground on the left side of frame in focus and there'd be a train coming into the station 200 yards behind him that was also in focus." Panavision and CinemaScope were widescreen, anamorphic systems used for big-budget, spectacle films at the time. Techniscope was also a widescreen technique, but the frames of the film were only half the height of a normal frame—it was two perforations high instead of four, so it used only half as much actual film. It was later stretched vertically so the final print had a 2:40 aspect ratio like other widescreen formats.

One problem with Techniscope was that filmmakers couldn't project dailies the following day because projectors ran at four perforations per frame and they were shooting two per frame. So the developed negative was put into an optical printer that stretched it vertically to a four-perforation frame. The optical printer was slower than a high-speed contact printer, so it took an extra day to deliver dailies and cost a little more. The process also made everything look squeezed. At movie theaters, the projectionists would take this squeezed print and use an anamorphic lens to stretch it out and make it look normal. So, while the filmmakers initially saved money by using only half as much film while shooting, the film was then blown up to four perforations for editing and projecting, therefore they didn't save money in post-production.

As they began to assemble a crew, the filmmakers were simultaneously talking to actors. For casting director, they hired Fred Roos, who also was a producer. Roos had produced two films that Hellman had directed, *Flight to Fury* and *Back Door to Hell*, which were made back-to-back in the Philippines and released in 1964. The two men would clash. In the case of *Two-Lane*, Roos brought in dozens of highly trained actors, including Bruce Dern, only to have Hellman shoot them down in favor of untrained, nonactor rock stars whom the director thought would be more natural and less mannered. Roos thought he was making a big mistake. "Monte always got on Fred's nerves," notes Laughlin. "I mean, he'd worked with him in the past, but he got on his nerves." As a casting director, Roos had worked on *Five Easy Pieces* (1970) and the television show *That Girl*, and would later achieve distinction for launching stellar careers and casting classic films such as *American Graffiti* (1973) and *The Godfather* (1972).

Casting lasted an "absurdly long" time, according to Laughlin, as Roos brought in many young actors whom Hellman rejected as not right for the roles. Although Hellman "saw lots of actors in his droning way," Laughlin says, "he was the kind of director who could turn a 'go' project into a development deal." This is literally true; Hellman was later slated to direct many pictures that either fell through or ended up being directed by others, including *Pat Garrett and Billy the Kid* (1973), *Midnight Cowboy* (1969), *Fat City* (1972), *Reservoir Dogs* (1992), and *Buffalo 66* (1998). The deals fell through for various reasons, but one is that Hellman is stubborn and unwilling to compromise if he feels that doing so would undermine his artistic vision. While he deserves praise for his artistic integrity and for sticking to his principles—without these courageous qualities he would not be the great director that he is—these traits can be hard on a casting director who can't find exactly the right actor to suit his boss. Although he wasn't working continuously, Roos submitted an invoice for casting services from October 1969 to June 1970. But his work didn't end even then; Dennis Wilson wasn't cast as the Mechanic until shortly before shooting began in mid-August of 1970.

In Hellman's defense, he did settle on an actual thespian for the Driver—the actor/playwright Sam Shepard. But when production was delayed, Shepard dropped out of the project because his wife was pregnant, he didn't want to miss the birth of their child, and, according to Hellman, "He doesn't fly," so he wouldn't be able to return home quickly for the event. As noted, Hellman hoped nonactors would be less affected and more spontaneous and believable than trained actors. According to Hellman, "It became apparent quite early on that there wasn't an actor, a professional actor, who was right for the Driver. I felt that we needed a star in the sense of someone who had that feeling about himself, who had that kind of authority. And there weren't any star actors in that age group who were right. There were some movie stars who were maybe thirty years old, but we wanted someone who was really young and couldn't find anybody. And I felt that a star from another field might be a possible way to do it. I felt it could have been an athlete or a singer or anyone who had experienced some measure of success and self-confidence." Additionally, as Roos notes, Hellman and Laughlin were interested in rock stars because they were considered more hip than actors in the late sixties and early seventies.

At the end of the hippie era, rock stars were the ne plus ultra of cool. The Byrds immortalized this hero worship in their 1967 song about the downside of fame, "So You Want to Be a Rock 'n' Roll Star," which warns that teenaged girls would mob rock musicians who had had a hit record, grabbing their hair and ripping their clothes. Although movies were catching up with the zeitgeist, teenagers hung posters of Jim Morrison, not Clint Eastwood, on their bedroom walls. Actors in general were not considered as authentic, sexy, intriguing and hot as rock musicians, with a few exceptions, such as Peter Fonda, Dennis Hopper, and Steve McQueen. After Elvis Presley started making (mainly dreadful) films, transitioning from a sexually provocative hillbilly to a bland singer/movie actor, he was no longer considered cool.

As Roos noted, "It was still basically the sixties—sex, drugs, and rock 'n' roll, and everybody at that time was feeling that real rockers were cool, much cooler than actors. And to some degree there was truth to that, but that isn't necessary to act. So a lot of rockers got shots in various movies because they were considered cool and hip, and we're not just casting the typical Hollywood actor. It's got to be 'Smarty Pants.'" Ringo Starr appeared in *Candy* in 1968 and *The Magic Christian* in 1970, and Mick Jagger acted in *Ned Kelly* and *Performance*, both in 1970. The Beatle and the Rolling Stone received mixed reviews. Roos concedes exceptions to the rule that rock stars with no theatrical training don't turn in good performances; he says he gave Kris Kristofferson his start in movies after he saw him perform at the storied Troubadour nightclub in West Hollywood. Roos brought in Kristofferson for Hellman to consider for the Driver, and thinks he would have done a good job; the singer/songwriter appeared in *Cisco Pike* (1972) shortly afterwards and has had a long career as an actor in films, with parts in *Alice Doesn't Live Here Anymore* (1974), *Convoy* (1978), and *Heaven's Gate* (1980).

Michael Laughlin always sought out actors and filmmakers who were hip or on the cutting edge, and he liked to discover and develop budding talent, so he says he supported Hellman's search for rock stars for the leading roles: "Singer/songwriters can be really good actors. I mean, they bring something that actors don't bring, especially in that time when singer/songwriters had credibility and were something new and authentic, in the world of the sixties, whereas Ryan O'Neal was not. And so, they were more the kingpins of the day than a plastic actor."

Although they tried to talk to Bob Dylan about a role in the film, he had no interest. Aside from Kristofferson, they interviewed Jerry Jeff Walker, who wrote the song "Mr. Bojangles," but Hellman didn't think either was right for the part. Finally, James Taylor came to their attention. Gary Kurtz remembers going to the Troubadour nightclub in West Hollywood to see Taylor perform: "His stage presence was very strong, and both Monte and I agreed that if we could capture that in this character that it would be great. We did do screen tests of several other people but none of them were as good as we thought he would be," Kurtz recalls.

Taylor, twenty-two at the time, was part of a new wave of singer/songwriters that came to prominence in the sixties and early seventies, which included Laura Nyro, Leonard Cohen, Carole King, and Randy Newman. Many were influenced by country, folk and blues music. They gained more mainstream popularity and made a lot more money than their predecessors, who included Pete Seeger, Woody Guthrie, and Billie Holliday. Taylor's career was just taking off, and during filming of *Two-Lane Blacktop* his first hit, "Fire and Rain," climbed the charts, prompting the crew to razz him for becoming famous. Although it had not yet reached the Billboard 100 when he went on the road for the movie, by the time the film wrapped, the song was in the top 20 and climbing; it would peak at number 3.

Taylor would have mixed feelings about becoming well-known and performing intimate songs about his emotions for a multitude of strangers. He had previously suffered from depression, and he had become hooked on heroin in the late sixties. He had yet to kick his heroin addiction, but he did not use hard drugs during the shoot. While Taylor was intelligent, informed, engaging, and a good conversationalist, according to his manager at the time, Peter Asher, of the sixties duo Peter and Gordon ("A World without Love"), in those days Taylor could be withdrawn around strangers. Tall, dark, and lanky, with finely chiseled features, Taylor had high cheekbones and was extremely handsome in a brooding, sensitive sort of way. He had the potential of projecting an iconic look when shot in profile while driving. Taylor joined the film production with absolutely no expectations, and he would be sorely disappointed.

Liking Taylor's look and keenly interested in him, Hellman sent the script to Asher. Laughlin remembers Asher as a particularly astute young man with "bright red hair. Kind of a nerdy guy, but hip." As Asher recalls, he had heard that Hellman was great and clever and the cool new guy. He says that he recommended that his client pursue the role. "My feeling was, if you were going to lurch into acting, this was clearly going to be, whatever else it was going to be, whether it came out good or bad, it was going to be interesting and hip and not like somebody casting James Taylor in a TV movie of the week or some crap." Since he had no experience negotiating contracts for movies, Asher asked the agency that they used for concerts to recommend an actor's agent. The agency suggested a bright new kid named Mike Medavoy (who would go on to become a studio head, co-found Orion Pictures, and produce films such as *Zodiac* [2007] and *Black Swan* [2010]). Asher told Medavoy, "Just get the best deal you can. You know movies, I don't."

In a deal memo, written on July 9, 1970, Medavoy offered Taylor's services as a singer/songwriter as well as an actor: "James Taylor will write the song, if there is a song to be written, which is yet to be discussed." Hellman declined. The director knew from the first that he did not want a soundtrack, only source music, or songs that the actors hear on the radio or that have their source in the on-camera action. Laughlin recalls, "The big creative decision and the dangerous one was no score." He went along with Hellman, who told him the lack of a score would make the film unique and more authentic.

Hellman offered Taylor the role over Roos's objections. "I was not for James Taylor. I didn't win that one," Roos remembers. Roos thought Taylor's appeal was hipness, not acting ability. "People like Monte would get to thinking someone like James Taylor would be cooler than any actor." The casting director tried to talk Hellman into hiring Kris Kristofferson instead. "I probably said, 'Monte, if you want a singer from music—Kristofferson, not James Taylor.' And I was right, wasn't I?" Roos explains why he prefers to cast trained actors in film roles: "I'm not generally a believer in casting rock stars when there are so many good actors who can do these things, who have studied all their lives to get these parts." Working at Laughlin's offices at Cinema Center Films, Roos talked to many actors, but didn't formally audition any of them. "I put great stock in just chatting with the actors in depth, at length. I can tell 70 percent of what I need to know just through in-depth conversation."

For the part of a gay Oklahoma hitchhiker, Roos was able to cast a fine actor, Harry Dean Stanton, who had appeared in a previous Hellman film, *Ride in the Whirlwind*. An angular-faced, wiry actor who brings an edge to his roles, he has often been typecast as bad guys, probably because of his looks, and in spite of a naturally sweet, endearing side that can elicit the audience's sympathy when he plays good guys. He was superbly menacing and creepy as Roman Grant, the villainous, lecherous boss of a polygamist community in the television show *Big Love*. But he also played an angel in a 1985 Disney movie called *One Magic Christmas*, albeit a somewhat degenerate-looking one. In his review of that film, Roger Ebert commented, "I am not sure exactly what I think about Harry Dean Stanton's archangel. He is sad-faced and tender, all right, but he looks just like the kind of guy that our parents told us never to talk to." Stanton was part of a crowd Roos hung out with in those days. "The circle was Monte and Jack Nicholson, Harry Dean, Carole Eastman, who wrote *Five Easy Pieces*, and Robert Towne," Roos says.

For GTO, Hellman chose Warren Oates, whom he'd worked with on *The Shooting*. Stanton says he knew Oates very well. "We knew each other for years. We're both from Kentucky. We were up for the same part many times." Stanton wanted Oates's part, a lonely, chatty character who has considerably more dialogue than any of the others. Stanton, who has played both leading roles (*Paris, Texas* [1984]) and supporting ones, "would get furious if you even said the word 'character actor,'" according to Roos. He would insist that he was not a character actor, that he was an *actor*. "He thought that was a demeaning kind of put-down. He didn't see that it was actually a positive statement. But he would always say, 'Oh, don't call me a character actor.' He would get his back up about that."

Oates was a highly regarded actor and an extremely personable man. Roos also knew Oates and had interviewed him many times; in a couple of years, he would cast him as the lead in *Dillinger* (1973). Gifted, spontaneous, and energetic, Oates also could be volatile and unpredictable. He used drugs to excess and sometimes drank too much. Leslie Caron, who appeared with him in *Chandler* (1971), calls him "a terrific guy. Very independent, very individual," and as an actor, "a natural."

Asked at a seminar at the American Film Institute about mixing professional and amateur actors, Hellman said, "There was a problem in the sense that whenever you have real people mixed with actors, as [Fred] Zinnemann had in *The Men* when Marlon Brando was acting with a group of paraplegics," the real people tend to look real and the actors tend to look like actors. But Hellman planned to have his wife coach the actors before filming began, and he didn't think the disparity would cause a problem.

For the role of the Girl, Hellman had chosen his own girl, Laurie Bird. "She was a very troubled girl who didn't have a mother" and who led an unhappy home life in Queens, New York, says the publicist Beverly Walker, who got to know Bird and became fond of her when they both worked on *Two-Lane*. The unit publicist Eileen Peterson saw Bird often in Manhattan in the late sixties and later when they were neighbors in Los Angeles after Bird moved there to live with Hellman, whom she married soon afterwards. The two had become friendly after Bird answered a call for extras for a movie called *Parachute to Paradise*, which no longer exists, directed by Peterson's then-husband, Floyd Peterson. His next project was a film directed by Robert Downey, called *Pound* (1970), for United Artists. It was about two dozen dogs, played by humans, in a pound, and all the scenes took place in an enclosed kennel behind a chain-link fence. Although UA executives had seen the script, they were dumbfounded by the movie, and not knowing what to do with it, they buried it, according to Eileen Peterson. After that the couple moved to Los Angeles to get assignments from MGM and Twentieth Century Fox in publicity and advertising. Peterson describes Bird: "She was very engaging, so people noticed her, she was beautiful, she had a sweet charm." With a gorgeous face and shapely figure, but loose-fitting clothes and long, honey-colored hair worn in the movie in an unflattering hairstyle that hung over part of her face when she walked with her head bent forward, Bird, as the Girl, would make a schlumpy siren as she shuffled along.

A kind and gentle girl, according to Peterson, "without being mature or educated, she was ramped into this world of fashion and film. I don't think she was at all prepared for it." Martin Landau also worried that she was in over her head and that some of the older, more sophisticated people she surrounded herself with presented a potential danger. "I thought she was very naïve, very young. I thought she was very vulnerable and very sweet, and could be taken advantage of easily if she wasn't careful." Bird did not have many close female friends, but "she was very aware of her sexual power," Peterson says. Like the Girl in the movie, who was based on her, Bird's world largely revolved around her relationships with men. But she seemed to be drawn to women who were a little older and whom she regarded as mother figures, such as Peterson, Walker, and Caron.

Many who knew her describe Bird as sweet, but she also often appeared nervous and unhappy. Leslie Caron, who spent time with her in Los Angeles, and when Bird and Hellman visited her and Laughlin at their home in Sardinia, describes her as a "very difficult, disturbed young girl." Caron says that the girl told her about her miserable childhood and family life, and adds that Bird was "really very distraught, very difficult."

According to his comments at a seminar at AFI shortly after the film was released, Hellman was struck by Bird when he went to New York to see Rudy Wurlitzer and audition actors. While he thought she was a good prototype for the character, she wasn't an actor, and he decided, "We would really have to find an actress who could be like she was. And I spent five months looking for an actress like Laurie Bird. And I finally said, 'Well, this is impossible. Maybe Laurie Bird can act, or at least do what you're supposed to do in front of a camera.'" Once again, Roos objected. "I was not for the Laurie Bird casting," Roos comments. "She was kind of a non-actress that Monte was just obsessed with. I mean, she gets by in the movie, but at the same time, there were twenty girls who could have really nailed that better. But he was just obsessed with her, obsessed or besotted."

The final leading role, the Mechanic, was filled by the drummer in the Beach Boys, Dennis Wilson. The band, which included Dennis's brothers Brian and Carl, secured their first recording contract and had their first hit record, "Surfin'," in 1961, when Dennis was seventeen, and they found fame with songs about surfing and cars. Despite the many popular songs they recorded about riding the waves, and several album cover photos that depicted them on the beach, walking along the shore and carrying a surfboard, Dennis was the only member of the group who could actually surf. The brothers had had a troubled home life with a tyrannical, abusive father. Whether because of childhood trauma, his early fame, or for other reasons, Dennis remained in many ways immature; he had trouble controlling his impulses and he was irresponsible. He got along very well with little kids who came along on the *Two-Lane Blacktop* shoot because he never outgrew his enjoyment of childlike play.

When hippie culture became trendy and surfing and hot rods went out of style, the Beach Boys changed their tune. They gave up singing about waves and rides and focused more on songs about romance and other topics that were not unfashionable. They also adapted their look to the new times, grew their hair long, sprouted beards and mustaches, and wore bell-bottoms and an occasional tie-dyed tunic and love beads. In their new incarnation, they achieved some popular and critical success, particularly with the 1966 single "Good Vibrations." They were trying hard to be cool.

But they were unable to completely shed their image of being square. Fred Vail, who was their first promoter and later their marketing and production manager, recalls that they had a couple of tours that bombed at this time. "People thought that they were still wearing white pants and striped shirts, and they were kind of looked upon as the establishment," Vail says. When they went on tour in 1968 with the Maharishi Mahesh Yogi, who had come to fame as the Beatles' spiritual advisor, they miscalculated, Vail says. "Nobody wanted to see the maharishi and talk about peace and love. They just wanted to hear the hits. So that wasn't a very successful tour. They canceled a bunch of dates on that one."

As the group's drummer, and its sex symbol, Dennis was accustomed to being observed. Vail remembers, "He was the star of the shows, he was the drummer, he was the center of attention, he was the one all the girls screamed for," and he was an unusually unselfconscious performer. Vail calls him "the Steve McQueen of the Beach Boys. He was Mr. Cool." He also retained a childlike curiosity, enthusiasm, and playfulness that many found endearing. But he was erratic, scatterbrained, somewhat unreliable, a womanizer, and, like Oates and Taylor, a substance abuser. When *Two-Lane* started production he was twenty-six years old and had just married Barbara Charren, the second of his five wives.

He demonstrated an appalling lack of judgment when he befriended the mass murderer Charles Manson and introduced him to the man who owned the house where the Tate murders that Manson masterminded were committed. In 1968, Wilson met Manson, and the cult leader and his followers, the Manson Family, moved into the large house Wilson was renting near the west end of Sunset Boulevard. Manson was trying to break into the music business and Wilson was willing to help him. His judgment clouded by heavy use of LSD and other drugs, Wilson admired Manson's spontaneity, and thought he had musical talent. Wilson introduced Manson to the successful record producer Terry Melcher, the son of the singer/movie star Doris Day. Manson wanted Melcher to record his songs, but the producer, after brief consideration, ultimately decided against it. Wilson also finally was realizing what a crazed, dangerous creep he'd hooked up with, and he moved out of his own house, leaving the Manson Family behind for his landlord to mop up. Furious at the music producer for dumping him, Manson got revenge by having his followers murder people at Melcher's house on Cielo Drive in Benedict Canyon, which he was renting to the film director Roman Polanski. Polanski was out of town, but on August 9, 1969, Manson's followers murdered his pregnant wife, the actor Sharon Tate, and others who were the house. The other victims were the celebrity hairdresser Jay Sebring, the coffee heiress Abigail Folger, Roman Polanski's friend Wojciech Frykowski, and Steven Parent, a teenager who had come to visit the caretaker.

Manson and his followers went on trial in Los Angeles in July 1970, just before filming began on *Two-Lane Blacktop*. The murders, and the subsequent killing of an audience member at a free concert at the Altamont Speedway in Northern California by Hells Angels who were providing security for the Rolling Stones, led to doubts about the ultimate consequences of drugs and the counterculture, helping to pave the way for a conservative backlash in the 1970s. Some fans of *Two-Lane* think the movie captures the lack of direction and randomness during this time of transition. This was the beginning of disenchantment with the hippie movement and the attendant popularity of marijuana and LSD, although drugs were still in widespread use on indie-minded movie shoots at this time. Similarly, *Two-Lane* would be a harbinger of the downfall of another form of idealistic experimentation—studio-financed auteur films that gave autonomy to the director.

∞

Meanwhile, casting had been dragging on for months, and Wilson was not hired until shortly before *Two-Lane* went into production in August 1970. Vail says that Wilson got many requests to appear on TV shows at the time because he was considered the sexy, cool Beach Boy. When he got the call to go to Cinema Center Films to try out for *Two-Lane*, Wilson telephoned Vail.

"He said, 'Why don't you go out with me to this thing? I don't know what it's about, I'm kind of nervous.'"

On the day of his appointment with Hellman and Roos at CBS Studio Center, Wilson went to pick up Vail at the Beach Boys' office on Ivar Avenue in Hollywood, above a drugstore and a smorgasbord restaurant. Vail, who has a prodigious memory for detail, recalls, "I had a big '68 Ford Thunderbird, that's when the T-Bird was a four-door, big car, so Denny got in. If you went with Denny anywhere, it didn't matter where, *you did not drive*. Denny always had to be the driver. So Denny hops in and he's driving and I'm shotgun, I'm riding in the passenger seat." About a mile or so north on the 101 Freeway, Vail recalls, "all of a sudden Denny said, 'I can't do this. I don't want to do this.' And I said, '*What?*' and he said, 'I can't go through with this. I just don't know what to do and I'm not sure I need to be doing this at this point in time.'" Vail managed to calm him down and deliver him to the interview. While Wilson went upstairs to meet with Hellman and Roos in Laughlin's offices, Vail waited for him in the lobby. After about forty minutes, Wilson came down, no longer nervous, and told Vail he thought he had done the best he could do: "I guess they're going to let me know," he said to Vail. Pondering why someone with daredevil tendencies, who raced Cobras at drag strips around Southern California, who was a seasoned performer, and who was even the focal point of Beach Boys' concerts, should get such cold feet about trying out for a part in a movie, Vail muses, "For whatever reason, he was out of his element. He was out of his safety, his comfort zone." A few days later they called Wilson to tell him he had the part.

∞

Earlier, Kurtz and Hellman had taken off across the country to scout locations. Having marked promising towns on a map, they started out on Route 66 from Los Angeles and drove through California, Arizona, New Mexico, Oklahoma, and Arkansas, ending in Tennessee. Although they began the trip on Route 66, at that time still a fairly major highway, they would film mostly on back roads because drag racers used smaller roads to avoid having other cars get in their way and to evade police. Kurtz remembers, "It was very colorful territory, but because the script was written the way it was, we realized that the only way to do the picture properly was actually to be in those various places and pick up the local color as much as possible." They stopped at each town they had mapped out, took a lot of still photographs, and assessed each practical location, such as exterior streets, and interiors of bars, cafes, and hardware stores. "Monte's then-wife [Jaclyn Hellman] went along with us because we felt that if we were approaching local people, especially local women, to be in the picture, we needed a female to do that, otherwise they would probably think we were weird," Kurtz notes. They told prospective extras and business owners that they planned to return in a few months to shoot the movie, and asked if they would like to participate. According to Kurtz, they took down "dozens and dozens" of names and phone numbers of people whom they would call on their return trip when they filmed *Two-Lane Blacktop*.

Everything seemed to be coming together. Jere Henshaw and other junior executives at Cinema Center Films were enthusiastic about the project. They gave the script to their boss, the company's chief executive, Gordon Stulberg, for final approval. According to Hellman, "We had gone on a location scouting trip and found the locations, we were most of the way through casting, and we were maybe three weeks or four weeks away from beginning to shoot when suddenly the last door was kept closed and the picture was dropped."

Jere Henshaw was the young executive who had been supporting the film, and "I think it broke his heart," says Floyd Mutrux. Mutrux and Laughlin dismiss the executive Gordon Stulberg as "an *attorney*" to explain his lack of imagination, failure to appreciate the script, and shortsightedness in deciding not to produce the film. "Gordon Stulberg didn't know what a car was and didn't want to make it," Mutrux says.

Despite the disappointment, the filmmakers were sanguine. They could take their movie someplace else to make it. According to Hellman, "I was very happy because I thought, 'Wow!' Everybody in town had said, 'If anything ever happens at Cinema Center, *please* bring it to us. We really want to do that picture,' and I thought, 'Well, we're going to have no problem at all.'" But when he and Laughlin pitched the project to executives at other studios, they were not enthusiastic. They thought Hellman was lowballing the budget. They told the filmmakers that the movie would be more expensive than they had previously thought. They said shooting so many scenes of people in a car would make the movie look too static. They said they had thought Hellman was going to cast a star like Elliott Gould.

The filmmakers began to fiddle with the budget and figure out how to do things more cheaply, hoping to make the project more attractive to studios. They laid some people off, including Billy Kincheloe, who had been advising Wurlitzer on the script. "Nobody liked it, so they were cutting back, trying to figure out ways to shave money to make it all work," Kincheloe observes. With the film in limbo and Laughlin and Hellman approaching other studios, some of the crew, including the production manager, began to jump ship. Sam Shepard, who had agreed to play the Driver, dropped out of the project because of the delay; he did not want to miss the birth of his child. Laughlin and Hellman were somewhat secretive about their unsuccessful efforts to find financing for *Two-Lane*, Kincheloe recalls. He remembers that they were indirect when they told him, "The film is kind of going on hiatus, and it's being perhaps bought out by somebody else and when we get ready to do it we'll bring you back," but he didn't hear from them again. He understands their reticence. "Some of that stuff I think they wanted to keep hush-hush so as not to scare anybody off." The filmmakers' mood changed from optimistic to discouraged. Their prospects had become bleak.

# 3

# A Jump Start

Like other Hollywood studios at the time, Universal had been losing money on movies that failed to connect with young audiences. Universal was so out of touch that it was releasing some feature films targeted to the youth market that were made from failed television shows. In May of 1967, on the eve of the Summer of Love, it released *Tammy and the Millionaire* starring Debbie Watson, composed of episodes from a TV show that aired for one season. Even worse, the studio promoted it with a poster warning: "Snooty Debutante! Wild Mountaineers! Uppity Millionaire!" The last in a tired series about a teenager that had begun in 1957 with *Tammy and the Bachelor* with Debbie Reynolds in the lead role, the film had little appeal. The same year, exploiting a TV show that didn't even make it on the air, Universal put out *The Perils of Pauline*, and touted the heroine as a "Rebellion Girl" on the poster. Starring crooner Pat Boone, the movie was a dud made from a pilot that didn't find a network or a sponsor. Universal's biggest movie of 1969, the bloated musical *Sweet Charity* starring Shirley MacLaine, cost $20 million to make but brought in only $8 million at the box office. Executives were perplexed because, in the past, Americans had regularly gone to their neighborhood theaters to view whatever the studios decided to present to them. No longer.

Meanwhile, New Hollywood films, which were hipper, more experimental, and more personal, were attracting acclaim and substantial audiences. *Bonnie and Clyde* (1967), *The Graduate* (1967), and *Midnight Cowboy* (1969) were groundbreaking movies that appealed to young viewers and did well at the box office. *Easy Rider*, the actor/director Dennis Hopper's 1969 film about hippie motorcyclists speeding across the country to a pounding rock 'n' roll score, cost $360,000 and grossed $41.7 million in the US. According to Daniel Selznick, who got a job reading scripts at Universal at about this time, "I think people have yet to realize and put into context how the success of *Easy Rider* shook the film industry. It was such an electric shock. They were asking, 'Who is this guy, Dennis Hopper? Is there a whole group of people now taking LSD, or heroin, or Christ knows what?' All the senior executives in the studios around town were saying, 'Are we losing the audience? Is there something going on in the younger generation that we don't connect to?'"

Hollywood studios had started to hire executives who were tuned in to the counterculture and to the innovative new directors and the French New Wave filmmakers who influenced them. Their job was to make movies targeted to youthful audiences. Universal was not the first studio to embrace, or at least grudgingly accept, American auteurs or counterculture filmmakers, but it was one of the stodgiest. Bert Schneider and Bob Rafelson, producers of *Easy Rider*, had teamed with Schneider's friend Steve Blauner to form BBS Productions with the aim of empowering filmmakers to work without interference. Even the name of their company, an abbreviation for Bert, Bob, and Steve, thumbed its nose at the establishment and signaled a departure from the conventional ways of conducting business, specifically the tradition of using more formal surnames instead of first names to name a production company. At Warner Bros., John Calley marginalized producers to give directors more freedom; he made deals with innovative young filmmakers and let them produce their own movies.

Calley didn't court young directors exclusively; he initially went after a legend. While dismissive of Hollywood hacks for hire who turned out bland studio fare, the new crop of filmmakers and executives revered the great directors of classic films. Brian De Palma emulated Alfred Hitchcock, Peter Bogdanovich lionized Howard Hawks. Orson Welles was put on a pedestal. Calley relates an anecdote that illustrates how much free rein executives were willing to extend to gifted filmmakers (and belies the conventional wisdom that Orson Welles was still trying to make movies but that the Hollywood studios shut the door on him).

The two knew each other well; Calley had given Welles a role in a film he had produced, *Catch-22* (1970), and Welles had stayed at Calley's house. The producer observed that the director had become cynical because he would never live up to his masterpiece, *Citizen Kane*, which he had made back in 1941. "When I took over the Warners' job, the first thing I did was call," Calley says, to ask Welles to come to Los Angeles to talk. Calley remembers he told him, "'Like most humans, I love your work, I think you're a genius, so I will make any picture that you want.' He had three projects he wanted to do. He was doing *Don Quixote*, which he'd been shooting for about 300 years in Europe with some old Italian guy, he had something he had not finished, a film called *Dead Calm*, which was later made with Nicole [Kidman] and Phil Noyce directed it, and that was shot with Jeanne Moreau, who was my lady friend at that time, and Larry Harvey. And he had never finished it, it was all sitting there. And there was another one called something about the wind [*The Other Side of the Wind*]. Bogdanovich was involved in it and John Huston was involved in it. And he mostly talked about not being able to finish these amazing things he wanted to do.

"So I said to him, 'Orson, you've got three projects.' He said 'Yes, and I don't think they'll ever be made.' I said, 'Why don't you do them? Make any one that you want.' I said, 'Let's start doing *Dead Calm*.'" Welles replied that he couldn't make *Dead Calm* because his dream project was *Don Quixote* and he wanted to finish it before Arthur Hiller's then-forthcoming screen musical *Man of La Mancha* was released so that the two films could be compared. Calley continues, "I said, 'Orson, when I tell you that I'd like to do *Dead Calm* I don't mean first. I don't give a shit. Do whatever you want, and do the wind thing, so there are three pictures.' And he started to cry a little bit. He said, 'I can't tell you how long I've been waiting for this conversation.' I said 'Well, sort it all out, and we'll make it all work.' And he said, 'Great.' He never called me back. Ever.

"And then a month or two later I saw him on the Johnny Carson show, and Carson was saying, 'Orson, I can't believe it'—I mean, this is when he was doing roasts and all that shit for Dean Martin, and wine commercials." Carson told his guest that he didn't understand why Welles, the great American director of the masterpiece *Citizen Kane*, wasn't making movies. Calley remembers that he heard Welles reply, "'Well, you know, Johnny, it's a small community and they closed ranks. William Randolph Hearst was offended and I've been blacklisted ever since.'" Meanwhile, he was shooting a pilot for a television show starring Lucille Ball. Calley muses, "It's one way to deal with that kind of anxiety—you're blacklisted. It's heroic, it's against the system, you're fighting the assholes who we all know can't be beaten, and it's just bullshit. And interestingly enough, there was a wonderful book written by an English actor about Orson, and he wanted to talk to me about Orson, and I told him the story. And he was astonished by it and wouldn't put it in the book."

∞

Calley's boss turned all of production over to his unit at Warners and gave him wide latitude. But the button-down corporate culture at Universal did not easily accommodate bare feet and love beads in the corridors of the Black Tower. The middle-aged executives did not appreciate cutting-edge filmmaking; it was a case of co-opting it to stay competitive. Lew Wasserman and his colleagues thought the new movies were in poor taste. The top brass would keep young filmmakers at arm's length and merely tolerate them, giving the impression that they secretly hoped their films would bomb and prove their elders right. They had been in the business of making films for the whole family, or in more recent years, at least little kids, squares, and adults. Smaller studios, such as American International Pictures (AIP) and Roger Corman's company, made exploitation pictures about drag racers and motorcyclists, juvenile delinquents, monsters, dope fiends, Martians running amok, and teenagers enjoying all the activities their parents warned them against. These pictures were made on the cheap and didn't need to do much business to make a profit; the big studios gladly ceded this market niche to smaller production companies.

Universal executives found New Hollywood films, such as *Midnight Cowboy*, *M\*A\*S\*H\**, and *Five Easy Pieces*, all released in 1970, equally distasteful. They considered the subject matter subversive, the dialogue dirty, the actors unattractive, the characters unappealing, and the plots mystifying or unsatisfying. These movies did not reflect the image of the company the higher-ups wished to project to the public. The studio was comfortable running a profitable operation making television shows for the three networks (ABC, CBS, and NBC) that appealed to middle-of-the-road viewers, shows that were not risky or controversial.

Universal had "built a huge, black tower in a community called 'Universal City.' They called it 'Universal City' to make sure everybody knew where it was," says Daniel Selznick, who worked for the company at the time. Lew Wasserman, a tall, imposing, autocratic former agent, was the chief executive officer of Music Corporation of America (MCA), which owned Universal. He ran the company with an iron fist, Selznick recalls, and ruled through intimidation. The tower reflected the studio's atmosphere at that time, he says, and "people were a little frightened of the Black Tower. It kind of symbolized Lew in a way, and the cold reserve and authority that he brought to that position."

To set up and run a new youth unit, Universal executives chose Ned Tanen. In 1966, they had hired him to start a record division, Uni Records, to appeal to young people. Although they gave Tanen only a small budget, he signed Strawberry Alarm Clock, Hugh Masakela, Elton John, Bill Cosby, and other acts, capturing "a real piece of the market, because he had ears for the youth market," according to Selznick. When they offered Tanen the job of film production executive, he told them he didn't like to read scripts. So Dr. Jules Stein, chairman of MCA, asked Selznick to join what would be called the Ned Tanen Unit, to read screenplays. Selznick had grown up in Hollywood, had learned about film from his father, David O. Selznick, and his grandfather, Louis B. Mayer, and was well-connected in the film business. He was literate and didn't mind reading scripts; he had been a journalist after college. As he recalls, Stein told him, "We're planning to create a new unit within Universal to make pictures for a younger audience and we're putting it together with a guy named Ned Tanen. The two of you are going to run this unit—no interference—and you're going to decide what you want to make. All the pictures ideally should be under a million dollars."

Tanen, according to Selznick, was sharp and funny, but accustomed to working in the record industry, "where the music tracks are three minutes long and then you listen to the next track." Selznick would read some fifteen scripts each weekend, but Tanen rarely had the concentration or inclination to read even one. Tanen, Selznick remembers, would ask, "'Danny, remind me, what was the script about again? I read it so quickly.' He hadn't read it at all." So, Tanen had a "fascinating attention span that only permitted him to focus for sixty seconds on each situation, and the phone lines were ringing all the time."

Both men were in their early thirties at the time. Selznick observes they were an odd combination; the hip, street-smart, whiz kid from the music industry and the literary, conservatively dressed descendant of Hollywood royalty. "Ned always looked at me as this straight guy from Harvard University who hadn't been exposed to the other side of America," Selznick recalls. "I thought it was a fascinating idea from the point of view of Universal's management to create this unit with two guys—sort of a hippie, Ned was a self-styled hippie and wore cowboy boots, and me in my Brooks Brothers suit—and we could presumably turn out some very interesting pictures."

Tanen was given the title of vice president and an office on the fourteenth floor of the Black Tower, the same as Wasserman's, conferring considerable status on him. Selznick remembers he asked Tanen, "'Do I have a title?' He said, 'No, you don't have a title. You don't need a title. People are going to return your calls. When they hear your last name they'll return your calls.'" Selznick's office was on the eleventh floor. They would sometimes meet filmmakers in the studio commissary, which they felt was less intimidating than their offices. To lure cutting-edge filmmakers, the Tanen Unit gave them unprecedented freedom—final cut and 50 percent of the profits—as long as they worked for scale and brought their film in for $1 million or slightly more. Selznick says he thought Tanen rather radical and daring in his absolute support for filmmakers. "Of course, they gave us their scripts, and we could comment on them, but Ned was very careful to say, 'Danny, I know you'd love to give some script notes. You can give script notes before the shooting starts, but we've really got to give these people final cut.'" Selznick thought they should play a more paternal and supervisory role, advising and guiding the filmmakers, and curbing their more impulsive, uncommercial, and potentially self-destructive tendencies. When reading scripts and viewing first cuts, Selznick always kept the audience in mind and what would please and displease them. But, he recalls, "Ned kept saying, 'Well, if they turn to us for help then we'll provide it, but we mustn't interfere.'" Tanen felt that they should choose gifted filmmakers and let them realize their visions.

Some established, well-known directors approached them with projects that Tanen and Selznick turned down because they wanted to foster emerging directors. This generated some ill will in Hollywood, according to Selznick. The first director they made a deal with was Frank Perry. Selznick had known him in New York and admired his first movie, *David and Lisa* (1962), which was much talked about at the time. Perry had a new project called *Diary of a Mad Housewife*, and Selznick thought it was interesting, fresh, and funny. He told Tanen about it. Tanen agreed, they made the film, it turned out to be a little gem, and it made a small profit. Carrie Snodgress even won an Oscar nomination for Best Actress for her performance in the film. The studio brass, Selznick remembers, said, "'These guys really know what they're doing.' So we got it rolling, and then I became completely swamped because the word got out that we were allowed to give 50 percent of the profits to these filmmakers if they could work for scale. Completely unprecedented in the business."

The next project was suggested by Dr. Jules Stein's daughter Jean, who was a friend of Dennis Hopper's. She told her father that Hopper had a new project called *The Last Movie*, and Stein asked Tanen and Selznick to meet with the filmmaker. It would be Hopper's follow-up film to *Easy Rider*, so Tanen and Selznick thought it sounded like a good bet; they gave it the green light. However, the unsupervised production went out of control. Hopper was a loose cannon, and he was shooting his movie on another continent with no one to rein him in. Selznick remembers, "Apparently they were smoking pot 11,000 miles up in the Peruvian mountains. Ned said, 'Do you want to go there?' and I said, 'Look, Ned, I don't smoke pot, I'm terribly square. No point in sending me to Peru.'" But as the production spiraled out of control, Tanen wound up sending an auditor, Reg Bisgrove, who describes himself as "the guy Ned chose to go on these shoots that weren't normal" because the filmmakers were taking drugs. According to Bisgrove, "I had to go down to South America because the girl who was handling the money ran off with one of the locals. All she left me was an adding machine and tapes."

When Hopper finished the film and showed it to them, Selznick says he told him that the ending didn't work. At the conclusion, Hopper's character was crucified by the community. "So you're thinking of Christ. And I said, 'Dennis, it's going to be very moving.' He said, 'I want to come down off the cross afterwards and tell the audience that I've just been an extra in a movie.' And I said, 'No, Dennis, please, you have to die on the cross.' And he said, 'No,

Danny, I'm not dying on the cross.' So, in my opinion, if he'd died on the cross it would have been a more moving picture, but he didn't want to die on the cross."

The erratic film's problems went beyond Dennis Hopper's character rising from the dead. In the finished picture, released in 1971, Hopper runs from pursuers and, apparently mortally wounded, assumes the crucifixion position, lying on his back in the dirt. We wonder if he is dead, but not for long before he gets up. He repeats this scene several times. In one of the shots he gets up and makes faces at the camera. But even if he had continued to play dead, that would not have saved the film, which is a real turkey. It is striking for a studio film, because it looks exactly like an experimental film, albeit with a bigger budget and some stunning views of the Andes. The movie doesn't cohere. Lacking a compelling storyline, the film jumps abruptly between unrelated— and sometimes incomprehensible—scenes. Hopper throws in some monkey wrenches, such as the lettering "Scene Missing" against a white background, and a clapboard at the beginning of a scene. Critics excoriated the film and audiences didn't like it either.

With a flop under their belts, Tanen and Selznick decided they'd have to choose their next project carefully. Tanen admired Monte Hellman and told Selznick to gather up all of his films. Selznick said, "Monte? Monte who?" Tanen replied, "Jesus, Danny I thought you were up to date on all that." Selznick suggested instead that a Czech director he knew of ought to make their third movie—Milos Forman, who had directed *Loves of a Blonde* (1966). Forman proposed a project about teenagers who run away from a town, and their parents who are left behind. Called *Taking Off*, it would star Buck Henry and Lynn Carlin, and it would be Forman's first American movie. *Taking Off*, Selznick remembers, opened in art houses in 1971 "and it really didn't do any business. It did not take off."

Now that they had two flops and a single success, they realized they would have to proceed with even more caution. Selznick knew Peter Fonda slightly from childhood because he had taken acting classes with Peter's sister, Jane. Fonda told Selznick that he wanted to direct a picture with a wonderful script by Alan Sharp: after wandering for seven years, a cowboy returns home. Fonda would play the cowboy, Verna Bloom would co-star, and Warren Oates would play a third part. Unlike his friend Dennis Hopper, with whom he had co-starred in *Easy Rider*, Fonda told Selznick, "I know what I'm doing and I'm not going to be smoking pot in the Peruvian hills." Fonda may not have been smoking dope in Peru, but the auditor Reg Bisgrove was dispatched once again and he says this shoot was even more out of control than *The Last Movie*. According to Bisgrove, Fonda and his pal Dennis Hopper got loaded and shot out the lights in a Native American area of Santa Fe, New Mexico. When the police were called in, the pair wanted to shoot it out with the law. After calming down Fonda and Hopper and placating the cops, Bisgrove recalls, "I was made an honorary captain" in the Santa Fe Police Department.

Just a few months after they green lighted this film, titled *The Hired Hand*, Selznick remembers, "Monte Hellman comes in and he's so lean. I said, 'Monte, are you eating now?' The guy looks like he's never eating. And then I met him socially and he had this really sweet girlfriend who didn't look more than seventeen or eighteen, called Laurie Bird." Selznick says he thought Hellman had a spiritual quality, almost like a monk. "I asked Ned at one point, I said, 'Do you think Monte's on drugs?' And Ned said, 'Of course he's on drugs.' He said, 'But you know a lot of artists are on drugs, Danny, you probably don't realize it.'" In Hellman's case, Tanen was off the mark. Since Hellman was a hippie who made artistic films, and since he sometimes projected an ethereal quality reminiscent of potheads, Tanen incorrectly assumed that the director was usually stoned. In fact, Hellman did not take many drugs or consume much alcohol. Laughlin remembers, "By the time I met him, he was about health food and those musty restaurants." *Two-Lane*'s publicist, Beverly Walker, agrees that "Monte was a health-food 'nut' who alienated or irritated people by telling them what he thought of the food on their plate." Additionally, she adds, "He is much too afraid of losing control to have done much in the way of trying drugs."

Hellman gave Tanen and Selznick the script for *Two-Lane Blacktop*. "I didn't perceive any weaknesses in the script as it was written," Selznick says. "I thought it was really very good, and Tanen was a huge supporter of Monte's." Hellman told them that James Taylor, who would star, was willing to work for scale. Another enticement, Selznick says, was "there was a leading role for this absolutely wonderful, wonderful American actor named Warren Oates," whom he and Tanen knew and admired from *The Hired Hand*. With Oates and Taylor pitted against each other in a race, Selznick and Tanen envisioned a terrific movie. "We were really quite elated about putting that movie into production," Selznick recalls.

To negotiate with Hellman, according to Selznick, Tanen put the brakes on his customary breakneck speed. Almost always in a rush, his mind on overdrive, making decisions with lightning speed, and juggling a dizzying number of phone calls and tasks simultaneously, Tanen reduced his hectic pace to deal with Hellman. Hellman, while no slowpoke, is a thoughtful man who moves and speaks at an unhurried pace. "I think back," Selznick says, "and think about Ned slowing down his speech and accepting that having loved Monte Hellman's work he then had to interface with Monte Hellman. I think Monte's a poet. He's a poet, and Ned was a shark. He just said, 'OK, listen, I see what the guy is and he's really special and I love him and that's the way we operate, Danny. I mean, you love Milos Forman, I love Monte Hellman, let's hope they both go on to more successful pictures.'"

However, Tanen was still impatient with others, and he had an explosive temper. He would become particularly annoyed with Michael Laughlin, who is accustomed to gracious living and is constitutionally unhurried. Selznick describes Laughlin as "this very lean figure with a Lincolnesque profile, who'd sit way back in a chair slightly stiffly and try to listen to everybody, and once in a while he'd make a comment." To Selznick, Laughlin appeared to inhabit a separate planet from Hellman. "He just seemed odd casting for the people he was working with," Selznick says. Tanen, with his limited attention span, had little patience for the producer, who is a gifted storyteller and can spin out his tales.

Tanen kept a round leather container of pencils on his desk. When he was angry, he would take a pencil out of its container, crack it in two, and hurl the pieces into the wastebasket. This violence to pencils intimidated visitors. Selznick explains, "Say you're sitting in an office and watching a guy break pencils. It's like, 'Oh, Christ, he could break my neck.'" People who knew Tanen well recognized the danger sign leading up to his pencil breaking, and would leave his office before his temper escalated. According to Selznick, "He had this very distinctive scowl, Ned, so if anybody knew him and saw the scowl coming on his face, they should have learned to get out of the office before the scowl turned into something fiercer." Laughlin, however, was not sufficiently acquainted with the executive to heed the warning scowl. One day, Selznick remembers, Laughlin was sitting in Tanen's office and "raised some picayune point, really. I mean, it was not really worth bringing up at that meeting." As Selznick and Laughlin recall, Tanen responded by taking a pencil out of his container and throwing it at Laughlin, hitting him in the face. "Tanen," according to Selznick, "was so annoyed. I mean, basically Ned was saying to him in so many words, 'I like Monte Hellman. I think he's really sharp. I'm making this picture with this guy because I believe in Monte Hellman, and he's dragged you in with him so I have to tolerate you, but there's a limit to how much I can tolerate.' That was the subtext of it." Afterward, Selznick says, Tanen told Selznick to take all future meetings with Laughlin because he had no patience for him.

Selznick, however, developed affection for Laughlin once he got to know him better. Like Leslie Caron, Selznick observed that Laughlin had good taste, and excellent ideas for projects, but lacked follow-through. "Growing up in Hollywood I didn't exactly have a normal childhood. I mean, if your mother's father was Louis B. Mayer and your father is David O. Selznick, you can't call that a normal childhood. And I remember my childhood now, and I'm still kind of doing second takes and third takes of all the things that I witnessed, but you see people like Laughlin, and they sort of come and go because they don't have that sort of aggressive push that you need to survive in the industry. You know that they're going to go on to something else, literary pursuits or something."

∞

Satisfied with the script, director, and cast, Tanen and Selznick were almost ready to give *Two-Lane Blacktop* the green light. But other executives in the production department had reservations, Gary Kurtz remembers. "We had decided before we started shooting that because there was so little money and time, that we would have to shoot pretty much in the Scandinavian Dogme style," which hadn't been formulated yet. In 1995, in reaction to technology- and-effects-driven big-budget Hollywood films, the directors Lars von Trier and Thomas Vinterberg came up with Dogme 95, a naturalistic approach to filmmaking. Dogme rules called for filming on location with no added props, no added sound or music, handheld cameras, and natural lighting, among other specifications. Also, the film had to be shot on color film and be set in the period of time when it was made.

*Two-Lane Blacktop* conformed to several of these Dogme criteria, Kurtz notes. The filmmakers thought that shooting in sequence would help the amateur actors with their character development. They didn't use sets, and often used natural light. Hellman insisted on using only source music, and the movie took place in the present.

This was not the way Hollywood made films in those days. Universal executives didn't think the filmmakers should shoot on the road while moving from location to location, and told them nobody had ever done that successfully. Kurtz says, "The studio was very uncomfortable with the idea of moving locations every single night, or every other night in some cases, and they wanted us to shoot the whole film in Southern California and just pretend it was across the country, which was a ridiculous idea. But we talked them out of that. Usually production people's first argument is, 'Well, there are no cover sets. What happens if it rains?' And so I told them if it actually rained then we would shoot in the rain and we'd make it work for the story because we were shooting in sequence, pretty much. I think 99 percent of it was shot in actual sequence as far as the story takes place. And because of that the weather isn't that much of a problem because you can do a scene in the rain and then the next scene can be after the rain and it's in the right order, so it's not jarring." (The problem the studio brass anticipated actually came to pass. When the film company was shooting in the rain in Boswell, Oklahoma, it stopped suddenly and the filmmakers had to create showers for a couple of days for coverage, or to film the scenes they'd shot in the rain from different angles.)

Tanen and other executives also doubted that the film company could shoot the movie in the eight weeks the filmmakers had projected. The studio made up its own schedule and estimated the picture would take ten-and-a-half weeks to shoot just in California, without going across the country, which would take even longer. Of course, Universal was accustomed to making studio movies, and Hellman and Kurtz were used to making Roger Corman movies. Kurtz finally convinced them that they would save time by crossing the country because they could take advantage of locations such as a drag racing track near Memphis.

Finally, executives feared that the filmmakers' appearances could cause problems in the Deep South, Kurtz recalls. "They said, 'You guys look like hippies. The long hair and all of this and that might not go down so well in Arkansas and Mississippi.'" Again, the executives had a point. Craig Pinkard, who worked as a driver on *Two-Lane*, says filmmakers were routinely hassled in some parts of the country in those days. "There are always idiots everywhere, especially back then when we did a lot of stuff in the rural parts of Texas. There were always these cowboy types that would think they were something, and they were just dumb yokels that would try, because we were outside movie people, they'd try to pull some stuff that didn't fly, but they always tried." Kurtz assured the executives that the film company could handle it. As it turned out, they did become threatened at gunpoint by some angry residents in Boswell, Oklahoma (after they had used up the little town's water supply to make fake rain for cover shots), but they left town quickly and lived to tell the tale.

With these points settled, Universal offered Laughlin a contract that gave his company complete creative control, including final cut, provided that the film avoided an "X" rating, wasn't longer than an hour and fifty minutes, was delivered by March 30, 1971, and didn't exceed its budget of $900,000. Universal would reimburse Michael Laughlin Enterprises the $100,000 it had paid Corry for the script (for the chain of title to the property) and $185,000 the producer's company had paid for pre-production. Given that Hellman had been making pictures for the notoriously cheap Roger Corman for less than one-tenth of that amount, "Ned thought this was exceptionally generous," Selznick says. But Kurtz had a different viewpoint. The budget "was just barely adequate," he says. Because they were spending less than $1 million, he continues, they were permitted to pare down the crew to a minimum. Then, since this made them short-handed, crew members were allowed to do jobs that were technically the province of other unions, which was unusual for the time.

The filmmakers spent about $35,000 on cars, which was relatively high at the time. They bought two brand-new GTO The Judge models for $8,849.46. Richard Ruth, of Competition Engineering in North Hollywood, charged approximately $20,000 to build three '55 Chevys. They also had to spend about $5,000 on spare parts to take on the road.

## CINEMA CENTER FILMS
### Feature Film Budget

Title: TWO LANE BLACKTOP          Date: _____

Est. Start Photo: _____          Prod. No: _____
Est. Finish Photo: _____         Producer: Michael Laughlin
                                   Director: Monte Hellman
                                   Script Date: _____

| Schedule | Days | Actual Days |
|---|---|---|
| Studio | 3 | LOCAL |
| Location | 48 | DIST. |
| Total | 51 | |

64 TOTAL DAYS
3 - pre. prod.    - shoot & travel
44 - shoot only   5 - travel only
                  8 - sundays

| Acct. | Description | Page | BUDGET to complete | Expended at C.C.F. | | | |
|---|---|---|---|---|---|---|---|
| 01 | Script | 2 | 1,360 | 125,216 | | | |
| 02 | Supervision-Direction | 2 | 125,050 | 74,525 | | | |
| 03 | Cast - Major | 2 | 81,922 | 1,500 | | | |
| 16 | A-T-L P/R Taxes & Fringe | 2 | 15,800 | 6,700 | | | |
| | TOTAL ABOVE-THE-LINE | | 224,272 | 207,941 | | | |
| 73 | Music | 3 | 25,000 | 4 | | | |
| 74 | Set Construction | 4 | 800 | | | | |
| 75 | Set Operation | 5 | 20,398 | | | | |
| 76 | Property & Set Dressing | 6 | 11,001 | | | | |
| 77 | Wardrobe | 6 | 10,301 | | | | |
| 78 | Makeup & Hairdress | 7 | 450 | | | | |
| 79 | Electrical | 7 | 33,890 | | | | |
| 80 | Camera | 8 | 72,946 | | | | |
| 81 | Sound | 9 | 33,632 | | | | |
| 82 | Studio Transportation | 9 | 1,000 | 1,185 | | | |
| 83 | Special Equip. & Animals | 10 | 14,405 | 32,806 | | | |
| 84 | Location Transportation | 11 | 97,015 | | | | |
| 85 | Location | 12 | 110,272 | 7,780 | | | |
| 86 | Special Effects | 13 | 2,168 | | | | |
| 87 | Miniatures | 13 | | | | | |
| 88 | Process Photography | 13 | | | | | |
| 89 | Trick or Matte Shots | 13 | | | | | |
| 90 | Stock Shots | 14 | | | | | |
| 91 | Film | 14 | 21,753 | | | | |
| 92 | Laboratory | 14 | 42,560 | | | | |
| 93 | Opt. Inserts, Titles, Trailers | 15 | 3,000 | | | | |
| 94 | Editorial | 15 | 28,220 | 1,540 | | | |
| 95 | Production Staff | 16 | 45,939 | 20,430 | | | |
| 96 | Tests | 16 | 8,000 | 8,150 | | | |
| 97 | General Production Expense | 16 | 67,784 | 4,126 | | | |
| 98 | Fees | 17 | | 1,900 | | | |
| 99 | Cast-Other | 17 | 27,184 | | | | |
| | TOTAL BELOW-THE-LINE | | 668,619 | 77,921 | | | |
| | TOTAL BUDGET | | 892,891 | 285,862 | | | |
| | CTF ADMINISTRATION | | | | | | |
| | TOTAL NEGATIVE COSTS | | | | | | |

Production Manager: _____          Producer: _____

Estimator: _____                    President, CCF: _____

Director of Finance: _____

A budget compiled by Gary Kurtz, who signed it as "Estimator." Tanen thought he was being magnanimous in giving Hellman a budget exponentially larger than he'd had on Roger Corman films. But the filmmakers found it skimpy for what they had to accomplish. The budget breaks down what the filmmakers spent when the project was at Cinema Center Films before that studio dumped it, and what they spent at Universal Studios to complete it. (Image courtesy of Michael S. Laughlin Enterprises)

The script was proportionately expensive; approximately $126,500 for the original and the rewrite. But the stars and the director worked for scale. Budget items that were unusually low were set construction ($800), since they shot on location and didn't build any sets, and makeup and hairdressing ($450), since the filmmakers got concessions from the union to forego a hair stylist and makeup artist. Laurie Bird, Dennis Wilson, and James Taylor did go to hairdresser-to-the-stars Carrie White on Brighton Way in Beverly Hills (White coiffed celebrities such as Elizabeth Taylor, Elvis Presley, and Ann-Margret).

Wardrobe expenses were $8,884; they managed without a costume designer. For the Driver's, the Mechanic's, and the Girl's costumes, they bought T-shirts and jeans at the Uniform Exchange on Melrose Avenue and London Britches in Manhattan Beach. Warren Oates needed a selection of V-neck, long-sleeved, cashmere pullovers in an array of colors for his character, whose wardrobe was based on Michael Laughlin's. Laughlin comments, "I dressed, as I do now, in jackets, ties, and suits from Savile Row. I would wear sweaters to the office. It was during the sixties and a lot of people were wearing bell-bottom trousers and looked like morons."

Product placement would help defray some costs for the low-budget movie. They made a deal with Coca-Cola, which would supply them with soft drinks for the cast and crew on the road in exchange for putting up about a dozen signs advertising Coke along the route as they shot. However, Kurtz recalls, "We never had to use them. There were too many Coke signs up all over the place, and we actually took some down because it looked silly."

∞

Since Dennis Wilson was hired at the last minute, his contract with Universal was dated August 7, 1970, just days before he was to start on August 12. Universal mailed the contract to Wilson, who could be absentminded and irresponsible, and he didn't sign it immediately. Two months later, the film having already wrapped by this time, Lawrence Jacobson, a lawyer for Universal, sent a reminder to Wilson in legalese, asking him to sign the damn contract already. In November, Jacobson sent the contract to Laughlin, hoping he could persuade Wilson to sign it. On January 7, 1971, an exasperated Jacobson wrote an irate letter to Laughlin regarding the flaky Wilson, who still hadn't gotten around to signing his contract.

Jacobson says he needn't have made such a fuss; he was a green young lawyer who didn't know that actors habitually signed off on deal memos, which were considered good enough to start production, and routinely put off signing their contracts. When he found out about this practice, he asked his boss what would happen if the actor reneged, since a deal memo wasn't a binding contract. His boss told him that if an actor reneged on a deal memo, that actor would never work in Hollywood again. This system worked because movies were made by a handful of studios, and if an actor screwed one studio, no other studio would touch him. All that changed in the early 1990s, when Kim Basinger backed out of an agreement, based on a deal memo, to appear in the movie *Boxing Helena*. By then, so many independent production companies were making movies that actors were no longer fearful of being unemployable if they reneged on an agreement, and contracts became important.

Jacobson says that in 1970, "I was the youngest lawyer on the legal staff, which meant that if it was really important, I didn't get to do it." But he paid attention to what his senior colleagues were doing. He remembers them talking about *Two-Lane Blacktop*. "It was an indie production, fairly low budget, 'Hey, these guys look like they might have some creative talent. Let's give them a couple of bucks and see what they can do.' The female lead, and I think her name was Laurie Bird, I remember there was some question that they wanted to absolutely confirm that she was eighteen or older because my recollection is there was a nude scene, or at least as close as you got to a nude scene back then, and Universal was absolutely adamant that there was no way on earth, or the universe for that matter, that Universal was going to have a nude scene with someone who was a minor. It wasn't going to happen. So they wanted to double-check and make sure" that Bird was eighteen, Jacobson says. Although he wasn't involved in the matter, "I was just told that was something they were concerned about."

Wurlitzer's script contains a few nude scenes and some explicit sex. And Bird was only seventeen. But the concerns never made their way to the producers. Gary Kurtz and Michael Laughlin say nobody from Universal ever asked them to make sure Bird was eighteen before they shot her unclothed. (Studios weren't actually all that strict about preventing even much younger girls from performing without clothes. In 1978, Paramount put out *Pretty Baby*, in which twelve-year-old Brooke Shields had some nude scenes in her role as a child prostitute.) As it turned out, Hellman filmed one scene of Bird skinny-dipping, but he told Kurtz he left it out of the movie because it brought the action to a halt. And Hellman didn't even shoot the rest of the nudity and sex in the script. In general, Wurlitzer's writing contains more explicit sex than Hellman's films, and the director would have been going against his sensibility and style if he had included the scenes as written. Also, they would have detracted from the romantic, almost innocent quality of the relationship between the Girl and the Driver.

Legally, Bird's guardian should have signed off on the scene where, frustrated that she can't get the hang of the Chevy's gearshift, she says, "Fuck it." Carrie Fisher, who also was seventeen when she acted in her first film, *Shampoo*, a few years later, was called upon to use the same obscenity and the producer made a real effort to talk her mother into allowing her to do it. Fisher's mother, Debbie Reynolds, had been America's Sweetheart and had starred in such wholesome films as *Tammy and the Bachelor*. Fisher recalls that in the script for *Shampoo*, "I had to say, 'You wanna fuck?' and she wanted me to say 'screw.' She didn't want me to say a really bad word." So, the film's star and producer, Warren Beatty, went to the house in Beverly Hills where the mother and daughter were staying to ask Reynolds's permission to let Fisher use the stronger language. "Warren came over and there was a piano downstairs, and he's a wonderful pianist, which I didn't know," Fisher recalls. To win over the conservative Reynolds, after Beatty played the piano for her, "he flirted with my mother," Fisher remembers, and "she agreed to it." Laurie Bird's father, however, was a staunch Catholic who would not have been swayed by such tactics.

Bird signed a contract that specified her salary as $1,000 per week. On the contract, she gave her address as her agent's office, CMA (Creative Management Associates) in Beverly Hills. However, on her tax withholding form, she gave her address as 6310 Heather Drive, a small residential street in the hills just below the Hollywood sign. Monte Hellman's wife, Jaclyn Hellman, gave the same home address on her contract to appear as a day player for $120 per day.

The producer inserted a clause about Jaclyn Hellman in her husband's employment agreement with Michael Laughlin Enterprises: "We agree to supply you with roundtrip transportation for your wife (first class and by air, if available) in the event that she accompanies you to location, provided however, if in our sole discretion the exigencies of our production schedule are such that we request you either not to bring your wife onto location, or in the event that she is already there, to return your wife from the location to your home." Laughlin notes that Jaclyn Hellman, the movie's dialogue coach, taught the novice actors exercises, which were intended to help them relax and get in touch with their emotions, for a few weeks before filming began. "Monte's wife worked with the actors in a kind of bullshitty way, doing exercises with them. And these were first-time actors, so it wasn't a terrible idea." But, he says, he added the clause giving him the right to send Jaclyn home at his discretion because "She was not particularly trustworthy and stable." Laughlin recalls the reaction of Monte Hellman and his agent, Mike Medavoy: "They were completely outraged" and "incredibly insulted." Medavoy fired off a letter asking Laughlin to change the language in the clause to make it less demeaning.

Just a few weeks before production was to begin, Bonnie Prendergast (now Bonnie Prendergast Freeman) and Walter Coblenz came onboard. Prendergast had worked as script supervisor on Michelangelo Antonioni's *Zabriskie Point* (1970), which, like *Two-Lane*, featured inexperienced actors in the lead roles.

She reminisces, "I believe that Monte Hellman hired me because I worked with Michelangelo, whose work he admired. He asked me lots of questions about how it was, working with Michelangelo." Fred Roos brought in the publicist Beverly Walker, who also had worked on *Zabriskie Point*, and who thought using untrained actors was a serious error in judgment that would damage both films.

Coblenz remembers he got the call offering him a job when he was on Mount Tamalpais near San Francisco shooting a film called *Thumb Tripping* (1972), a car-centric movie about two hitchhikers in California who accept rides from oddballs. He had interviewed for the position of first assistant director eight or nine months previously when *Two-Lane* had been at Cinema Center Films. But they had hired someone else instead. When Cinema Center dumped *Two-Lane*, the original first assistant director quit. Coblenz says he was surprised to receive the call: "Even though I didn't get the job the first time, they asked me to be both the production manager *and* first AD when it was with Universal." Coblenz hesitated, telling them he thought the two jobs would be too much work for one person. They replied that Gary Kurtz had done much of the preparation and said they would send him up to San Francisco to brief Coblenz. "Gary came up to the San Francisco area to spend the day with me going over all the particulars that had already been prepared by him, which were extensive. And then we talked about the crew. Well, they had the cameraman, they had wardrobe people, certain people already had started. So what was left for me? Well, two very important things. I said, 'You know, it's a very heavy car picture and there's a lot of action with cars and there are some safety issues that will have to be dealt with,' and so I suggested that we hire the entire grip and teamster crews who I was working with on the picture called *Thumb Tripping*. And so I brought that whole group over three weeks prior to the start of the picture, and why they called me again, I have no idea."

Laughlin says he called Coblenz again because the production manager had experience working on a big Hollywood movie, *Downhill Racer* (1969), starring Robert Redford. Hellman and Kurtz, on the other hand, had worked exclusively on small, low-budget movies. Moreover, Hellman and Kurtz, says Laughlin, "were a little sort of hippie-dippy for me," and he didn't have confidence they could keep the show on the road, on time, and on budget. Laughlin thought that Coblenz was energetic, sharp, and reliable. According to Laughlin, "Walter was the grownup."

∞

Since Sandor would be the cinematographer, and he wasn't a member of IATSE, Coblenz learned that they would need a standby cameraman who belonged to the union. He figured they could just pay somebody and leave him in LA. "But they said, 'No. The standby *has* to come with us.'" Coblenz would occasionally use him to shoot second-unit footage, but the standby cameraman, Jack Deerson, wasn't happy about it. "He said it wasn't the way he was supposed to be used, but I said that was how we were using him, and persuaded him to do it. And unfortunately, oftentimes he gets the credit for being the cinematographer, and he was not the cinematographer," Coblenz says. John Bailey, assistant cameraman on *Two-Lane*, also thinks it's a shame that Deerson gets the credit for Gregory Sandor's work. Bailey says he didn't think much of Deerson: "He was a boob."

Coblenz remembers that they had to hurry, especially to prepare the picture cars (the cars the actors are filmed in), which involved a somewhat complex task of devising rigging. Plus, they were operating on a fairly low budget. "We had to get these cars ready and we had to get these cars properly rigged so that we could mount cameras on the cars," and they had to make sure that it would all be safe, Coblenz recalls.

Gary Kurtz devised a scheme to rig the cars. On big-budget Hollywood movies, they take the wheels off a car and mount it on a very low trailer. Although this is a safe method of shooting, Kurtz says, "it means the car is a little bit higher on the horizon than it would really be, and we decided we wanted the cars to actually be on the road." Kurtz had worked on Roger Corman movies where the cars were rigged so they could be driven and filmed simultaneously. On these films they used suction cups and straps to attach the rigs to the cars, but to save time Kurtz started to weld brackets to the frame of the car underneath, so they couldn't be seen when they weren't being used. He used this method on *Two-Lane*. "Before we started, we welded these brackets and tested positions for the camera using pipe, scaffolding pipe that you would use on a building. And it worked pretty well because Monte wanted to not just mount the camera, but in some cases he wanted to be able to ride along on a kind of outboard on the passenger side outside the car, and so we set it up so we could put a little platform out there and you could sit on the pipe, and the camera operator could, too, so that you could actually move the camera, so that it wasn't just in one position. So that was quite successful. It worked fine. The local police sometimes weren't so keen because it stuck out about two feet from the car." The platform was large enough so that they could mount the camera on a normal tripod head, providing some flexibility to adjust it a little back and forth, and it wasn't locked in position.

Another advantage was increased realism. "Except for those front-angle shots, if we mounted the camera on the back three-quarters on either side, or in the middle of the back of the trunk, the actors could actually be driving. James could actually drive the car rather than pretending to drive, so it worked really well," Kurtz says.

Meanwhile, Laughlin had to decide whether to go on the road with the film company. Looking back, he remembers that it was a tough decision; in a way, he would have loved to go on the trip. But he was committed to letting Hellman try to realize his vision and did not want to interfere. He muses, "If I had gone out, I would have objected to too many things." Additionally, he says, he thought the film company was "a glum and depressed group. Not light-hearted and fun." Finally, he has always been wealthy and lived in luxury. When he married Leslie Caron, they had their honeymoon at Frenchman's Cove in Jamaica, the most expensive hotel in the world at the time. It is hard to imagine Michael Laughlin voluntarily spending a night, or being in his element, at a Holiday Inn in Durant, Oklahoma.

From outward appearances, the filmmakers would be on their own, without interference from the producer or the studio. But, once again, Tanen sent along the auditor whom he designated to monitor drug-taking, hippie filmmakers, Reg Bisgrove, to manage the money (although Hellman was not a doper, Oates, Wilson, and others would get stoned day and night). And Laughlin considered Coblenz his proxy: "Walter was my eyes and ears."

# 4

# On the Road

The opening scenes of *Two-Lane Blacktop*, of street racers milling around, getting ready to race, and taking off, were filmed in and around Los Angeles on August 12, 13, and 14 of 1970. The first day they shot on the Sunset Strip, the second day at Alameda Street and Del Amo Boulevard in Los Angeles County, and the third day at a Builders Emporium and Safeway parking lot at Soledad Canyon and White Canyon Roads in Newhall in northwestern Los Angeles County. For the crowds, they used members of the Los Angeles Street Racers Association and their leader, "Big Willie" Robinson, the one who had organized street racing downtown. Robinson, an imposing 6'6" with a proportional circumference, had been a body builder and had competed in Mr. America and Mr. Universe contests. A highly respected figure, he took charge of street racing in Los Angeles to make it safer and to promote peace among the blacks, whites, and Latinos who participated. At the time, there were no drag racing strips in Southern California. Big Willie and his group held races in the dead of night and closed down roads so passersby and motorists wouldn't stumble into a race and get hurt. Billy Kincheloe, who sometimes went to these races, remembers, "These things were clandestine events that would come about at like 1:30, 2 o'clock, 3 o'clock in the morning, and they would go down to some industrial park, and they would rope off the area, cordon it off. They'd have guards out there somewhere all looking for cops, and everybody would arrive and they would race, and then everybody would disperse." For *Two-Lane*, they staged a race for the cameras.

The film company paid the LA Street Racers $2,000 to act as extras. Gary Kurtz remembers, "I knew about the LA Street Racers because they had been in the news, and I did some research when I first talked to Monte about the project, and so we were very keen that we actually would be able to shoot that opening scene with the real street racers group. As I recall, they were very wary of having a film crew around because they didn't get along with the police very well. We had to assure them that we actually, on the evening we were filming, we were filming the setup which was in the car park at a Ralphs supermarket late at night, and we weren't actually asking them to do any street racing when the police were there, and so they were fine with that." Coblenz also recalls that the street racers were scared of getting busted and remembers persuading them. "We were saying, 'What you were doing that was illegal—tonight it's legal.' I bet a lot of things may not have been 100 percent legal, but we did them."

Although James Taylor is shown in the driver's seat as he prepares to peel out, Jay Wheatley did all of the actual racing in the '55 Chevy race car, except for the film's last shot, when Taylor is at the wheel. Taylor liked Jay very much and the actor sometimes drove with the mechanic from location to location. During the shoot, when he talked on the phone to his manager, Peter Asher, Taylor singled out Jay as someone he liked and was friendly with. Jay also endeared himself to some of the Hollywood filmmakers, and several in the film company remember him as the most interesting member. He was serious, knowledgeable, and dedicated to his job, but he also had a sense of humor. According to his brother Buck, Jay had an eclectic and playful fashion sense and would mix and match mechanic overalls with the legs rolled up, black-and-white saddle shoes, and porkpie hats or hippie headbands; other times, he would dress like a country boy in a cowboy hat, cowboy boots, blue jeans, and, in a nod to the fashion of the times, a leather wristband. Jay nearly always smoked a cigar at a time when young men customarily smoked only cigarettes or joints. "He walked to the beat of a different drummer," Buck recalls. The script supervisor, Bonnie Prendergast Freeman, remembers Jay fondly: "What a neat guy he was; not a crew member, he was on his own level as the main person tending to the show cars and helping actors with same. The most unpretentious person on the set, in my mind."

In addition to being generally personable, Wheatley was by all accounts an excellent mechanic. He was charged with keeping the three Chevys and two Pontiacs in good working order. The Chevy racing car was particularly difficult to maintain. It was built for one purpose: to go at lightning speed for a quarter mile. Richard Ruth explains: "It didn't want to just putt along," and when it was driven at normal speed down city streets, "it was a little temperamental."

Being a drag racer, Jay knew how to fix cars quickly when they broke down. Gary Kurtz says he was impressed with Jay's speed. When they were filming at a race track near Memphis, he won a race, and when the transmission broke he replaced it and had the car back on the track in half an hour. Although he took along a lot of spare parts, and Richard Ruth sent him even more when he found he needed them when he was on the road, Jay could improvise if he didn't have precisely what was needed. As Ruth recalls, "He was a good MacGyver kind of guy."

The key grip in charge of rigging the cars so they could put camera mounts on them was Chuck Record, who was very good at his job. He was also, according to the transportation coordinator Jim Thornsberry, a "character" who "burned the candle at both ends." Thornsberry says, "I loved Chuckie, but he was really a wild card." An extremely competent key grip, he was lively, mischievous, and high-spirited after work—and outgoing at all times. He is recognizable in photos taken on the shoot as the blond guy without a shirt on. At night, he would drink and take drugs with cast members, then regale the crew with his exploits the following day.

Record, according to Walter Coblenz, "had pretty good control of the people who worked for him. He made certain these rigs were on solid on the cars." The rigging on the picture cars had pipes that screwed into each other and the screws needed to be tightened with an Allen wrench so they wouldn't get loose and cause the whole contraption to fall apart. Record not only gave Allen wrenches to his grips, he passed them out to the electricians and even to Walter Coblenz. "Chuck Record gave people in the crew a wrench, and every time you'd go by it, you'd give it a little twist," Coblenz reminisces.

Record recalls that when he was hired for *Two-Lane*, he flew down from San Francisco, where he was working on *Thumb Tripping*, for an interview, got the job, then flew back. "I fell asleep on the plane, and I didn't get up when they stopped in San Francisco and I woke up in Washington," Record recalls. "I got out, I didn't know I was there, I figured I was in San Francisco. I went to look for my car where I had parked it and it wasn't there."

∞

The film company of thirty-four people, plus some family members and Monte Hellman's dog, took to the road on August 17, leaving at 9 a.m. and arriving in Needles, California, around 4 p.m. The following day, they would shoot at a Shell gasoline station on Route 66 in Needles, one of the few times they would film on the iconic highway. (The other locations on Route 66 were in downtown Flagstaff; in Two Guns, Arizona; at a Fina gas station restaurant at the junction of US 54 in New Mexico; and in San Jon, New Mexico.) The film is now a time capsule of Route 66 and smaller roads when they still had roadhouses, diners, drive-ins with jukeboxes, and service stations where attendants pumped gas and washed windshields, and where customers reached down to get bottled drinks out of horizontal coolers full of Coca-Cola, before the small businesses were razed to make way for mini-malls, monoculture, and Muzak.

On August 18, the temperature rose to a high of 120 degrees in Needles. As Richard Ruth, who had a small role as a garage mechanic, recalls, "The cars were overheating and the people were overheating. It was just a giant bad thing." First, James Taylor was having difficulty getting the race car, which was temperamental at the best of times, and not designed for unhurried city driving, or for scorching temperatures, into the gas station where the scene would be filmed. When the car was driven slowly in the blistering heat, it was uncooperative and exacted revenge on the filmmakers, knocking and bucking when it was turned off. Also, Taylor was not yet familiar with the car's gear shift and the coordination between the clutch and throttle and brake, and Jay Wheatley and Dennis Wilson were trying to teach him how to operate it. Taylor, according to Ruth, "kept lugging it, and it would buck back and forth." It would have been preposterous to show the Driver, who was supposed to be supremely competent at handling the Chevy, pull into the gas station only to have the car jerk about and make a racket. Finally, Taylor got up enough momentum to put the car in neutral and coast into place at the gas pump.

The actors did not stick to the script for the scene, Ruth remembers. "It was ad-libbed in part. I said something different every time we did it." In a line that made it into the movie, Ruth says his Thames panel truck is having transmission trouble. He came up with the line because he was actually building a Thames truck, which was an old Ford made in Great Britain, "a tiny little thing," he says. Hellman, he says, gave little direction. "As far as the car coming into the gas station, he knew what he wanted to see, but he didn't really care about it as far as any kind of lingo went."

Shooting was "good until garage mechanic's entrance," according to the script supervisor's script. Ruth and Wilson rubbed each other the wrong way. Dennis Wilson, by all accounts, was frequently stoned or drunk, and on this day, Ruth says, the drummer and some others were "Louie, Louie," high and giggling, from "smoking pot in the corner" between takes. As Wilson smoked more joints, he flubbed more lines, getting too stoned to perform properly. Ruth became progressively irritated at the delay. Ruth, a perfectionist, was in the sun, changing a tire over and over, and wanted to get the scene right, get it over with, and get out of the heat.

Still rankled over Hellman's comment that "drag racers are dirty," Ruth hadn't wanted to act in a scene but was persuaded by some friends of his who thought it would be fun to be in a movie and wanted to come along. Ruth also wanted to keep a promise to his friend Richard Cholakian that he would give his business a plug by wearing a Glendale Speed Center T-shirt. Now Ruth found that the cast and crew were mistreating his carefully crafted Chevys, slamming the doors and sitting on the fiberglass hood to take publicity photos. "I was a drag racer and I was very hot-headed kind of guy at the time," Ruth says, and the combination of the intense heat, the sight of crew members brutalizing the cars he'd painstakingly crafted, and the annoyance of Dennis Wilson getting more and more stoned, laughing, and flubbing lines so they had to do take after take, warmed Ruth up to the boiling point. "I was ready to turn the car over," he says, because Wilson wouldn't take the work seriously. "I could have strangled Dennis, and he knew it too." Finally, Ruth says, he warned Wilson. "I said, 'The next time you screw this up I'm going to pinch your head off.'" Ruth was a strong man in his youth who would make wagers, for hamburgers, that he could lift up the front ends of cars and win the bets, so a threat from him would have been menacing. But Wilson was evidently too stoned to be frightened, plus a car separated him from the angry hot-rodder. In a take that made it into the movie, after Ruth's off-screen threat, the garage mechanic looks somewhat exasperated and says that his panel truck is having transmission trouble, hardly a cause for hilarity. Wilson laughs, puzzling the viewer because it seems a peculiar response in a conversation between two auto mechanics about parts and car trouble.

Jaclyn Hellman, who was observing the proceedings, stepped in, Ruth remembers. "The only person that impressed me was Monte Hellman's wife," Ruth says, "because she could see this was going to come to blows." Ruth remembers that he wasn't alone in having a smoldering temper. "It wasn't just me being ornery, everybody, the cast, the crew, everybody was kind of sideways," so she lined everybody up against a chain link fence in the shade, had them sit down, and took them through some yoga exercises. It was Ruth's first experience with Eastern techniques to relieve stress. "It was pretty hard for a welder/hot-rodder/fabricator/let's-go-fast kind of guy to sit down and do the Ujjayi breath." But even though Jaclyn was a hippie with "giant bell-bottoms" Ruth says, "I was real impressed with her." Afterwards, he says, he was calm and so were most of the others, so they went back and finished the scene.

After shooting was completed for the day, and the temperature had dropped to about 110 degrees, Ruth and his friends who had accompanied him went back to their motel looking forward to cooling off in the pool. Ruth remembers,

"And so, we all got our swim trunks on and jumped in the pool and jumped right out because the pool was like 95 degrees."

∞

The film company next took Route 66 to Flagstaff, Arizona, where they shot downtown, on residential streets, and then on US 89 outside of town. Sometimes they shot on the road when they drove from location to location, Kurtz remembers, "and we couldn't have the production cars be in the shot, so we would have to let the camera and the picture cars go ahead so that they could shoot while the rest of the cars were behind and out of camera range until they stopped and we needed to change film or change the camera angle or something, and so it was logistically probably more difficult than most pictures like this."

Most scenes shot on the road were filmed on smaller highways, with less traffic than 66. John Bailey remembers the sight of the camera operator, Hugh Gagnier, perched precariously on the side of the car with a camera as they zipped down country roads. Gagnier, according to Bailey, "insisted on riding the camera with his eye to the eyepiece, so the key grip had to build very sturdy pipe mounts on the car." The Chevy was rigged so that the pipes slid into the chassis and were bolted on, sort of like Tinker toys, Bailey says. "We'd have the camera and then we'd have a 175-pound camera operator riding alongside it, and I thought, 'Oh my God, this is so dangerous. He's hanging out in space.' We were shooting a lot of times on narrow country roads with traffic coming in the other direction. And I used to worry so much about it, and he said, 'In case somebody moves and I have to pan correction or something with the camera.' He was very responsible and very methodical, but I also thought he was a little off his tree for doing that." Gagnier received $75 per week for "hazard pay."

Gagnier was "an old-guard, studio camera operator," according to Bailey. Prematurely white-haired, and with impeccably manicured fingernails, Gagnier belonged to a golf club in Palm Springs and, like GTO, always wore a cashmere sweater. Bailey remembers, "He showed me, he had a whole pile of these cashmere sweaters, long-sleeved sweaters, they were in all different colors." Gagnier also impressed Bailey with another collection he kept. The camera was mounted on a Worrall Geared Head, with wheels to do pan and tilt. Bailey explains, "The wheel that would do the pan on the left side here or the tilt from behind, these wheels would essentially screw into the main part of the head. This camera operator had his own wheels. He didn't keep them with the regular rental head we had because he said they could get bent and then they would kind of be out of line. And so he had his own. And he kept them in a handmade wooden box with a lid on it with his name on it. And he would come in the morning with his box, his camera would be set up on the head, and he would make a big sort of display of opening the lid, taking the wheels out, and screwing them on the head. And at the end of the day, he would take them off, put them in the box, close the box, and go home. And I had never seen anything like it. I've never seen anything like it since. But I started in the business at the very end of the old studio days, the old studio-era contract cinematographers, operators, and assistants."

The old-guard studio camera operator Gagnier admired the old-school cinematographer Gregory Sandor. "I was just starting my career at the beginning of the American New Wave," Bailey remembers. "That camera operator, he liked Greg very much because he respected that Greg was not one of these hotshot kids that wanted to shoot everything hand-held and with flares in the lens, that Greg was really a classical cinematographer." *Two-Lane Blacktop* straddled two eras, the old, tradition-bound, studio system with people under contract, and the new, more independent system where people had more freedom to make multi-picture deals with studios or jump around from studio to studio. The "above-the-line" principals on *Two-Lane* and many other Hollywood films were in general younger, more drawn to hippie dress and philosophy, and more inclined to make youth-oriented, experimental movies that reflected the counterculture. The "below-the-line" crew members were nearly all union guys highly experienced in working on more traditional Hollywood films.

"Above the line" and "below the line" are budgetary terms. For example, in a budget summary for *Two-Lane Blacktop* prepared by Gary Kurtz, he lists Script, Supervision-Direction, and Cast-Major as "above the line." They are on top of the page, separated by a line from everybody and everything else, which are labeled "below the line." So, the screenwriter, producer, director, and stars are generally considered above the line, with the rest of the participants below the line.

Those above the line tended to regard the crew, at best, as old-fashioned, by-the-book traditionalists, and at worst, reactionary, closed-minded, beer-guzzling bozos. For their part, the crew regarded those above the line as snooty, arty, inexperienced hippies who took more drugs than were good for them and didn't know what they were doing. The film company was roughly divided into above-the-line pot smokers and below-the-line beer drinkers, and they didn't mix much socially. Some described the factions as separated into divided camps. Monte Hellman, Gary Kurtz, Rudy Wurlitzer, and the stars inhabited Camp Above the Line, and most of the remainder were relegated to Camp Below the Line.

People who straddled or breached the line included Warren Oates, Jay Wheatley, Chuck Record, and Beverly Walker. Oates, by all accounts, was extraordinarily friendly and democratic. Teamster Rick Mercier, who drove the car carrier, remembers Oates as approachable. "Some actors are not very close with the crew, but this guy was." Teamster Craig Pinkard compliments Oates by describing him as "a regular guy." His daughter, Jennifer Oates, visited him on *Two-Lane* and other films, and notes that he was just as friendly, if not more so, with the crew as with the other cast members. He had no airs about him, she adds.

Jay Wheatley, according to Bonnie Prendergast Freeman, "bridged the above-the-line caste because he was so integral to the show and the actors." The publicist Beverly Walker was so well-connected she seemed to transcend the line; she became very fond of Laurie Bird, and she also became a lifelong friend of Monte Hellman's. Like Hellman, Gary Kurtz had brought along his family and his own van, and the director continually conferred with him, but Kurtz made an effort to socialize with the crew. The key grip, Chuck Record, was an extrovert; he bulldozed across the line.

In general, however, "There wasn't a whole lot of contact between the cast and the crew, let's say," Bailey remembers. According to Prendergast Freeman, the divide was more pronounced than on the previous movies she'd worked on. "To my memory, none of us were invited to the parties or gatherings with the cast and out-of-town visitors. This was different from my previous road film, *Thumb Tripping*, where the cast and crew mingled together on location." Some time after the Criterion Collection DVD of *Two-Lane Blacktop* came out, Prendergast Freeman watched it, and she remarks on Hellman's commentary: "I had to snicker at the notion that filming on the road was like a family affair. Maybe it was for him and his group, but it was always two camps, no communal picnics or gatherings, not that we cared much, that's just the way it was. Every project is different. This was just a job. No hugs after the last take in the camera was shot." Jim Thornsberry, *Two-Lane*'s transportation coordinator, worked on many Hollywood films, and he thought the divide was unusual. On most other movies, the writers, actors, and filmmakers would talk to the crew, he says. But not on *Two-Lane*. "They really didn't have much to say to any of the crew. We didn't take well to that. I mean, it didn't bother anybody, because to be real honest, nobody wanted to be in their camp."

In Gary Kurtz's view, "The shooting crew was very kind of what I'd call conventional Hollywood guys for the most part." They were, he continues, "kind of down-to-earth, working-class guys who do this work day in and day out and year after year." Kurtz, unlike Wurlitzer, Hellman, and the stars, had extensive experience doing many different below-the-line jobs on Roger Corman movies, and he mingled with the crew more than the other above-the-line participants.

The crew mostly regarded James Taylor as withdrawn, quiet, and distant. Peter Asher, Taylor's manager at the time, explains, "He always did seem like a very shy, reserved person until he got to know you, so I guess the nature of the movie set, or the whole experience or whatever, had him in his shell perhaps, a little bit. I mean, at first, when you met James, he always used to be staring at his feet. But then when you got to know him, you realized how unbelievably smart and well-read and funny and stuff he is." The crew did enjoy listening to Taylor playing his guitar and composing songs during downtime. "When we were in between takes, he'd pick on the guitar and make up songs," remembers Rick Mercier.

Jim Brubaker, who worked as a teamster on *Two-Lane* and went on to become a prominent film producer, remembers that the actors "were really amateurs." Since the actors were untrained, and since Hellman didn't instruct them on how to shape their performances or tell them what he wanted, the director sometimes called for take after take.

Bonnie Prendergast Freeman remembers, "After working with nonactors on *Zabriskie Point* it became even more clear to me that it was highly risky to place the potential success of a movie on the shoulders of unknown or untrained actors. But it was only in my thoughts; I never had a discussion with Monte about this and frankly, hoped that what I was seeing on a daily basis was going to be much more interesting when Monte cut it together." The transportation coordinator Jim Thornsberry thought Hellman, while intently focused on the film, was not a nuts-and-bolts kind of guy, and he says the transportation department, made up of experienced teamsters, worked with little supervision. The crew also regarded Hellman as aloof, someone who kept his distance. Thornsberry remembers, "He was a very quiet guy, very into the picture. Not a ton of chuckles." Thornsberry thought Hellman was "a nice man." However, he says that Hellman and Wurlitzer were unapproachable "in their own little world." He also notes that Hellman's distant manner contrasted with that of the director's English sheepdog, a rambunctious pooch that, says Thornsberry, was "totally opposite" in personality from the director.

Gary Kurtz recalls the split between the crew and Hellman. "It felt like he was from an entirely different world," he says. "Monte was kind of an erudite intellectual from a kind of hippie world. He and his wife were quite counterculture, and it was kind of a divided thing." Additionally, Kurtz, who had known Hellman for some years because he had worked on two Westerns with him, says Hellman has "always been a bit shy" and "he didn't like talking to the crew. He wasn't the kind of director who would stand up and give a little talk at the beginning of each day on what he wanted to do." Instead, Hellman would meet with Kurtz and Coblenz early in the morning and leave it up to them to organize the day's activities and to supervise the crew.

In his defense, Hellman can be open and charming when not under pressure. During the shoot, he was intently focused on making an unusual film, with inexperienced actors, on a tight budget and schedule, and he didn't have time for idle chitchat. "He's just not a chitchatty kind of guy, a small talk kind of guy," says Beverly Walker. He talked to her during the shoot and they have remained friends. He is not a snob, she says, and he was taciturn because he was absorbed in his work. She describes him as somewhat withdrawn and extremely controlled. "He's pretty warm and open, within the limitations of what his personality is, to people he likes and trusts." Hellman is much beloved by a number of younger filmmakers and he has quite a few loyal friends who have known him for years and who describe him as generous, funny, brilliant, and wonderful company.

Due to the low budget, the crew was smaller than usual. Rather than hire an extra teamster, the studio asked the auditor, Reg Bisgrove, to drive James Taylor from location to location. That didn't work out too well, since Taylor thought that Bisgrove was a slowpoke and a fuddy-duddy, and neither man enjoyed the arrangement.

"Universal asked me, because it was a low-budget movie, they wanted me to drive James Taylor, and I didn't even know who James Taylor was. I got a car from somewhere and rented it, and I drove him, but after a couple of days he thought I drove too slowly and he thought I was too straight," Bisgrove says. By the second day, Bisgrove continues, "He was so fed up, he wanted to drive. I quickly got rid of that obligation, either by his own hand or by mine." It really should have been a teamster who drove him, Bisgrove adds.

The crew helped one another in ways not permissible under union rules on usual Hollywood movies. Gary Kurtz says crew members "normally weren't supposed to do anything but their job, but we were away from Hollywood and we didn't have any union reps around, and everybody agreed to help out. So the drivers would pull cable for the electricians, and that would never happen in Hollywood, it would be just an absolute no-no." At one point or another, he adds, everybody on the crew worked as an extra. When the caterer prepared consistently inedible food and Walter Coblenz fired him, teamsters took responsibility for providing meals. Coblenz was struck by the sight of cast and crew so repelled by the unappetizing look of the food that they wouldn't even taste it. "What was happening was they were going down the line and picking up a piece of chicken, they'd look at it, and after they'd pass the line, they'd throw it in the trash." After Coblenz fired the caterer, he couldn't get an immediate replacement. He asked Jim Thornsberry, the transportation coordinator, to get food in the meantime. Thornsberry recalls that they were in a remote location, far from a city. The film company, he says, "was almost ready to rebel, and I couldn't blame them because I had to eat the same thing, we all ate the same thing, and it was horrible, and the guy was horrible, and Walter and I talked about it." Thornsberry says he took off and tracked down a restaurant, then "I came back with my station wagon full of food and it was a hit, and I remember telling Wally, 'This is the beginning and end of my catering career.'"

Since they didn't have stunt drivers, John Brumby, the driver of the bus that transported cast and crew, jackknifed a semi. Brumby would start his trips by putting a cooler filled with Coors beer next to the driver's seat. Then he'd climb in and pop the lids and drink the beer as he drove, gradually working his way through the entire cooler. In those days, cops would often wink at drivers who were a little drunk but not totally smashed, and Brumby always delivered his cargo safely. Although Brumby successfully jackknifed the semi, as Coblenz looks back on the decision to ask the hard-drinking bus driver to do something so dangerous, he says, "I did a few stupid things which I wouldn't do anymore, but I did then."

Since they didn't have a production designer or art department, the prop master would do any necessary set dressing. Driver Jim Brubaker remembers the crew's, and the transportation department's, cooperative spirit: "Everybody helped the electricians and the grips, there wasn't any, 'Oh, I don't do that because I don't belong to that union.' Everybody was getting along with everybody." In the spirit of cooperation and sharing, Coblenz even gave one of his credits to second assistant director Ken Swor, who had worked with him as a trainee on the TV series *The F.B.I.* Coblenz explains, "I gave him the assistant director credit because I was getting production manager credit, and I didn't need two credits."

∞

The publicist Beverly Walker was given a car to drive. "I had a hairy experience," she recalls. "I was taking Laurie to the set on a curvy road with a long drop-off when the passenger door swung open. I had to grab her with my right hand to prevent her tumbling out while maneuvering around a sharp curve with my left. I had learned to drive only a little more than a year earlier. I've never forgotten the near-catastrophe. She was such a trouper. She turned white as a sheet but said very little. And I don't think she ever told a soul because it was never mentioned to me."

Reg Bisgrove also had a car and Jim Thornsberry had a station wagon, but most of the crew traveled in a Greyhound-type bus. In the back, Thornsberry put a table and an upholstered, dinette-style booth that wrapped around it. The table was used for playing poker. On the first days of the shoot, the actors commandeered it, Thornsberry says, and "stayed to themselves, and they were playing cards." But the crew resented the actors' monopolizing the poker table. The actors "had the wrong group, because the crew spoke up and said, 'Look, we want to play cards, too.'" The crew didn't merely integrate the card table, according to Thornsberry, "They took it over," although sometimes they let Dennis Wilson play poker with them.

One bright, sunny day on a two-lane road, Rick Mercier, who was driving the car carrier that held the Chevys and GTOs, was in a hurry, and his vehicle was a little faster than the crew bus ahead of him. Mercier decided to pass the bus full of cast and crew on a small country road, according to Thornsberry. Brumby, who had already had a few beers, didn't want to let him pass. So the two raced down a "teeny little road," as Thornsberry describes it, while terrified cast and crew on the bus tried to find an emergency exit so they could try to bail out.

Although the crew was competent and cooperative, its small size was sometimes a problem, according to Coblenz, especially in scenes at the racetrack. "We were working very short of crew. I had one assistant director helping me, and sometimes we had as many as 3,000 extras in some of these scenes. I would just get on the bullhorn and be the loudest person there." The script supervisor, Bonnie Prendergast Freeman, says that Coblenz made the best of the circumstances. He served as both production manager and first assistant director, so he coordinated crews and equipment and met any of Hellman's unanticipated needs, plus he coordinated logistics, confirmed locations, supervised the extras, and made sure the actors were where they were supposed to be. According to Prendergast Freeman, this entailed "corralling Dennis Wilson," who would frequently wander away, and was usually somewhere else goofing around when a shot was being set up.

Coblenz gives Gary Kurtz a great deal of credit. He describes Kurtz in such superlatives as "absolutely brilliant" and "extremely knowledgeable," and adds that he was "tremendously helpful on location." (After *Two-Lane Blacktop*, Kurtz went on to produce two critically acclaimed and highly successful movies for the director George Lucas, *American Graffiti* [1973] and *Star Wars* [1977].) One reason Kurtz was so competent is his exceptionally comprehensive training and experience. First, he went to film school (at the University of Southern California) before the auteur theory caught on, and the few students in some technical classes would work on several student films each semester. Then he went on to labor for cheapskate Roger Corman, who had Kurtz perform two or more tasks on each movie he worked on.

Kurtz attended film school just before it became popular. Before 1966 or 1967, Kurtz says, "it seemed to be kind of a poor relation to the various other art courses that were around—performing arts, and theater, and other things."

He remembers that one semester he and another student were the only ones enrolled in the advanced cinematography class. "We had to do three films, each, because there were six projects and they had six directors, and they had other crew, but in the cinematography class, there were only two of us," he says. "It was quite a chore, actually."

In quasi-desperation, he and his fellow cinema majors, he recalls, "would commandeer other people. We'd go over to the drama department, and we needed to get actors for some of the projects, but we also said, 'Why don't you take a couple of cinema courses and be on the crew, and get some credits, and learn about film?'" (One of the recruits was Dorothy Alsup, Kurtz's future sister-in-law, who would babysit his children during production of *Two-Lane Blacktop* and work as his assistant during post-production.) The next semester, he says, "there were enough people to do the key jobs without having to double up, but it was tricky. And I did a lot of different things."

After film school, Kurtz went to work for Roger Corman. He says he learned to perform many jobs working on Corman's low-budget, often schlocky movies. (If some of Kurtz's word choices sound unusual or pretentious, it is not because he is quirky or arrogant. Kurtz has lived in London for many years, and he now sounds like a Brit—not the accent, just the vocabulary.) "After being at university during the early sixties, I must have worked on forty or fifty films. They were all 35 mm feature films, but most of them were absolutely terrible. I mean, they were low-budget exploitation films that were used as third features or for late-night television and various other things that he had an automatic market for, so he could make whatever he wanted and they would be accepted, but some of them were better than others. It was really good experience because on one film I would be the cameraman and maybe the editor, and on another film I'd be the assistant director and the production manager, and on another film do the sound work and on another film do the visual effects, and so on."

Kurtz probably soaked up more knowledge than most people would in similar circumstances because he is exceptionally curious. Billy Kincheloe, who worked on the cars and helped Rudy Wurlitzer put realistic automotive lingo into the script, remembers Kurtz grilling him about mechanical equipment. Kincheloe says Kurtz quizzed him about the innovative features Richard Ruth added to the '55 Chevy, such as Koni coilover shock absorbers—shock absorbers with coil springs around them, which were just starting to be used on professional race cars, but not yet on street-racing cars. Kurtz, Kincheloe remembers, "was always asking questions: 'How does this work?' 'What does this do?' 'What does that do?'"

Coblenz says that although he would usually have prepared the schedule, Kurtz prepared it. Coblenz looked it over and couldn't find anything wrong with it. When they needed a second camera, Kurtz operated an Arriflex several times. Monte Hellman considered Kurtz the de facto producer, as well as editor, cameraman, and director of some second-unit footage on *Two-Lane*. When Hellman was ill for a day, Kurtz even directed a few shots with James Taylor and Laurie Bird. Often, when cast or crew members had delicate personal problems or were bothered by bad behavior—unwanted sleeping arrangements and a cast member becoming drunk and abusive—they went to Kurtz as well as Coblenz to help set things right.

Some members of the film company thought Kurtz was a hippie because he had long hair and he traveled from location to location with his wife, Meredith, and children, in a Volkswagen van. Kurtz explains, "I did look very much like a hippie, with very long hair. I was just out of the military—I'd been drafted into the marines during Vietnam—and so when I got out I kind of went to the other extreme. And it was a VW van on the whole road trip with a flower on the front." Kurtz elaborates that he cut a flower that resembled a daisy out of wood and bolted it on the cover of the tire on the front of the van. So, with long hair, a flower, and a VW van, Kurtz associated himself with three icons of the hippie movement (others being marijuana and free love).

Beverly Walker thought Kurtz and his wife looked a little like Amish or Quaker people. "Meredith, who was quite plump, wore long skirts or dresses all the time, as I recall. She also looked like anyone's image of 'Mrs. Santa Claus.' She had blonde ringlets and a merry face with apple-red cheeks. She was—and probably still is—a very merry, delightful person. Their children were beautiful—two daughters."

Hellman also traveled in a van with his wife and children—plus his sheepdog and Laurie Bird. Although Bird was seventeen when they left California, and had her eighteenth birthday near the end of the shoot, the crew thought she was sixteen because of her looks and immaturity. "She did look very, very young," Kurtz comments. "I thought she was sixteen." Initially, the film company had the impression that Monte and Jaclyn Hellman were taking the role of surrogate parents to the girl, whose mother had died when she was very young and who didn't get along with her father. They also thought Monte Hellman was taking her under his wing for good reason, since she was performing a lead role in a major studio release and she had had no acting experience.

Warren Oates traveled in a van that had been modified to put a captain's chair in the driver's seat, and Hopi and Navajo rugs decorated the back. Walter Coblenz and James Taylor say they particularly enjoyed riding with Oates. Taylor recalls, "Warren had his own—like a Winnebago—motor home, and he sort of used it as his dressing room, and traveled between our sites in the camper. So I spent a lot of time riding along with Warren and talking to him and hearing his stories. We had some amazing adventures on our days off, too." On one of those days off in Flagstaff, their next location, Oates, his two children, Taylor, and the singer/songwriter Joni Mitchell, who lived with Taylor at the time and was visiting him, went to a snake dance at Hotevilla, Arizona. Taylor was profoundly impressed. Recalling the experience forty-five years later, he says, "It was amazing to see, and it's just stayed with me for the rest of my life. I think about it all the time." Taylor says he was told that Hotevilla was the oldest continuously inhabited town or village in North America, and Hopis had lived there for at least 3,000 years. This was the last year the public was admitted to the snake dance. Taylor recalls that the Hopis gathered snakes and kept them in underground rooms called kivas and spent time with them. "Then they do this amazing repetitive dance all around the square of this ancient village Hotevilla, and at the end of this two-week ceremony they've communicated something, somehow to the snakes who take it to the environment in a way that I don't think I could ever understand. It was kind of a human existence and a kind of consciousness that I just have never seen since or before." Moreover, Taylor adds, Joni Mitchell "had a phobia, and has had for many years, of snakes. So there was, for her, a sort of level of courage to it that was remarkable."

While Taylor says that the snake dance, and the time he spent with Warren Oates and Joni Mitchell, were the high points of the shoot, the lack of a script and Jaclyn Hellman's coaching were low points. Although Oates insisted on having a script, Hellman thought his amateur actors' performances would seem less forced and rehearsed if he withheld their lines until the last minute; he would dole them out the night before, or the morning of, each scene. Taylor resented this and thought it implied a lack of confidence in the actors. Accustomed to being in control of his music and his performances, Taylor was uncomfortable being left in the dark and would ask crew members to show him their scripts. Taylor comments, "It was as if he was shooting a documentary because we were living in the car. We were driving it all day long and essentially he just herded us through it, and I found that really vexing after a while and insisted that he give us the script, which he did, finally, toward the end. But it was an odd technique. I'd never heard of it before and I basically think that he didn't trust us to act."

Another technique Hellman employed to try to help the novice actors improve their performances was to have his wife, Jaclyn, take them off into the bushes before a scene and try to elicit memories that would stir up their emotions to keep their performances from becoming wooden. To do this, she used her idiosyncratic version of the sense memory exercises she'd learned from Martin Landau in his acting classes at Monte Hellman's theater in Los Angeles. The novice actors, according to a talk Hellman gave at AFI not long after the film was released, "worked with my ex-wife for about two weeks before we began to shoot. She's a writer and an actress and a coach, and she put them through a series of exercises to prepare them for the task of beginning to act for the first time in their lives." Once shooting started, she gave them "basic tools" according to Hellman, "to learn to deal with their emotions, primarily to, there's a term that's used in describing an actor's work. You refer to an actor's 'instrument,' which is his basic physical and emotional equipment that he has. It's like a musician plays his violin but an actor 'plays' himself. The exercises were really designed to reduce inhibitions and give them certain techniques to call upon their emotions."

Gary Kurtz remembers that Jaclyn Hellman told him several times that her exercises didn't always work. In fact, they backfired. Taylor confided to the script supervisor, Bonnie Prendergast Freeman, that the coaching, which was supposed to make him relaxed, made him uncomfortable. Prendergast Freeman recalls, "At one point, he asked me if it was normal for the dialogue coach to be doing these emotional 'exercises' with the three of them (Laurie, Dennis, and him), but he didn't know how to complain as the coach was Jaclyn, Monte's wife. I assured him that he could talk to Monte about this, and I don't know if he did, but since I had been involved with classes at the Actors Studio West (plus having actor friends) and exposed to this style of preparation, I knew how it was affecting him. But it was not my place to coddle him, but rather to refer him to Monte."

Looking back, Taylor indicates the coaching had the opposite of its intended effect: "I think that rather than trust us with coming up with our own character and rather than take a chance on our acting, he basically gave us a page of script at a time, or a page and a half, whatever sort of constituted a scene or a shot, and basically a lot of his technique was just to try to drain us, like flatten us emotionally, so we would rehearse it over and over again, and then also, his wife, Jackie, would take us through these sort of desensitizing kind of exercises to try to just basically sort of emotionally exhaust us before most of these scenes."

Gary Kurtz observed Taylor's discomfort. "James was, as far as I could tell, a kind of control freak kind of person who wanted to be in charge of everything about his life. He was in his music, and what he did in performances, and so it freaked him out a little bit that he was at the mercy of a director and a film crew and not understanding what was going on." For these reasons, he adds, Taylor "was a reluctant participant in the project."

By contrast, people in the towns where they filmed often wanted to be in the movies. In 1970, before multiplexes degraded the experience, moviegoers would go to high-ceilinged, stand-alone theaters, formerly called "palaces," designed to impress and to convey grandeur, to see a double-feature. The theater was a destination in itself as opposed to a multiplex in a mall with a wide choice of movies that makes each of them less special, plus nearby stores and restaurants and other distractions that compete for attention and the customer's dollar. News about movie stars was published in magazines, which often spun stories, stage-managed by publicists, of romantic, fairy-tale lives. Actors didn't so often betray their less-than-glamourous attributes in the days before they could tweet off the top of their heads, and before they were hounded by paparazzi whom they sometimes punch in the nose. Before CGI made it possible for special effects to render nearly everything imaginable believable onscreen, and before the internet explained how it was all done, before hordes of amateur filmmakers inundated YouTube with their homemade videos, the movies still held a unique magic for the general public. The tradeoff for having a truly scary monster instead of a guy in a phony-looking monster suit was that movies lost that magic and their mystery. When audiences were bombarded with an overabundance of spectacular and elaborate special effects, they knew a computer had produced the mayhem, and they became jaded.

In 1970, however, in the Middle American towns where *Two-Lane Blacktop* was filmed, recalls teamster Craig Pinkard, "Everybody wanted to get into show business." Locals were happy to work as extras for very little money, he continues. "A lot of them just donated the time so they could tell their grandmother, 'Hey, look grandma, see, that's me!'" John Bailey found that locals were friendly and generous. "People were very curious," he says. "In the middle of the afternoon, they would come by with brownies or cakes and things like that. In these small towns I don't remember any hostility at all." Bailey also remembers that the residents were fascinated by the filmmakers and found mystique in their most mundane chores: "It was still kind of a magic realm, and you would go into a town with a movie crew, and people would just come out and watch you unload the trucks."

Even police and firemen agreed to be in the movie. In a scene shot in Flagstaff, the Driver and the Mechanic are being chased by cops. They pull into a driveway in front of a house and the police car goes by. Then they look into a window at a family (portrayed by Gary Kurtz, his wife, and their little kids) in a scene intended to show them observing a normal life that they will never have (the sequence was cut because of length). Hellman first shot inside the house, then Kurtz left to operate a camera while Hellman shot the Mechanic and the Driver outside the house looking in. Coblenz had to get a second unit to shoot the police chasing the Chevy through Flagstaff. To play the cops in pursuit, "We got the police to do it for us," Coblenz recalls. Kurtz and Jack Deerson shot second-unit footage, going from block to block, filming actual police speeding after the Chevy. Teamsters were holding hoses to simulate rain. In one scene, a fire truck drove next to the car with firemen holding hoses to provide the illusion of rain. Coblenz was greatly impressed with the city's cooperation in allowing a film company to race through the streets of Flagstaff with real firemen making fake rain and real cops chasing the Chevy.

In many towns, residents would shake down the filmmakers. Some members of the film company filled out vouchers for reimbursement of cash they paid to "buy off nuisance people" who would interfere with filmmaking. They also had to shell out cash to "prevent use of noisy equipment" by people who were trying to extort money from them in Santa Fe, Tucumcari, Durant/Boswell, Little Rock, and Memphis. The amount of the payoffs seemed to vary with the size of the town, plus the number of troublemakers. In tiny Durant, they bought off extortionists threatening to use noisy equipment for $60, whereas in Tucumcari they paid people $135 to quit being a nuisance. But in Flagstaff, the film company merely paid residents to reimburse them for trouble the filmmakers caused—interfering with their business and making noise at night.

∞

After leaving Flagstaff, the film company shot on US 89, then on Route 66 in Two Guns, Arizona, on their way to Santa Fe, New Mexico. Like several other locations, Santa Fe had not been on their itinerary. Teamster Rick Mercier, who drove the car carrier, remembers they would sometimes stop spontaneously at unscheduled locations. "When we stopped and shot, it wasn't necessarily planned all that well sometimes, and they'd say, 'Why don't we shoot here instead of doing what we were going to do?' and the director liked it and, boom! We'd stop and shoot." John Bailey also remembers that Hellman would take advantage of opportunities that presented themselves on the road. "Some of the local casting was done as we went along. There was a certain amount of improvisation. I couldn't begin to tell you what scenes might have been rewritten, or were partly improvised based on what we saw when we got to certain places, but it was not a hard script" in the sense that "there was a certain flexibility, as there was for all films at that time. It was a time of a certain amount of experimentation and looseness in American filmmaking that the studios wouldn't begin to let you do today."

Gary Kurtz and several others had visited Santa Fe before and thought that the big square in the city's center, Santa Fe Plaza, was quite colorful and would be a good place to shoot, so they diverted from their scheduled route. There, Laurie Bird had to panhandle, which unnerved her, while cameras out of sight across the street filmed the scene. A lot of hippies panhandled at the time, and a lot of their elders would react with disapproval and censure, admonishing them with: "Shame on you" or "You should be ashamed of yourself," or telling them to "go get a job." Kurtz recalls that "Laurie was petrified of doing that scene because all of the traders that were sitting there around the square were real, and the tourists were all real, and we had one plant, one guy who was a local artist, but he was a plant to give her money in case nobody else did. And we filmed it from the hotel window, so there was no camera crew in the square, and she had to have a couple of drinks to loosen up a little bit. And several people gave her money, and in the end I had the production people, I said, 'You've got to go give this money back to these people because otherwise we'll get arrested.'"

Kurtz says this was probably the most complicated scene in the movie to shoot. They had cameras in two hidden locations, the people in the square didn't know they were being filmed, and the filmmakers weren't sure what would happen. Scenes on the road, or in bars or restaurants, had been staged and were easier to organize and control, Kurtz recalls. Hellman, he says, was interested in logistics. "Monte liked to talk about some of those things, and he wasn't always clear about how to do them, or exactly what he was after, so by talking it out, and looking at the technical problems, and saying, 'Well, we can't really do that because we just don't have the resources to spend the time to set it up, so how about doing it this way?' So I was usually put in the position of suggesting alternatives to get what we needed without spending much more extra time."

In Santa Fe, the filmmakers also shot the scenes of Rudy Wurlitzer, who played a street racer, challenging the Driver to a race and later arguing with his girlfriend (played by Jaclyn Hellman) at a table in a cocktail lounge while the Driver has a drink at the bar. Hot-rod authority Pat Ganahl cites this episode as one of the most realistic in depicting street racers, who would go looking for a patsy to bet $100 or $200 on a race: "They'd go somewhere to a new town where they didn't know how fast the car was, and find a guy who thought *he* had the fastest car, which was that guy with the hot rod at the bar [Wurlitzer], who Monte Hellman's wife was with. He thought for sure he could beat this old '55 Chevy with his little hot rod. Well, he didn't know that this '55 Chevy had this big-block engine in it and was built specifically for drag racing," Ganahl says. Wurlitzer's character was just the sort of sitting duck the Driver and the Mechanic were hoping to find. "The other guy's car was just a regular hot rod that cruised the drive-in and made a lot of noise, and everybody ooh'ed and aah'ed over it, but he didn't really race it."

After he loses the race to the Driver and the Mechanic, Wurlitzer's character has a fierce argument with his girlfriend or wife. Furious at him, she gets up from the table and storms out of the cocktail lounge. According to Monte

Hellman, the purpose of the scene was to show its effect on the Driver, who is sitting at the bar observing the couple from a distance. "It's really an argument about their relationship and about his being a thirty-two-year-old drag racer, and she splits. You get the feeling it's a really serious argument that's going to end the relationship." This scene foreshadows another near the end where the Girl, disgusted that the Driver has neglected her to focus on his car and drag racing, walks away from a table, out of a café, and out of his life.

Wurlitzer deviated slightly from his script in both scenes he acted in—the challenge to race and the argument with his girlfriend at the bar—and ad-libbed a few lines. Hellman explains, "I always encourage actors to make slight alterations to make the dialogue more comfortable for them. The dialogue in *Two-Lane* is so minimal, this was rarely necessary." Wurlitzer says he had never acted before. "I was very nervous, but then on the other hand I wasn't alone, because for a lot of the other actors it was their first experience, too." The crew compared Wurlitzer's arrival on the traveling set to the second coming of Christ. As Bonnie Prendergast Freeman remembers, "From the beginning, you heard so much about Rudy Wurlitzer, whether innuendo or secondhand gossip passed on by the publicist on the show, that by the time he showed up in person, some of us were in awe without really knowing why. He seemed like a nice man, but he was definitely 'above the line,' so I really never had a conversation with him. Which is unusual as never did a writer come on a set and not want to talk to me about how the dialogue was going, how were the actors doing with their lines, etc."

Had Laughlin come along, he would have chatted it up with the crew and found out their favorite movies, their hobbies, and the names, professions, and health of their relatives. While the producer notes that Hellman was "never one of the guys," Laughlin brags that a crew member on a film he later directed said, "Not only does Michael Laughlin direct the movie, he hosts it." But since Laughlin wasn't there, and Hellman didn't mingle with the crew, Kurtz took it upon himself to try to build some rapport with the beer-drinking faction. "I never have been a drinker, so I didn't actually participate with the crew much, except there were certain nights when I'd go down and hang out and chat about how things were going, and drink lemonade or Coke. But with a small crew, you can't appear to be too standoffish, I don't think. With a small crew you need the kind of support and cohesiveness of their take on what we were doing." But if the crew thought Hellman was snooty, they thought Kurtz had a pointy head. Jim Thornsberry describes Kurtz as a *"nice guy.* But, I mean, he was just one of those kind of guys that if you were sitting having dinner or something, and said, 'Would you please hand me the salt?' or 'Pass me the salt,' he would give you the origin of salt, the chemical makeup of it, how it's processed, what the effect is on the body. A real bore." Kurtz had an inkling of how the crew regarded him. "Monte was not always the most casually friendly, either, to crew people, so it was 'us' and 'them' in a way that I tried to bridge some of the time, but I'm not sure how successfully."

∞

On their way to their next destination, Tucumcari, New Mexico, the filmmakers shot on State 104, a 110-mile highway. Richard Ruth had designed the cars so that many of the parts were removable and the filmmakers could put the camera in the Chevy; sometimes they put it in the trunk. The script supervisor, Bonnie Prendergast Freeman, remembers that the sound mixer, Charles Knight, would sometimes scrunch down inside the quiet Chevy they used for filming and hold a hand mike. When the camera operator, Hugh Gagnier, was on the camera mount, his hindquarters protruding out into the highway on small roads such as State 104, Gary Kurtz recalls, "we would usually run one of our production vehicles behind them out in the middle of the road so if there was anybody else coming the other way, they would see it and get out of the way. We never did have an accident, but it was scary on some of those roads."

Warren Oates joined the film company here, and his first scene was shot on State 104 between Santa Fe and Tucumcari, where he picks up the actor Bill Keller playing a hitchhiker. The car his character is named for, the GTO, first made in 1964, was one of the original muscle cars, emblematic of the establishment co-opting a quasi-outlaw, often blue-collar hobby. The guys who built cars in their back yards with spare parts from the junkyard now competed with wealthier, fancier guys who bought ready-made fast cars off the showroom floor. Oates's character talks car but doesn't know car. Serious hot-rodders could build shabby-looking cars with powerful new engines inside and beat the new factory-built muscle cars. Ganahl comments, "That's what Warren Oates didn't know. He figured he could go buy one of these factory hot rods and it would be faster than any of these junky-looking hot rods. He didn't know that the '55 Chevy had a bigger engine than his car because he didn't know anything about engines."

But his character pretends to know. Warren Oates told students at the American Film Institute about his first day shooting, in the GTO, when he tells the hitchhiker what the car has under the hood. "That was a gruesome day. First of all, I had a lot of nomenclature to understand about the automobile that I'm not familiar with. Even though I served time in the US Marine Corps as an aviation mechanic, I closed out that aspect of my life. And I didn't understand, so I had to learn that dialogue first, and it was brutal." At first, Hellman treated Oates as he did the novice actors and gave him only his dialogue for each day instead of the entire script. Prendergast Freeman says Oates resented being treated this way. "He complained to me that he was not used to working that way and it really upset him. He said they could do that to the nonactors, but he wasn't going to put up with it for himself." Hellman relented and gave him the script.

By all accounts, Oates and his professionalism elevated the proceedings. Walter Coblenz comments, "Warren Oates was a really great actor and he brought so much to this because he got Dennis and everybody else to play off him, he played his part so well." Gary Kurtz says his most vivid memory of the shoot is the way that Oates interacted with the amateur actors. Oates was the type of actor who liked to rehearse and hone his performance, finding nuances, and by the fifth or sixth take, he would have reached his peak. "Whereas when you're working with nonactors, you pretty much have to get it the first time around, the first or the second take because otherwise they start to get self-conscious, so we were worried about that," Kurtz recalls. He cites the scene at the gas station where the race begins as an example of Oates playing off the other actors' untrained performances.

John Bailey thought that Oates was the "lynchpin" of the film. "Because Laurie and James Taylor and Dennis Wilson, they weren't actors. Dennis and James were public performers so they had a sense of how to present themselves, but Warren was right on all the time, so he not only was an inspiration but he was kind of a challenge to the younger kids, you know, 'Come on, get with it.' He would bring them along. He was never critical of them, he was always very supportive. But when you have somebody that is that 'on' and is that good, it's like a musician who's really riffing, he lifts everybody. Warren was like that."

Gary Kurtz during pre-production in his neatly organized office that overlooked the historic lot at CBS's Cinema Center Films. Even though the movie eventually ended up at Universal Studios, the film company continued to operate out of their suite of offices at Cinema Center, where the producer, Michael Laughlin, had some other deals. Other people working on the lot would come by the office to play the director James Frawley's pinball machine. (Photo courtesy of Gary Kurtz)

The leading lady, Laurie Bird, looked very young, which led some in the film company to feel parental and protective towards her and others to avoid her because they thought she was immature. She had left home early to escape a tyrannical father who was a religious fanatic, and friends say she was unprepared for a life mingling with more educated, sophisticated, and high-powered men in the worlds of modeling and moviemaking. (Photo courtesy of Gary Kurtz)

"Big Willie" Robinson, who organized Los Angeles street racing and was synonymous with it, appeared in the first scene in the movie and lent it credibility with car guys. Big Willie was 6'6" and towered over Dennis Wilson, who, being from Southern California, was also a gearhead. (Photo courtesy of Gary Kurtz)

The production manager and assistant director Walter Coblenz was amazed that they were able to persuade real policemen and firemen to appear in the movie. Here, a state cop, along with Dennis Wilson, kneeling beside him with his head lowered, endures the tedium, endemic to a film set, of waiting for a shot to be set up. (Photo courtesy of Gary Kurtz)

The rigging was sturdy enough to allow both the cameraman and Monte Hellman to ride on the car. Kurtz took quite a few photos of the rigging, and members of the film company described him as a geek who, instead of indulging in small talk in social situations, shared his technical knowledge with cast and crew. (Photo courtesy of Gary Kurtz)

Gregory Sandor, shown here with his hands in his pockets and wearing his trademark Panama hat, was an excellent cinematographer from the classical school. A tragic, overlooked figure, he wasn't sufficiently gregarious and aggressive to get into the IATSE union for cinematographers of major feature films and didn't even get credit for shooting *Two-Lane Blacktop*. (Photo courtesy of Gary Kurtz)

Gregory Sandor holds a light meter on a cloudy day. His assistant on the movie, John Bailey, remembers, "Gregory worked at a very low light level compared to the big studios—what Gordon Willis called 'flamethrowers.'" Gary Kurtz, nervous that the light might not be sufficient, sometimes would be on the set with his light meter checking f-stops right next to Sandor, and the crew had the impression that this caused friction. (Photo courtesy of Bonnie Prendergast Freeman)

Jaclyn Hellman, who served as the dialogue coach, would take the actors off into the bushes, or in this case, weeds, before a scene and take them through relaxation exercises, then try to get them to think about their families and painful memories to elicit emotions for the camera. James Taylor, in particular, resented these sessions, and thought they had nothing to do with his character. (Photo courtesy of Bonnie Prendergast Freeman)

Both Jaclyn Hellman and Monte Hellman would call for take after take, hoping that the non-professional actors would come up with something better. Laurie Bird, who had had no experience acting or performing, seemed bewildered and nervous. James Taylor found the repetition draining and numbing. (Photo courtesy of Bonnie Prendergast Freeman)

Hoping for spontaneity and naturalism, Monte Hellman didn't tell James Taylor and Dennis Wilson how to shape their characters, but relaxation and sense memory exercises, as well as rehearsals, tired the actors and made them uncomfortable. Some fans of the film say the actors acquitted themselves well, but others like the film partly because they find the acting so inept and, thus, unique. (Photo courtesy of Bonnie Prendergast Freeman)

Gary Kurtz was so experienced in filmmaking that he did a little bit of everything on the film, except drink and take drugs, which left him out of the divided camps of beer drinkers vs. stoners. Having grown up in Southern California, he also knew about cars and had modified the first one he owned, making him technically a hot-rodder. (Photo courtesy of Bonnie Prendergast Freeman)

Universal executives told Kurtz that he and Hellman looked like hippies and might provoke conservative people in the South. In this photo taken on the Toad Suck Ferry on the Arkansas River, the assistant cameraman, John Bailey, wearing a headband with a floral pattern, and Hellman, with his Afro-style hair, could pass for hippies, but Kurtz, in a white short-sleeved shirt with a pen in the pocket, looks like a nerd. (Photo courtesy of Bonnie Prendergast Freeman)

Walter Coblenz was the competent production manager and assistant director. He kept the picture on schedule and made sure the cast showed up every day. He did not involve himself in the politics, the beer drinker/drug-taker divide, or the after-hours shenanigans; he kept his eye out for trouble and tried to patch it up before it affected the film. (Photo courtesy of Bonnie Prendergast Freeman)

James Taylor and Dennis Wilson sit in the car while Monte Hellman hunches over it, with other crew members behind him. The serious filmmakers, or those "above the line," largely thought the skilled crew were, at best, conservative oafs who had gotten into their unions through nepotism; at worst, reactionary and racist drunkards. The below-the-line crew thought the filmmakers were drug-befuddled, amateurish, arty poseurs. (Photo courtesy of Gary Kurtz)

From left to right, Gary Kurtz, Monte Hellman, Chuck Record, and James Taylor look over a wrecked car. The low-budget film was shorthanded, so for a scene of a fatal accident, teamsters did the stunt driving and a crew member played the dead body. (Photo courtesy of Bonnie Prendergast Freeman)

Local residents were mostly friendly to the traveling film company, and would come out to watch the proceedings and offer homemade cookies. In the days before the computer made possible super-realistic special effects, amateur movies on YouTube, and celebrities making fools of themselves on social media, motion pictures and their stars still held mystique. Here, the car with all its rigging, the actor Warren Oates, and the trailer with the Universal Studios logo lettering have attracted two local women. (Photo courtesy of Gary Kurtz)

James Taylor holds the wheel of the '55 Chevy, but he didn't feel like he was in the driver's seat on the film, unsettling the singer/songwriter. During the shoot, while he waited around between takes, he wrote his song "Riding on a Railroad" about being caught up in a creative project where he didn't run the show, and where the person in charge, Monte Hellman, had an out-of-control infatuation with Laurie Bird. Ironically, although Taylor had initially offered to write and perform a song, he didn't sing in the film and the only person who did was Bird, who couldn't carry a tune. (Photo courtesy of Gary Kurtz)

By the side of the road at the end of the day. When they were not shooting at night, the film company separated into divided camps in the evening: the above-the-line principals retired to smoke pot while the crew went to the local bar to drink beer. (Photo courtesy of Gary Kurtz)

Joni Mitchell was living with James Taylor when he was making *Two-Lane Blacktop*, and when she visited him they spent much of their time playing the guitar and singing. Although he was just becoming famous, she had already won a Grammy for her album *Clouds*, with the song "Both Sides Now," and had released *Ladies of the Canyon*, which included her iconic songs "Big Yellow Taxi" and "Woodstock." (Photo courtesy of Bonnie Prendergast Freeman)

Unused to participating in a group creative endeavor, James Taylor recalls that he felt off balance: "I do live and work in a musical community, but a film is another whole thing entirely, where your creative process is so dependent on other people doing their jobs right, too." (Photo courtesy of Bonnie Prendergast Freeman)

Monte Hellman cast Warren Oates in four films. Critics raved about his performance in *Two-Lane Blacktop*. The film's publicist, Beverly Walker, says, "Warren should have had a supporting actor Oscar nomination for his performance but didn't get it because the film was such a public failure." (Photo courtesy of Bonnie Prendergast Freeman)

Warren Oates, shown here focusing on a page, insisted that he be shown the script. Oates was extremely endearing and somewhat mischievous; he attempted to turn the "straight" members of the crew on to psychedelics, including Bonnie Prendergast, who took this nice photo of him anyway and didn't hold it against him. (Photo courtesy of Bonnie Prendergast Freeman)

John Bailey was so overwhelmed with his work as assistant cameraman that Walter Coblenz noticed, and hired an assistant for him. Bailey recalls, "It was such an intense and demanding work experience because it was such a low-budget film and I never was able to raise my head above the sand, so to speak." Bailey went on to have an illustrious career as a cinematographer on major motion pictures, and has always felt sad that his mentor Gregory Sandor, the de facto, uncredited director of photography on *Two-Lane Blacktop*, never achieved the recognition he deserved. (Photo courtesy of Bonnie Prendergast Freeman)

James Taylor had been driving cars since his early teens, but the real race car that Richard Ruth built for the movie was a speed demon that Taylor needed to learn to operate. It was built to go like hell for a very short distance, but wasn't good for much else. A full-time mechanic, Jay Wheatley, went along on the shoot and stayed busy. (Photo courtesy of Bonnie Prendergast Freeman)

Gary Kurtz modified and improved a system of rigging cars for a camera that he had devised for Roger Corman films he had worked on in the 1960s. According to Kurtz, "It allowed us to shoot from many positions around the car even when it was not being towed. We had special brackets welded to the frame of the Chevy and the GTO that were not visible if the pipe was removed, and that made the cars usable as second picture cars to do two units as necessary." (Photo courtesy of Gary Kurtz)

From left to right, Monte Hellman (seated), director; John Bailey, assistant cameraman; Chuck Record, key grip; Hugh Gagnier, camera operator; behind Gagnier, a little bit of Jay Wheatley, auto mechanic; Gene Clinesmith (seated), truck driver; Bonnie Prendergast, script supervisor; Dick Bruno (leaning on chair), wardrobe man; Gene Booth (in cowboy hat), prop man, in Boswell, Oklahoma. To match scenes shot during a downpour, the film company used up the little town's water supply to make fake rain. (Photo courtesy of Gary Kurtz)

The untrained lead actors sit with Warren Oates in a café, surrounded by crew, the actor Alan Vint (smoking), who plays a menacing country boy that GTO placates, and a young local woman who plays the waitress. Since the film company was shorthanded, they had no production designer, and used practical locations largely as-is, local color and all—for example, the "No Dancing" sign. (Photo courtesy of Gary Kurtz)

Photo portrait of Laurie Bird taken by Monte Hellman. Hellman's friend Steven Gaydos remembers, "Laurie was just absolutely gorgeous in a life-force way, not just a pretty girl, just a dynamic, lovely ball of energy and openness and humor and gentility—she had kind of a wonderful native elegance to her—and very, very, very neurotic, a very troubled person, and her own worst enemy in many ways. And she was just so young." (Photo courtesy of Monte Hellman)

# 5

# The Fast Lane: Sex, Drugs, and Rock 'n' Roll Stars

In Tucumcari, New Mexico, where they spent two weeks from August 30 to September 14, their longest sojourn in one place, the film company shot the extended, complicated scene at the gas station where the race for pink slips is set up. They stayed at the Pow Wow Inn on Route 66, a U-shaped building with a pool in the center. Beverly Walker remembers it as "a motel that had a lounge with a lounge singer." For Warren Oates's daughter Jennifer, it was close to heaven, largely because of heartthrob Dennis Wilson. While some adults, such as Bonnie Prendergast Freeman, found Wilson "infantile" and irresponsible, he had manic energy and made a terrific playmate for children. Jennifer Oates, who was ten years old, found him childlike in a playful, companionable way: "He was such a kid and it was just so much fun. It was so much fun being a kid in that moment in Tucumcari." She describes Wilson's magnetism, especially to women and children: "He was fun, he was adorable—I mean, even to a ten-year-old girl he was cute as a bug." To the delight of Jennifer, her brother Timothy, and other children, Wilson would pick them up and throw them part way across the pool. They ate it up. "He was kid-tossing. It was great, we loved it. We'd swim back for another kid-toss."

Joni Mitchell visited Wilson's more sedate co-star James Taylor in Tucumcari, and many cast and crew members have fond memories of them jamming together in the motel rooms, at the bar, and around the pool. Gary Kurtz describes Taylor as coming out of his shell one weekend: "James got a little more relaxed. There was one Sunday afternoon where his girlfriend at the time flew out and was hanging around for a couple of days, and it was Joni Mitchell. Anyway they sat around the pool all afternoon with their guitars and played and sang all these songs, and the crew was really enchanted because up till that time James had pretty much kept to himself and was a little self-conscious about talking to anybody off the set, so it was great." Bonnie Prendergast Freeman remembers the times when Joni Mitchell was visiting Taylor: "We [the crew] could hear the music wafting through the corridors of our motel, along with the strong smell of weed."

One night when they were shooting, Jim Thornsberry was sitting with his wife, Sheila, in their station wagon with the tailgate down. It started to rain, and as Sheila remembers, "these two hippies got in the back. And I was trying to have a conversation with Jim, and they were singing and playing their guitars, and I whispered, 'Can't you make these hippies leave?' And he told me to be quiet and he said, 'You don't know who they are, do you?' And I said, 'No.' I said, 'They can't even sing.' And it was James Taylor and Joni Mitchell."

Many wives and girlfriends visited in Tucumcari, and Thornsberry drove to a nearby airport one Saturday morning to pick them up. John Bailey and his future wife, the film editor Carol Littleton, witnessed their arrival. "On the road, a lot of guys were having flings, and a busload came in from whatever the closest airport was," Bailey recalls. "And a bunch of wives piled out of the bus to come and visit their spouses for the weekend on Saturday morning, and somehow word had passed out through the teamsters that a busload of wives was coming in. And Carol and I were sitting there having breakfast at the restaurant, and all of a sudden front doors of a lot of the motel rooms opened up and women started running out and getting into their cars."

Despite these breaks, the crew was working six-day weeks with frequent shooting at night, and tensions had been building from the beginning of production. Bailey, the assistant cameraman, had so much work that he couldn't keep up. He had never had a second assistant or a camera loader. On this show, he was loading all the magazines, keeping the camera reports, doing the slating, and unloading everything and packing it for shipment—and they were shooting a lot of film. They were using 400-foot magazines, and he had about thirty magazines, and because he couldn't reload during the shooting day, he would load them at night after they wrapped and go through them during the day. But when they reached Tucumcari, Hellman started calling for a lot of takes, and he would have to load and unload magazines at lunchtime. Consequently, he never had lunch.

Walter Coblenz noticed, Bailey says, "and he said, 'John, I've been watching.' He said, 'You really need somebody to help you.' And I said, 'What do you mean?' because I'd never had anybody. And he said, 'Well, don't you need another assistant?' And I said, 'Well, Walter, I've never had another assistant,' and he said, 'Well, I can see you need one so I'm going to bring somebody in.' It's the only time in my entire career of forty-five years where a producer or a production manager has ever come to me and suggested getting another person on the crew." The assistant they chose was a young man named Robert Stradling, the grandson of the great, founding master cameraman Harry Stradling Sr., who was nominated for 13 Oscars, and the son of Harry Stradling Jr., who was nominated for Academy Awards for *1776* (1972) and *The Way We Were* (1973). "So here I was doing my first studio film, not knowing anything about how the system worked, and they brought in an assistant to help me who was third generation Hollywood royalty. So it was very bizarre," Bailey says.

Robert Stradling recalls that he, too, was overwhelmed with work in his new position as film loader/second assistant when he started on September 7. Then nineteen years old, he was new to the business. He remembers they were shooting inside the Chevy with a handheld camera and had to use 200-foot magazines, which held 200 feet of film, just a few minutes' worth. On one shot, Monte Hellman called for twenty-five takes, and they could only get about one take per magazine, which meant he had to reload twenty-five times. "I think there were even times when they had to wait for me before they could go shoot the scene because I couldn't keep up with what they were doing," Stradling says.

A number of times, Hellman called for twenty or more takes; more often he called for thirteen or fifteen or seventeen. This is not surprising, since three of the lead actors were novices. Jaclyn Hellman also sometimes asked for many extra takes, as she tried to get the actors to improve their performances. Finally, Walter Coblenz got fed up: Jaclyn was calling for a lot of repetition and nothing was improving. They were getting behind. He called Michael Laughlin in Hollywood. Laughlin remembers, "I had anticipated what we could be in for. I had it in Monte's contract that she had to leave if we decided, 'That's it!'" Laughlin told Coblenz to send Jaclyn home. But although many people on the traveling set objected to Jaclyn's erratic, unhinged behavior, nobody, including Coblenz, was willing to confront and alienate Hellman by complaining about his wife, and Coblenz did not banish her from the film.

On the other hand, several people felt sorry for Jaclyn, whose forty-one-year-old husband was having an affair with the seventeen-year-old leading lady—while they were all traveling in the same van and sharing a hotel room. They thought she had reason to behave emotionally. Jim Thornsberry says he liked Jaclyn: "She was really sweet and nice, and I just looked at her and I thought to myself, 'How in the world can you stand that?'" Craig Pinkard and several others thought that Bird's age was misrepresented (which it wasn't) because of her adolescent looks and immature behavior. "Laurie was younger than I think they said she was. She was underage and she acted it," he says. "There was some strange stuff going on there, it was a strange deal. And it looked to me like they were protecting him from her being underage, was what it was. They had to make it look like she was just a friend, that's what I think. I mean, these people were *weird*."

Kurtz reflects that Hellman's having his wife coach his mistress to try to improve her performance misfired. "I think that, in Laurie's case, she just made her nervous." Peter Asher spoke to Taylor regularly while the singer was on the road, and often called the film's publicist, Beverly Walker, to ask about Taylor's welfare, because he knew his client felt constrained and frustrated. Asher received reports that Jaclyn Hellman's dialogue coaching was becoming more aggressive and hostile. "These acting exercises she made them do apparently got fiercer and fiercer every day," Asher says. "And that's when they found out, finally, that what was going on was that she was so furious that he was having an affair with Laurie Bird." Finally, it came to a head and the husband and wife had a blowup.

Kurtz recalls when the simmering situation boiled over. "There was this kind of family squabble thing about Monte's involvement with Laurie, and then that blew up too during the shoot, and that was a mess. I don't like things like that because I think they actually take away from what you're trying to get done every day." Many in the film company felt uncomfortable with the ménage à trois in a motor home. Taylor recalls, "The line was crossed, and she was too young. She didn't have enough personal experience or personal gravity, I guess, to be able to handle this thing on her own. She really depended upon Monte, and I guess these sorts of things happen, that people are working close together and they kind of get involved like this, but that was really unfortunate, I thought. It just seemed to me as though Monte, he was the director, he was in a position of authority and power over us and control, but I didn't feel as though he himself, he was a little bit out of control himself, personally and emotionally."

These days of "free love" were permissive times of experimentation and crossing sexual boundaries. A 1969 album by Blind Faith featured the nude torso of an eleven-year-old girl on the cover. "Child molestation" did not receive the attention and condemnation that it does now. Laurie Bird was seventeen, and would turn eighteen late in the shoot, and she was willingly having an affair with Hellman. After the film wrapped and he divorced his wife, she would marry him. He adored her. However, by several accounts, Bird was cowed by Hellman, dependent upon him, and afraid to confront him. Bonnie Prendergast Freeman says that Bird seemed to feel uncomfortable in both her work and personal life on the shoot. "She did not know the process, and seemed out of sorts most of time. Not very interesting as a cast member, I felt she was lost and very insecure. We knew she was very tightly controlled and under the protective wings of Monte, maybe his wife's as well, because at some point it was known that she was living in the motor home with Monte and was rumored to be like a part of his family. I always thought she was stoned, but it fit the character if she was, so it didn't matter." Beverly Walker, who says she thought of Bird almost as a surrogate daughter, remarks, "He did keep her very close to him." A health-food enthusiast, he tried to control what Bird ate, according to Walker, and the girl would sneak off to indulge in forbidden foods such as orange juice and bacon. Walker continues, "She became his very young sidekick in a Hollywood scene he knew how to handle but which would've had to be challenging for her—parties at Jack Nicholson's house, etc."

In one scene that was shot, despite the rattled lawyers at Universal, the Girl goes skinny-dipping in a lake as the Driver and the Mechanic sit on the bank and look on. Walker remembers the controversy that ensued. On the day of the shoot, the still photographer Jack Hamilton came along, and he took pictures of Bird swimming nude and frolicking in the water. Walker recalls, "Hamilton is, in fact, a good photographer, but he focused on the potentially salacious visuals inherent in the story. He was avid to take photos of that scene, which was subsequently cut. He did not have permission to release those photos. I argued strongly against letting him be on the set at all that particular day, but Monte said OK." Walker explains, "I was convinced that Hamilton would go right out and sell the photos, which is exactly what he did." Several of the photos appeared in a *Show* magazine article about *Two-Lane* published in March, 1971. Bird also was concerned about the photos. "Laurie expressed that she didn't want nude pictures of herself floating around, primarily because of her father, as I recall," Walker says. When the pictures were released, Hellman was angry, she adds. "After the photos were published, Monte blamed me!"

Kurtz remembers, "Laurie was very nervous about that scene. It was almost an ad-libbed scene because we found this location that looked good for that, but it didn't end up in the movie because Monte felt that the movement of the story was just kind of stopped for too long."

Kurtz learned that Bird was not happy to be traveling in Monte Hellman's trailer with him and his family and sharing hotel rooms with them. Kurtz says, "She came to me a couple of times and said, 'Listen, I've got—I want my own hotel room,' and I said, 'Sure,' but she was almost reluctant even to say it." On August 31, Bird got sick and went to the emergency room in a hospital in Tucumcari. She was diagnosed with gastroenteritis and mesenteric adenitis, which causes temporary pain in the stomach, and usually affects children. On some of the forms, her age was given as seventeen, on others eighteen, but she was born on September 26, 1952, so she turned eighteen on the road with *Two-Lane*, in Little Rock, Arkansas. Bird's friend Eileen Peterson wasn't surprised to learn that Bird had been ill at the time: "Well, if things got emotional, tense on the set, that's a good default. So your body breaks down and suddenly everybody feels sorry for you, and you get some attention, and you get a break from all that." Walter Coblenz visited Bird in the hospital and evidently it meant a lot to her; years later, when she ran into him at the Cannes Film Festival, she thanked him for coming to see her when she was sick. For a few days, they shot around her, postponing some scenes until she was released from the hospital, on September 3.

∞

While Laurie Bird was unnerved by Jaclyn Hellman's dialogue coaching, James Taylor also was troubled by it, as well as by what he saw as the lack of trust implied in Monte Hellman's decision not to give him the script. Finally, Taylor refused to work unless he got a copy of the script, so Hellman relented and gave him one. Asher remembers he was concerned about his client. "The reports I was getting from the road, of how crazy it was, were unexpected; it was all a bit fraught," Asher says. "I got the impression it was kind of nuts, and I do remember saying, 'Shall I come out there?' And the general feeling was: no. I know Monte very much wanted him to be left alone, and I never wanted to be the interfering manager who shows up and is annoying. But I did say, 'Look, if you really need help or something I'll come and make a fuss,' but his reaction, as I recall, was, 'No, we'll get through it.'"

Dennis Wilson wasn't visibly upset by the coaching, but he was troubled by (and sometimes caused) his own problems. He was impatient, for example, and unwilling to wait around until a shot was set up and they were ready for him. This was partly because of his immature temperament, but also, Coblenz thought, because he wasn't allowed to see the script and didn't know where his character was going. He didn't have the opportunity to become involved in a continuing process of formulating a character; he did it on the fly.

As befitted a rock star who was besieged by groupies, Wilson was a womanizer who, according to Beverly Walker, "was screwing everything that walked," including one of the magazine writers who visited the set. Wilson told Walker later that the reporter had begged him, "Please don't tell Beverly," and she says, "He was right about that. I would have had a fit." Walker, however, had sympathy for Wilson, who told her "horrors" about his brutal father. Wilson, she says, "really had a kind of sweetness about him. And lost-ness." His womanizing (at least when his wife wasn't around), she says, "was relatively inoffensive because it was so clearly a habit borne of being a drummer in a big rock band."

Wilson was a newlywed who brought along his pregnant bride, Barbara Charren, whom the film company describes as a sweet young woman. Wilson's father had been abusive, and Dennis was prone to getting drunk and becoming violent. The teamsters despised him. Craig Pinkard recalls, "He was a druggie and he hit his girlfriend at the time or whatever, he punched her out, and I don't like men to be beating on women. And I let him know it, too. He was a nasty dude." Wilson's wife-beating upset others in the film company, who complained to Coblenz and Kurtz. Chuck Record recalls that one time after Wilson beat her up, Charren had a black eye. "Everybody was talking about it," Record remembers. "Everybody was really uncomfortable about that," Kurtz agrees. "That was ugly. He had a really bad temper and it was quite uncomfortable sometimes. And other times he'd be sweet as you can imagine, and that's true. It did happen several times, and I think he was going through an awful lot emotionally, not only with his relationship with his family, but with the group as well at that time, with his brothers and the rest of the band," Kurtz remembers. Charren did not stay for the entire shoot; after one beating, she needed medical attention and returned to Los Angeles.

Jim Thornsberry almost came to blows with Wilson; Thornsberry thought he was an "idiot" and a "total jerk" and told him so. Thornsberry was fearless when confronting stars, directors or other big shots, even when it could cost him his job. Pinkard often worked with Thornsberry, and relates, "We used to do some really big movies with some really big people, and some of those really big people are really big asses. They would try to pull something on him, and Jim would see right through it and call them on it immediately and make them look like fools. It was the greatest thing to watch." Pinkard says that although Thornsberry didn't go to college, he was extremely smart and knew immediately when someone was trying to fool him, take advantage of him, or deflect blame onto him. "He was brave enough to just call them on it. We got kicked off a couple of shows because he called these idiots 'idiots.'"

Wilson didn't take his job too seriously, and would forget or flub lines. When he was needed on the set, he was nowhere to be found, Bonnie Prendergast Freeman says, and she found it "amusing when he was aggravating the assistants trying to track him down." Sometimes Hellman would call for additional takes because Wilson's performance wasn't up to par. James Taylor, a perfectionist, would become annoyed when Wilson was unprepared. This tension sometimes carried over into the movie, pleasing Hellman, who strove for authenticity. Jarod Hellman says that in *Road to Nowhere*, made forty years later, his father went so far as to actively create confusion among his actors to promote spontaneity. According to Jarod Hellman, his father instructed one actor to improvise, while telling other actors in the same scene to follow the script to the letter.

John Bailey remembers "lots of times when Monte would shoot ten, twelve, fifteen, even a couple of times he would do over twenty-five takes," and these were often scenes, he continues, "with Laurie Bird, the Girl, because she was young, she was a child," and she wasn't professionally trained. Sometimes she would hum, or she would come in too early. Bailey gives her credit for working hard to learn her lines, "but she had no discipline. And she had no ability to know how to shape a performance. And Monte was reluctant to give her line readings or to tell her what to do, so we just kind of had to keep going and going until she would get pieces that he felt would be right."

Another reason for additional takes was that Hellman didn't tell the other actors, either, exactly what he wanted. "I never discuss acting with actors," Hellman says, since he strives for realism. Warren Oates, a seasoned professional, didn't require much direction, but the amateurs were at sea. Bailey says, "There were times when it was hard to know what he wanted by doing another take because he wouldn't necessarily say anything. And there are directors like that who will say, 'Well, let's just do it again,' and not really give any directions." Bonnie Prendergast Freeman observes, "I recognized the style of keeping the inexperienced actors a little off-balance so as to get a natural or un-groomed performance."

By withholding the script, Hellman intended to give them leeway to be spontaneous and unaffected; ironically, their insecurity from not knowing where the script and their characters were headed, their resentment at the director because they thought he didn't trust them, and their ignorance of just what was expected of them caused some of the nervousness, self-consciousness, and woodenness Hellman was trying to avoid. At the beginning of the shoot, Jaclyn would coach them, but that tapered off because it clearly wasn't working. Walter Coblenz says, "Monte set the tone, and gave people the directions of pretty much what they wanted to do, and then after he'd let them go to see what they'd come up with." Robert Stradling, who was reloading film, says Hellman was often dissatisfied and the technique was time-consuming. The strain, tedium, and frustration of doing repeated takes without understanding what was wanted of him drained James Taylor of emotion, and he figured that that was what Hellman intended. "From the point of view of what Monte wanted out of us, the sort of emotional flatness—shooting it over and over again, doing a lot of takes—that sort of helped him get the feel out of us that he wanted."

While some viewers criticize the awkward performances, others say they are not so bad, and still others say the nonprofessional acting distinguishes the film and makes it unique. Warren Oates gave Hellman credit for helping shape his performance, which many viewers say elevates the efforts of the amateurs. "Monte would sit on me, in a sense, if I began to get too large," he said at an AFI seminar. "Because of the position of the character in the drama, as I say, he represents a comic and a tragic figure. You have to walk a very tight line to achieve this. So if I got a little too large in one area, Monte pulled me back and if I went the other way, Monte pulled me back."

While many in the counterculture at the time thought drugs stimulated creativity, dope could also slow the proceedings down. On at least one occasion, the gas station scene in Needles, Dennis Wilson repeatedly screwed up because he got so stoned. Nearly everybody who worked on the movie remembers that Wilson was usually drunk or high on drugs. In those days, drugs were pretty much de rigueur if you were a rock star, or even if you just wanted to be considered cool, but Wilson overdid it; crew members say he was usually high and behaving peculiarly. Buck Wheatley, who visited his brother Jay on the set several times, reminisces, "He was stoned all the time. He was loaded. JT [James Taylor] and everybody else was smoking dope and stuff, but they weren't loaded, like he was, on whatever he was on at the time." Bonnie Prendergast Freeman says that Wilson "seemed stoned or somewhat infantile in his behavior" when she saw him. Teamster Rick Mercier remembers that Wilson "did a little bit of everything; he drank, he smoked, he partied, he was a wild guy."

Warren Oates also had trouble regulating his alcohol and drug consumption, although he was more mature, professional, and in control of his behavior and emotions than Wilson. His daughter, Jennifer Oates, remembers an incident on the way back from the snake dance in Arizona. "When we were leaving, because my dad was smoking pot obviously, I asked him, 'Please don't smoke on the way home.' I took him to the back, outside of the motor home while everybody else was getting in. I said, 'Please don't.' But he did, anyway," she says. Warren Oates mischievously tried to turn on the non-drug-taking members of the film company. Bonnie Prendergast Freeman says he constantly invited her to accompany him, at the end of filming, to the Four Corners region to visit the great Native American territories and score peyote; although she enjoyed his company, she didn't use drugs and she declined. The auditor Reg Bisgrove says Oates offered to put mescaline in his beer. Bisgrove also declined. "They all thought I was Mr. Square," says Bisgrove, who although he is British and dresses conservatively, and had a button-down job in the finance department of a corporate Hollywood studio, nevertheless is lively and entertaining and had been around the block more than once by that time.

James Taylor would not kick his heroin addiction until years later, but at the time he was not using. He does recall, however, "There was some drinking, there was some dope smoked," and he remembers dropping mescaline with Oates and Joni Mitchell, but this was common at the time. He continues: "It was just sort of typical low-level recreational drug use." Peter Asher remembers hearing about dope on *Two-Lane*: "I know they were taking acid a lot during the movie, and that it was Warren, I think, who brought the acid."

Coming from small-town Maryland, Buck Wheatley and his brother Jay were unaccustomed to Hollywood- or hippie-style drug consumption. Buck says, "We were from the country. We weren't used to people partying like that. My God, they partied. Jiminy Christmas, after the thing was over, at nighttime we were sitting in the hotel drinking and smoking and playing guitar and singing." Like several others, Bisgrove observes, "What affected that show more than anything was drugs," because they impaired performance and judgment. "I did wonder who was paying for the drugs," the auditor adds.

∞

The gas station scene, the most lauded sequence in the movie, took two days to shoot at a Ute Station on Highway 54 in Tucumcari. The filmmakers liked the look of the location, but too much traffic passed by on the busy highway. For the appearance and to minimize noise, they wanted the highway semi-deserted, so they ran two traffic breaks some distance from the station. Consequently, shots could not go on too long, Kurtz recalls, because they had to release traffic, which built up quickly. They would have to stop shooting and wait for the traffic to pass. Kurtz says, "We'd have to wait fifteen minutes for another shot, even if it was just another take of the same camera angle."

The scene begins when the GTO pulls into the station. The camera is stationary as an attendant approaches the driver's seat from the right while a kid approaches the pump, on the passenger's side, from the garage, which is to the right and behind the car. Then the attendant circles around the back of the car to the pump on the left, while the hitchhiker circles around the front of the car to the right, and GTO walks from the driver's side to a cooler full of Coke on the right. The camera pans to show the hitchhiker walking to the rest room. Then the film cuts to show GTO leaning against the cooler in the foreground as the Chevy approaches from the highway in the distance. The camera pans a little to show the Chevy stop at the same pump as the GTO, on the other side. The three passengers get out, the attendant circles around to the front of the GTO to check under the hood, and the camera pans to show the Girl circle around the back of both cars and head off to the right to the restroom. As she is on her way, the attendant passes her going in the opposite direction. The film cuts to the restroom, then cuts to the Driver, then pans a little as he walks from the back of the Chevy to the pump and leans his elbows on it. It cuts to GTO, then the hitchhiker passes him on the way to the GTO to pick up his stuff. Then the camera pans as GTO walks to a gas pump directly across from the Driver. The hitchhiker passes them and continues off across the road to resume hitchhiking.

The long scene continues in this fashion. There is little dialogue but lots of activity—mostly people moving at an unhurried pace. The four lead actors, the gas station attendant, the kid, and the Texas hitchhiker appear, circle the cars, and weave in and out of frame. They go back and forth, around and out. Characters come and go, moving around almost like skaters in an ice show. The camera doesn't move much, but people walk in various directions across the frame, and the shots continue for quite a long time. Characters play their parts and leave, then other characters enter the stage.

To explain and put into context his mentor's style, John Bailey describes Gregory Sandor as a creature of habit who adhered to rituals in his personal as well as professional life. Every night, no matter where he was, Sandor would finish his dinner by eating one scoop of vanilla ice cream and smoking one Delicados cigarette, and then he'd go to bed early. Bailey observed him follow this routine without fail on all the movies they worked on together. "And the ritualistic way that Gregory led his personal life off camera is also the ritualistic way he worked. And for any cinematographer that really understands how you put shots together and everything, there is a tremendous sort of discipline and coherence and continuity to the way Gregory worked. If you look at a lot of the other American New Wave films of the early seventies and how chaotic they are—lots of zooms and flares in the lens and handheld and all this sort of thing. Greg's work isn't like that." Bailey describes the gas station scene as the result of a meshing of two similar sensibilities: "Monte's a classicist, too, Monte Hellman. But so was Gregory. So the two of them working together, those two interlocking classical disciplines, made the film look very controlled and planned, as it was. It was very stately."

Referring to the gas station scene, Gary Kurtz says, "Greg was really good at setting up shots." He continues, "Greg should really get the credit for the look of the film, because he did most of the photography, and he was very good at framing." The graceful photography clashes with the awkward, wooden performances, particularly Laurie Bird's, at the end of the sequence when the Driver and the Girl sit on a fence and talk. Bird walks with her head forward, looking down, her hair falling to cover her face as if she's trying to hide. Her timing is off, and she seems nervous, awkward, and self-conscious.

On a highway outside Tucumcari, Harry Dean Stanton played a small role as an Oklahoma hitchhiker who makes a pass at GTO. In a poignant scene, GTO rebuffs his advance, stops the car, and tells the hitchhiker to get out, in the rain, at night, in the middle of nowhere. When GTO rejects him, the hitchhiker weeps a little and stutters as he asks if they can still be friends. Although the role is small, Stanton is memorable. In those days, homosexuality was not acceptable to most people; a review of *Two-Lane* by Jay Cocks in *Time* magazine, then an extremely popular publication that reflected mainstream thinking, called Stanton's character "a faggot cowpuncher." Still, Stanton's character is sweet and his scene is moving. When GTO, repulsed by the hitchhiker's timid advances, tries to dump him by the side of the road in a remote location on a rainy night, we feel empathy for the man who fears he will be stranded. Although brief, the sympathetic portrait of a gay character is to the film's credit. Stanton had worked with Hellman before, in *Ride in the Whirlwind*, and the actor had agreed to play a role in *Two-Lane Blacktop* without seeing the script beforehand. Stanton did not know he would play a gay character. "They didn't tell me till I got there, which pissed me off," Stanton says. "Maybe I wouldn't have done it if he'd showed it to me."

Stanton brought along a guitar, an old Martin. Stanton says that James Taylor "borrowed it and he loved to play it, and I think he wanted to buy my guitar." Stanton remembers Taylor using his guitar when he was composing "Hey Mister, That's Me up on the Jukebox." But, Stanton says, "I didn't sell it to him."

Jarod Hellman says his earliest memory is of being four years old and going with his family to pick up Stanton from the airport when he flew in to Albuquerque to join the film company. Then the Hellmans took him out to dinner. Stanton, Jarod recalls, "was flirting shamelessly with the waitress," really laying it on strong. The little boy was impressed when Stanton tipped her $100.

∞

In a later scene, back on the road, when a cop pulls GTO over, the Driver stops nearby and makes up some stories to try to get him in deeper trouble. After the cop releases him, GTO catches up with the Driver, and he is angry. As a peace offering, the Driver and the Mechanic offer him a hard-boiled egg. Hellman wasn't satisfied with Oates's performance when he ate the egg; Oates thought he should become like Hamlet, and it affected his performance. Hellman thought it wasn't coming out right. Oates told an AFI seminar, "If he likes it he prints it. If he doesn't, we go again. I eat another egg. *Eighteen eggs.*" After each take, according to Oates, the director would say, "Once again, please," quietly and firmly.

# 6

# Potholes

On the way to their next destination, Durant, Oklahoma, the teamster Dick Austin lost his way. Austin worked for Universal, and drove a Does-All, which carried camera and electrical equipment, "and just heavy stuff," according to Austin. It was an old Crown bus that had been converted for this use, and it weighed fifty tons and was on air rides, or air bags used to cushion the suspension. "It was kind of an unusual ride. It rocked back and forth like a boat, and the crew, the actors liked to ride with me because they liked that. I don't know why, unless they'd smoked a joint before they got in."

When Austin got lost on the way to Durant, he spied a child by the side of the road and pulled over to ask directions. "We stopped at this little town just before Durant, and there was this young boy about seven years old, eight years old, and we asked him where Durant was, which way Durant was, and he was chewing tobacco, and he spit and he said, 'Y'all mean *Du*-rant?'"

The film company stayed at the Holiday Inn in Durant while they shot in nearby Boswell. Reg Bisgrove, the location auditor, had to take some money out of the bank and wanted a police escort because shady characters were lurking around the hotel. Bisgrove worked in finance and production at Universal. "On any show, they always try to spend more than they should," Bisgrove says, and Ned Tanen had sent him to safeguard the funds on Peter Fonda's picture *The Hired Hand* and Dennis Hopper's *The Last Movie*. "They allowed people to have money that really were druggies," Bisgrove says. "Would you trust your money to these people?" he asks, referring to pot-smoking, counterculture filmmakers suddenly given charge of Hollywood-studio, feature-sized budgets.

"I had to call Ned if they were doing anything stupid." Tanen chose him for the job, Bisgrove says, because "he knew I had worked with some of the drug people in Hollywood and I left them alone. I wasn't too righteous, although they thought I was." Since Tanen had the mistaken impression that Monte Hellman was a druggie, he sent Bisgrove along on *Two-Lane Blacktop* to keep an eye on the money.

Bisgrove tried to look up the office number for the chief of police to ask for protection from suspicious-looking characters and was surprised to find it was unlisted. "That shows you how much crime there was," he says. "I had to physically go find him and make sure a cop would go to the bank with me because they were just waiting for me to go get $50,000." Since the film company was on the road, they needed access to more money than they would have in Hollywood. Credit cards were not widely accepted then, particularly in the small towns where they filmed. Buck Wheatley, who had never been on a movie set before, was impressed. "There was a man with a suitcase full of money on the doggone movie." Wheatley recalls that a radiator broke on one of the cars, and he and his brother Jay went to get it repaired. "You didn't take the radiator into town and say, 'Well, these people in Los Angeles are going to send you a check. We need it fixed in fifteen minutes because we've got 100 people standing around.' Well, that doesn't work. You go into town and you say, 'Here's $200, can you fix it?' Because you couldn't have somebody say, 'Well, we're not going to get a check from Los Angeles for six months for fixing this thing.'"

Bisgrove observed that Gary Kurtz and Walter Coblenz were responsible and diligent, and he says they helped him keep track of the funds and keep costs down. Like many others on the shoot, Bisgrove didn't talk much to Hellman. The director has an ascetic quality and is not materialistic; he didn't immerse himself in financial details and was preoccupied with realizing his vision on film. But when Bisgrove did speak to the director, he says, they didn't communicate well. Hellman "had no concept of money," Bisgrove says. "I thought he was wacky."

∞

It was raining in Boswell when they were scheduled to shoot a scene at a gas station where the Mechanic steals a license plate and GTO passes out drunk. The forecast was for continued rain, so Walter Coblenz decided to proceed. "I just did a lot of things that if I had been an executive I wouldn't have let me do," Coblenz says. "An example would be certain weather decisions on what to shoot." He made the best decision he could based on the information available. But after they had filmed the master shots when it was raining, it suddenly stopped. So they needed to fabricate some more rain to complete the rest of the shots.

The driver Craig Pinkard describes Boswell in those days: "It was just a little town along the railroad tracks, and it was kind of a dying town. At that time, the railroad had shut down and there was no work, and it was just a little rural community with this little town." It had only a volunteer fire department. Gary Kurtz arranged for a fire department in a nearby town to bring a fire engine to help the filmmakers. For two days, firemen and teamsters held the powerful fire hoses vertically, two or three men per hose, shooting water up into the air so it would pour down to simulate rain. There was rain in the scene where the characters come into town, and rain at the gas station. For shots that were supposed to take place after the showers had stopped, they wet down the streets downtown and in the residential neighborhood surrounding the gas station so it would look like it had rained recently. They used water from the town's water tower, which is visible in the distance, behind the Chevy, in a scene where the Driver returns to the gas station with the Girl.

Although townspeople in Oklahoma were for the most part gracious, friendly, and helpful, some of them, watching the proceedings, thought the filmmakers were wasteful and irresponsible to use so much water, and some were irked. According to Craig Pinkard, some of them were "redneck types and we were in their territory. And there was a guy, an old man, they called him 'the judge,' and he didn't like us at all. And he was like ninety years old, he wore bib overalls, but he was the judge there, he was the local magistrate, I guess. He'd wear bib overalls and stand in the local market where we were shooting, and he'd get in the way. I mean, he was there so he could get in the way." The filmmakers placated the old man sufficiently to get the footage they needed.

Unfortunately, they depleted the town's water supply. The elevated tank they were using to get their water held 30,000 gallons, and they emptied it. That made some of the locals angry. Jim Thornsberry recalls a threat from two men in a pickup truck. The day after the film company used up Boswell's water, Thornsberry relates, he was driving his new car with California plates. "The people were kind of upset with us, and we were just about ready to leave then anyway, but it's understandable they would be upset with us, and I had my station wagon, and it was a new vehicle so it kind of stood out in this little town with usually older pickups and older sedans and things, and I was going out to the set, and two guys came driving up next to me," Thornsberry remembers. "They pointed a shotgun out of the window toward me." Thornsberry says the concluding scenes of *Easy Rider*, in which the rednecks shoot the hippie motorcyclists on the highway, flashed in front of his eyes. He continues, "And, anyway, they did that, and obviously nothing happened, they didn't shoot the gun." Coblenz adds, "A bunch of the younger townspeople were riding around in their pickups, which of course in Oklahoma have guns mounted inside, and how real a threat it was, I don't think it was that real, but I decided to get out of there sooner rather than later."

Pinkard recalls the sad, befuddled looks on the residents' faces as the film company left: "We left and they were standing there, 'What just happened here?' It was pretty sad, really, but that's the way they did it." The filmmakers reimbursed the town for the water, but if a fire had started, the residents wouldn't have been able to put it out, Pinkard observes. "We shot in these towns with these poor people. We'd come into town and just destroy the place and then move on, and they'd go, 'What the hell happened here?'"

Film companies are notorious for leaving a mess behind, and the people in Boswell were justified in their indignation. And the threat from the thugs with a shotgun was an aberration. "My wife was born and raised in Oklahoma," John Bailey says, in the state's defense. "Even in 1970 it wasn't a red state. Oklahoma was an agrarian, workers' state" that had voted Democratic for many years. Gary Kurtz says that people in rural areas and in the South accepted the filmmakers despite their hippie appearances. In Arkansas and Tennessee, he says, "the people were very friendly. They were very car-conscious people. They loved hot rods and they loved talking about cars, and how to customize cars and things, and that was the common thread. They didn't really care that we were from California and in the movie business. The link was the cars."

After Durant, the next stop was Little Rock. Nearby, at the Bright Spot road house on US 70 at Percy, they filmed the scene where a menacing young man delivers veiled threats aimed at the Driver and the Mechanic, before GTO defuses the situation and charms him. The key grip, Chuck Record, was proud that Hellman asked him to play an impatient motorist on a highway near Little Rock. He honks at the Chevy and tries to pass, but the Driver refuses to pull over and let him by. In the next scene, the Driver swerves off the road to avoid cars that have collided in a fatal accident. Dorothy Alsup, Gary Kurtz's sister-in-law and babysitter, remembers how the accident was staged. "One of the crew members lay down being dead." Later, the film company shot the scene outside the graveyard, where GTO lets out the old woman and the girl, at the Memorial Gardens Cemetery on US 70, west of Hot Springs.

∞

As the film company moved across the country, James Taylor's song "Fire and Rain" climbed the charts. He became famous during the shoot. On October 3, the song reached number 30 on the Billboard charts, and on October 10, the day after the film wrapped, it hit number 10, on its way to number 3, where it peaked. Gary Kurtz remembers, "He was just becoming popular as a recording artist—as a matter of fact, 'Fire and Rain' was just starting to show up on the jukeboxes in some of the towns we shot in, so just to annoy him sometimes the crew members would put his song on the jukebox while we were setting up." Taylor was not used to his newfound fame and felt uncomfortable. Kurtz adds, "I think he was embarrassed about it." Harry Dean Stanton and Chuck Record remember Taylor writing the song, "Hey Mister, That's Me Up on the Jukebox," which Taylor says is "a song, and I've written a number of them actually, just sort of about the experience of taking a very private process public."

Taylor's budding fame was an added draw to journalists who visited the set. Writers from *Show*, *Rolling Stone*, *The Realist*, and other magazines came and wrote feature stories. The writers would stick around for a few days. "There was nonstop press," says the film's publicist, Beverly Walker. Their feature stories, published months later, would raise expectations for the film before it came out.

Ned Tanen visited, but not in the role of a meddling studio executive. "It wasn't like, 'The studio executive is coming today!' It was just that 'Ned Tanen is coming down,' and he spent a few hours with us, or maybe even a day or two," Walter Coblenz says. "It was one day when we were doing a big car racing scene at night. It was a very friendly visit, it wasn't, 'You're over budget, you're overspending, you're this, you're that,' because we weren't any of those anyway." Hellman said Universal kept its word not to interfere. "Nobody bothered us at any point. It was really terrific," according to Hellman. "A marvelous way to make a movie."

When Tanen returned to Hollywood, he told Selznick he had high hopes that the picture would be a hit. "He came back and he said, 'It really looks terrific.'" Aside from Tanen's brief visit, and the watchful eye of Reg Bisgrove, who had instructions to monitor expenditures and to report back if the filmmakers ran amok, the two executives relied on the film's producer, Michael Laughlin, to keep them apprised of the movie's progress. Selznick says, "Laughlin was presumably our voice of stability on this project and so it was Laughlin's duty to kind of check in with us periodically and let us know what was going on." Laughlin mentioned to them that James Taylor, although not using at the time, had not yet kicked his heroin addiction, and that he was upset about not getting the script, as well as about the ferocious dialogue coaching. "Ned and I said, 'Well, is there something we should do about it?' He said, 'No, I just want you to know that it's under control.' So if Laughlin was saying it was under control, Ned and I looked at one another and wondered whether Laughlin had a full picture of what was going on." They had been worried that Laurie Bird might not be capable of giving a competent performance, but the producer reassured them. Laughlin told them, "'I just want you to know we're on budget, we're on schedule, everything looks well,' and then he'd leave the office, and Ned and I would look at one another and say, 'Well, we let this ship go out from the harbor, and now that we let it loose from the moorings there's nothing we can do about it.'"

The two executives found Laughlin and Hellman an odd pairing. Selznick recollects, "I said to Ned at one point, 'How did Michael Laughlin get attached to this project?' Ned said, 'Damned if I know.' And I said, 'Well, somebody put him on to Monte Hellman. Do you think he really understands Monte Hellman?' Ned said, 'You tell me.' I said, 'I don't know.'" The executives also found that Laughlin could be opaque. Selznick was designated to take his phone calls. Tanen asked Selznick, "Are you getting anything cogent from these phone conversations?" Selznick remembers he replied, "Well, I'm trying. Michael keeps me on the phone for a long time, and I'm trying—I get to the end of the conversation and I say 'Michael, so in essence, what is it that you want to tell me in this call?' And Michael will say, 'Well, I said it all.' I say, 'I know, but what's the *essence* of what you were trying to tell me?' He'll say, 'Well, I can't put it into a few words.' So he had the inability to address what he wanted to say cogently." In essence, Selznick says, Laughlin was "completely indirect."

Laughlin himself felt perfectly competent; he points out that he had produced two films made in England not long before this time. And the people he was dealing with were hardly seasoned veterans of the film business. "The executives at both Cinema Center, as well as Ned, were just setting up shop," and were administrators who had never physically produced a movie, he points out. Additionally, although the director and performers hadn't made studio films before, Coblenz had, and Laughlin relied on him to keep the movie on track. He was not worried about Taylor's heroin addiction, which turned out not to be a problem. "Monte's wife was the only worry," he says, and he had forestalled any disasters on her account by insisting on the right to send her home if she became too troublesome.

∞

Just outside Memphis, they filmed the day at the races at the Lakeland International Raceway on Interstate 40. They couldn't afford to stage the scenes, so they just integrated the car and actors into the action on an actual day of races. This necessitated moving extremely fast with much cooperation, John Bailey remembers. "We tried to fold ourselves into it. And so there were times when it was like trying to shoot a concert, a live concert when it's going on and you have to shoot it whether you're ready or not, and if the camera breaks the concert still goes on. We had a lot of times where people were just jumping in and running around at these stock-car or these racing events, drag strip events, so everybody would suddenly get very involved in moving whatever had to be moved because it was a ticking clock."

They entered the Chevy in one of the races. With Jay Wheatley driving, the real race car that Richard Ruth had built won in its class in one of the competitions. Gary Kurtz also remembers a mishap. "Jay Wheatley was our ace stunt driver—a race car driver and a mechanic—and I remember at one of the runs at Memphis he came out and got about half way down the track, and the transmission blew up and threw pieces of metal all over the place. We towed the car back to the pit, and he put a new transmission in it and had the car back on the track in about thirty minutes."

For the racing scene that ends the film, James Taylor would have to be at the wheel, and Wheatley instructed him. Taylor says, "Jay definitely did show me how I should drive the car, how to drag race, how to come off the line, how to burn the tires, and at what rpm to shift." Although almost all of the rest of the movie was shot in order, this, the last scene, was shot second to last. The filmmakers shot the scene where the Girl departs with the young motorcyclist at Crafton's Restaurant in Deals Gap, North Carolina, after they finished the racing scene at the airstrip at McMinn Airport in Athens, Tennessee.

For the final shots, where Taylor takes off in a race on the airstrip, Jay Wheatley put the car into position for him. Taylor vividly remembers what happened next: "We were doing takes of racing down this runway, and after a couple of runs the car overheated. So when that happens they turn the car on, let the motor idle, and then spray down the radiator to speed the cooling of the engine so that we could do it again. So there was this puddle of water in front of the car, and so they backed the car up, drove it around the puddle, they shifted it into reverse to back it up to the starting point, and they left it in reverse. And in that car, reverse and first, you can't tell the difference from just looking at the gear shift. They're right next to each other. And so I didn't realize when I got in the car—I had left it in first gear when I turned the car off—I didn't realize it was in reverse.

"So the cameraman was in the back of the car, they'd taken out the rear seat and they had, with a chain, had sort of cinched the camera tripod down in the back of the car, and he was shooting high speed as I was going down so that they could slow the motion down later. So the cameraman was in the back, we had a chase car that was following us in case anything happened, and up until that shot someone had been right in front of the chase car, between the two cars, sort of photographing it as we got off the line. But he ran out of film, so he wasn't behind the car when this happened.

"The typical way to start a race, to come off the line in a car like that is you take the rpms up to about 6,500 when you can feel the valves start to float in the car, and it's about as fast as it can go and develop any power, and then you just dump the clutch, so it's just full out, you're floored. And the car is sprung to go forward but not to go backwards. So when I dumped the clutch in reverse, all hell broke loose. The front end of the car came off and jumped up into the air, the car—basically, it was like a big sumo wrestler stamping its feet, first one rear wheel and then the other would hit the ground. It was basically just hopping up and down, and it climbed up the front hood of the chase car behind it. If there had been a photographer, if he hadn't run out of film, he'd be dead for sure. And the poor cameraman was in the back with his eye on the finder there on the lens, and it totally blacked his eye out. It ruined the car."

Buck Wheatley, who witnessed the accident and can't even find words to describe the wreckage, says the mishap "broke everything under the car," but they had spare parts and could use parts from the other Chevys to replace the broken ones.

∞

After the film wrapped, many people heard James Taylor say that he would never act in another movie—and he never has. Craig Pinkard, Gary Kurtz, and Peter Asher all remember him telling them that his career as a film actor was over. "Afterwards, he said, 'I'm never doing another movie as long as I live,'" Asher recalls. Taylor says he enormously enjoyed meeting Rudy Wurlitzer and Warren Oates, and Dennis Wilson and Harry Dean Stanton. "It was enjoyable and compelling and engaging, certainly, all along, and at the end of it I just said to myself, 'Look, James, you've got the best job in the world. What you do, you basically are in control of it,'" Taylor says. "I was just happy that I was a singer/songwriter/recording artist and performing musician. It just sort of re-emphasized to me how great a place I was in."

∞

Some in the film company continued to shoot additional footage on the way back to Los Angeles, some took advantage of the return trip for personal reasons, and some were just happy to escape the discomfort of driving from town to town on a traveling film set and the seemingly endless tedium of waiting around for the shots to be set up and completed.

The script supervisor Bonnie Prendergast Freeman remembers that she worked out a deal with the transportation captain Jim Thornsberry to drive the normal '55 Chevy picture car used to shoot interiors from Maryville, Tennessee, back to Hollywood, trading her airplane ticket with the teamster who had been assigned to drive the car back. She remembers, "I rented a medium-size storage carrier which I towed, stopping in the cities where we had filmed, buying antiques that I brought home to Sherman Oaks. I stored my purchases while looking for a home to buy, which I bought on first sight for $32,000 with 10 percent down ($3,200 I had saved from per diem on various shows) and furnished it with my purchases on the way home from *Two-Lane Blacktop* locations."

While most of the cast and crew, except for the teamsters, flew back to Los Angeles, Gary Kurtz also drove. He reminisces, "I came back across the country with the cars and a couple of drivers and we shot footage, just incidental footage—pretty shots of driving into the sunset and racing along back country roads and things, filler shots that we used scattered throughout the film."

Jim Thornsberry was one teamster who did not drive back to Hollywood; after weeks on the road, he was sick of driving his station wagon. "The last day, we were in Tennessee, and we'd finished the last day's shooting. And my fondest memory was, I told my guys to load my station wagon on one of the auto carriers, and they did, and then when we took off in the plane, all my boys were on the road. And the plane took off and banked, and I saw them all driving down the road, and I thought, 'Oh, am I glad I'm not in that car!'"

∞

A year later, James Taylor appeared at the Hollywood Bowl and performed the song he had written about Monte Hellman and the experience of making *Two-Lane Blacktop* on the road, "Riding on a Railroad." Gary Kurtz was in the audience. "I remember going to the concert, Monte being there and James playing the song," says Kurtz. In the song, Taylor uses the metaphor of being a passenger on a train to convey the experience of being an actor in a movie. He writes of being carried along, performing another person's music instead of his own. He says that the man at the front of the train who thinks he is in charge is actually fettered, and is being swept up and borne along by his circumstances.

# 7

# The Wreck

Monte Hellman, who had extensive experience as a film editor, cut *Two-Lane Blacktop* in Rooms 225 to 227 at the Studio Motor Inn, across Lankershim Boulevard from Universal. Many rooms of the motel had been turned into offices or into editing suites, and were used for spill-over tasks such as script analysis. Gary Kurtz says Hellman wanted to work outside the studio so that executives wouldn't try to meddle. "Monte wanted to edit the film himself, and he didn't want to be in the editing building and have people around that would want to see it all the time. So they gave us a space across the street and never bothered us. So it was pretty quiet, the editing." But Dorothy Alsup, who worked as Kurtz's babysitter during production and as his assistant during post-production, remembers that the editing rooms were constantly noisy with the sounds of machinery and loud voices. Not only did the Moviola make noise, a clackety racket. But Hellman and Kurtz, who was helping with the editing, "had many discussions between them" and, when the Moviola was running, they had to shout at one another to make themselves heard over the clatter.

Hellman says the motel wasn't his first choice of a place to cut the movie: "We edited near the studio because Michael didn't want to schlep to my house, which I would have preferred. He never came to the cutting room." Laughlin, who had watched the rushes when the film company was on the road, says he didn't try to interfere with the editing because "I felt Monte was entitled to put his film together." But he says he did stop by the cutting room from time to time. "The editing room, like anywhere else Monte might be, was not a fun place. It was obvious that the film was going to be languid—not a lot of vitality."

In Arizona, they had shot a scene where the Driver and the Mechanic try to outrun the cops; they go into a residential neighborhood, pull into a driveway, get out of the car, and look through a window at a family played by Gary Kurtz, his wife, and his little kids. But they cut that and other scenes to keep the length down. Kurtz remembers that Hellman cut out the scene with Laurie Bird swimming because he felt that it stopped the momentum of the story for too long.

Wurlitzer's 118-page script, Hellman told an AFI seminar, "crams a lot on a page," and, filmed in its entirety, and edited with the director's leisurely pacing, would have made a four-hour movie. "We found, sometimes to the dismay of the writer, that we would use three lines out of a two-page scene, and that really got the scene across. Sometimes part of a scene is as good as the whole thing." Hellman added that writers and audiences have become used to overclarification. "The screenplay was very clear in ways the film was not. The film gets across similar ideas more economically and perhaps more intimately."

In editing, Kurtz recalls, "Monte had a routine that he liked to use, and he didn't want to rush things. A lot of people would watch a sequence on the Moviola and say, 'Well, you could cut that down a bit, it's playing a little slow.' But he had a particular rhythm in his mind that he liked to use. So I think it works, definitely, to the advantage of the film because it's not intended to be a high-energy type film like a recent one, like *The Fast and the Furious*, for instance, films about street racing which are just ludicrous. They're full of outrageous stunts that probably cost a lot of money but are unbelievably complicated and would never actually work in real life."

When Kurtz wasn't helping Hellman edit, he was shooting additional footage. "Back in LA, we shot some incidental shots like the opening titles of the film, which is just a photograph of the yellow line down the middle of the road at night. I shot that when we were in editing. I bolted the camera to the front bumper of a car and drove down Riverside Drive at 4 o'clock in the morning to shoot that title background shot." For the title sequence, Hellman used the sounds of someone turning the dial through various radio stations, which they had recorded during the shoot.

It also fell to Kurtz to figure out how to produce the movie's final shot of the film catching fire. Hellman said that the ending brought the audience out of the movie and also made a statement about speed—the speed of the film in the projector. Kurtz says, "I had spent a whole day shooting that last shot of the film burning up because in the days before digital effects the only way you could actually do something like that was actually just to do it. So I think I had six or seven copies of that final shot printed, and then we rented a screening room and I set up a camera and we projected that image on the screen and then stopped the projector to see. We knew definitely it would burn the frame—I mean, we knew it would disintegrate—but we couldn't tell how, so we just did it over and over and over again until we got one that looked pretty good."

Meanwhile, someone had to clear rights to the songs used in the movie, all of which are examples of "source music" that supposedly emanates from radios or jukeboxes or a character (such as the snippets of tunes the Girl sings off-key). At the time, Billy James was a successful talent scout and publicist who took on the job of music supervisor. James shared Kurtz's office as he made endless phone calls trying to clear the rights to the songs in the movie. James, who is extremely well-spoken, says of himself: "I am sort of a footnote in rock 'n' roll history, is what I am." As he recalls, he was "working for my dear, departed friend Terry Melcher as the publicity director of *The Doris Day Show*—Doris was Terry's mother." The *Doris Day Show's* offices were in the same building as Laughlin's at the studio on Radford Avenue in Studio City. James used to stop by Laughlin's offices. "Cindy Williams was his receptionist, the actress Cindy Williams—short, pert, sort of cute actress, high-energy," James continues. "Michael had a pinball machine in his office, and I used to go over there and use his pinball machine, and at some point or other I was retained."

James received a script with the tunes specified, so he didn't select them. Instead, his job was to determine who held the rights—that is, the publishers and the record companies—and to negotiate terms and conditions and secure permission to use the songs. He was supposed to negotiate favored-nations agreements with all the publishers, meaning nobody would be paid more than anybody else. As he recalls, this arrangement was made to keep the cost down. "I think there were some budgetary constraints, that's the impression I had." He would call music publishers and tell them that he wanted rights to use the music in a low-budget movie and that he had very little money to spend to secure them. He had no problem clearing the rights to the Doors song "Moonlight Drive," a fragment of which is played at a drive-in in Santa Fe when the Driver and the Mechanic challenge a drag racer played by Rudy Wurlitzer. James explains that the Doors were happy to cooperate because, "I got those kids their first record deal."

Only one holder of music rights balked at the favored-nations agreement, and maintained that the singer was too famous and the song was too celebrated to license for the fee the others were receiving. So, James asked Monte Hellman to step in and negotiate for the rights to Janis Joplin's version of "Me and Bobby McGee." Hellman approached Kris Kristofferson to ask if he could use the song he'd written about life on the road. Kristofferson misunderstood and thought Hellman wanted to use the songwriter's own version of the tune he'd written, and Hellman didn't have the heart to set him straight. Although Kristofferson had tried out for a role in *Two-Lane*, he hadn't gotten it, despite the backing of the casting director Fred Roos. But Kristofferson agreed to license his version of "Me and Bobby McGee" for favored-nations terms, and it became the song most associated with the movie. The song is the story of a man on the road with the young woman he loves. He allows her to disappear despite himself, just as the Driver helplessly watches the Girl take off with the motorcyclist.

Billy James's job entailed "dozens and dozens and dozens of telephone calls that I had to make to make this thing happen." It wasn't a creative job, where he chose the songs, it was a matter of calling people who were busy or out of the office, waiting for them to call back, calling them again to remind them he wanted to talk to them, missing their call when they did call back because he was on the phone with somebody else, and finally reaching them. "It did take a tremendous amount of time. It was quite tedious. It was not my idea of a good time. It's just the phone calling back and forth, back and forth that I'm not constitutionally disposed to enjoy."

James found the job so distasteful that when Gary Kurtz approached him to secure music rights on the producer's next film, James turned him down. "After I did the job for *Two-Lane*, he asked me if I wanted to do another picture and I declined, saying that it wasn't my idea of a good time to be doing it. And that other picture was *American Graffiti*."

Meanwhile, the film's publicist, Beverly Walker, had sent *Two-Lane*'s script to *Esquire* magazine and pitched a story. Editors are inundated with press releases, most of them self-serving, and most of which they toss out. In a public relations coup for Walker, the magazine printed the entire screenplay, and devoted its cover to the movie. Under the headline "Read it first! Our nomination for the movie of the year: *Two-Lane Blacktop*," the magazine's editors ran a picture of Laurie Bird hitchhiking on a country road. "I was a hot publicist," Walker recalls, because she had previously promoted innovative, critically acclaimed films. Before *Two-Lane*, Walker had worked on *Zabriskie Point*, which, while a flop, was directed by the celebrated director Michelangelo Antonioni. "Before that, I headed the PR staff for the New York Film Festival, as well as individual films that were hot-hot-hot like *Bonnie and Clyde* and *The Graduate*." Walker, an extremely bright woman who went on to write for *Film Comment*, *Sight and Sound*, and *Premiere*, and authored the book *Jack Nicholson: Anatomy of an Actor*, was well-connected with Hollywood filmmakers and New York editors. So, with her track record, when she pitched an idea, editors listened. "I was heavily credentialed and totally in tune with the New York media. Everybody knew me, and I knew everybody."

Also, the media tries to anticipate trends and be the first to spotlight music, books, and movies before they become widely popular. Editors, as well as studios, were looking for the next hit movie, and Tanen, Selznick, and many others hoped *Two-Lane* would be *Easy Rider* with a hot rod and a muscle car. Finally, *Esquire* appealed to a hip audience, and, as Walker points out, Rudy Wurlitzer was considered cool. "Rudy also had a certain sort of underground reputation, but chi-chi. He's the scion of the Wurlitzer family, the Wurlitzer organ people. So they decided they wanted to publish his script." *Esquire* ran the story in April of 1971, when the movie was still in post-production, three months before its release. This prominent plug in a hip magazine led studio executives, the filmmakers, and the public to expect that *Two-Lane* would be a hit.

However, Monte Hellman was cutting together a dreamy, slow-paced film with long silences, which was nothing like *Easy Rider*. From its first scenes, *Easy Rider* is an eye-catching crowd-pleaser. As the movie opens, characters snort cocaine, duck low-flying airplanes, drive a Rolls Royce. The protagonists are hippies who dress in leather and fringe, smoke joints, freak out on acid, talk about astrological signs, and end their sentences with "man." The landscape in the background, as they speed along on their motorcycles, is spectacular. Dennis Hopper stands up one-legged on his bike, Jack Nicholson mugs for the camera. The film is filled with "wow!" moments. And the score is made up largely of loud, fast, then-recent rock 'n' roll hits. *Two-Lane* is much more sedate and unembellished. Characters dress in jeans and T-shirts, don't take drugs, and don't talk much. Most of the time, they don't even drive very fast. The story takes place on dusty country roads, not Monument Valley. The music is minimal and is played quietly.

Once Hellman had assembled a first cut, he went across the street to show it to Ned Tanen and Daniel Selznick. Selznick explains, "Filmmakers are just so tense when they're dealing with studio executives. We tried to create this relaxing atmosphere. In fact, we'd deliberately come down from the Black Tower, we didn't want any people going up to our offices." To avoid intimidating Hellman by inviting him to Selznick's office on the eleventh floor or Tanen's on the fourteenth floor, they met Hellman in the commissary, "so that we were at least human-size and not tycoons," Selznick continues. Then they went to a screening room on the lot. Hellman showed them the movie, and Tanen gave his usual response: he said he'd talk to the filmmaker the following day. Tanen was proud of Hellman; in the end, the film came in at $875,000, a little under budget.

After Hellman left, Tanen and Selznick discussed what they'd seen. "I said, 'Ned, there's a real problem.' He said, 'What is it, what's the problem?' I said, 'The movie is about who's going to win the race and who's going to get the girl.' He said, 'Yeah.' So I said, 'Well, the film is about one but not the other.' I said, 'The other half has been dropped by Monte for reasons I don't understand.' He said, 'Well, do you want to talk to Monte about that?' I said, 'I will, absolutely.' So he said, 'Let me know whether you succeed or not because,

Danny, don't forget, we give them final cut. And if he says no, Danny, I'm not prepared to change it. Then we'll release it as is.'"

The following day, Selznick met with Hellman. "I said, 'Monte, here's what I believe. I'm sorry I didn't mention it before when I read the script, but it's very clear to me now. And I think we could give you a little more money to shoot some new scenes if they could be written so it's very clear that there's a complete resolution of the story.' And he looked at me in that lovely, dazed quality that Monte has—a sort of dazed, dreamy quality. He said, 'Danny, I honestly don't know what you're talking about.' I said, 'Well, I really think this picture has tremendous potential if you just get these two storylines resolved.' He said, 'I don't see any way back. I don't see any way back. You know, I had this vision of the film and I've edited it the way I saw it, and I don't embrace your vision.' And I said, 'Well, Monte, I don't think it's going to be a *success* if you don't do that.' He said, 'Well, then in the end I'll know that you were right and I was wrong.'"

Other Universal executives were not happy with the movie, and tried, in vain, to persuade Hellman to change it. "They were expecting a totally different kind of movie—the suits, the Wassermans," Laughlin says. "In other words, they were thinking it would be much more action-oriented—I mean, teenagers being teenagers." Gary Kurtz also recalls their complaints. They objected to the film catching fire at the end, he says. "They didn't like the ending. They thought it was too weird." Also, under the opening titles the filmmaker ran footage Kurtz had shot in the middle of the night of the yellow lines in the center of Riverside Drive in the San Fernando Valley. And, instead of music, he says, "Monte wanted to use the radio for the titles, but it's not music, it's actually turning the dial, turning through multiple radio stations which we found and recorded on the trip, to get an idea of someone changing the stations on the radio. And the studio didn't like that much, either."

Studio executives were particularly peeved that James Taylor, or at least Dennis Wilson, didn't sing in the movie or even contribute a song or two to the soundtrack. They had hoped the two rock stars would lure young viewers, but fans who came to see Taylor and Wilson would want to hear their music. Taylor had initially offered to write a song in a deal memo written by his agent, Mike Medavoy, but Hellman declined; he had decided from the first that he wanted only source music and Laughlin backed him. "The agreement we had with James from the beginning was that we weren't exploiting his music," Laughlin says. "Monte thought the engine should be the score, and that was going to make it unique and make it different and make it more authentic" than a more conventional movie with a musical score, Laughlin adds.

When they saw the first cut, Universal higher-ups suggested that the actors contribute some tunes to juice up the movie and, in James Taylor's case, to take advantage of his newfound popularity. Although he had not been famous when he agreed to do the film, he had become so well-known that *Time*, then one of the most widely read magazines in the country, put him on the cover of its March 1, 1971, issue. Gary Kurtz remembers that by this time, Taylor was no longer willing to contribute music to the film. "They suggested that maybe he could do a song or two on the soundtrack and then put it on one of his albums, but he didn't like that idea, and he was a reluctant participant in the project anyway. He wasn't really an actor."

The executives didn't want to take "no" for an answer. They thought a James Taylor song or two was crucial to attract a large enough audience to make the movie a commercial success. "The issue of music was heated at the time," Beverly Walker remembers. Danny Selznick recollects pressure from Universal's head of distribution, Hy Martin. Martin, Selznick recalls, "was a guy with a great track record of being able to distill what a movie was in a trailer and in the ads, in the text in the ads and the pictures in the ads so that audiences would know what to expect of a film." Martin leaned on Selznick. "He said, 'You know, I think this has an audience, but we've got to tap into James Taylor's popularity. We've got to feature songs on the soundtrack and there's not enough of James Taylor on the soundtrack.' I said, 'Hy, we've got a delicate issue here.' He said, 'Well, what is it?' I said, 'Well, we're not supposed to look at James Taylor and Dennis Wilson and listen to their voices on the soundtrack because they're supposed to be characters in the film. They're not singers in the film.' He said, 'That's not important.' And I said, 'Well, there's an authenticity to Monte's work. You really believe these characters are living through this.' 'They're going to have all kinds of other music on the soundtrack. We can't have James Taylor on the soundtrack?' I said, 'I don't know. I'll review it with Monte.'"

Selznick took Martin's request to Hellman. "I said, 'Monte, I'm sort of embarrassed to raise this issue with you, but I had this conversation with Hy Martin.' He said, 'So, tell me.' And I did, and he laughed, and he said, 'Danny, I hope you told him to go take a flying fuck.' I said, 'That's not my language, Monte. I said I'd raise the issue with you and I'd get back to him.'" Hellman was adamant that the music in the film would flow from the action, and the audience would only hear music the characters heard. At Universal, Beverly Walker recalls, "People were furious."

However, no matter how angry they got, Tanen intended to honor the contract. Tanen had given Hellman final cut as long as he avoided an "X" rating and delivered a movie that ran one hour and fifty minutes or less. According to Hellman, "I must say that they tried to influence us, particularly in the area of cutting down in length, and they had the final right to insist, of course, but they didn't even exercise that right—they wanted to work through persuasion."

The studio wouldn't have needed to pressure Hellman to shorten the film; he was naturally inclined to do it himself. His original cut was twice the length of the final cut. Hellman says the final cut was so much shorter largely because he tends to go overboard when he is cutting; he jokes that he practically has to have "my hands tied behind my back" so that he doesn't eliminate too much.

His second cut, to show to preview audiences, was about two hours and five minutes. The sneak preview was held on May 6, 1971, at the College Theater on Park Boulevard in San Diego. Michael Laughlin thought the movie was much too long, and remembers that many viewers walked out. Rudy Wurlitzer also attended. "I remember the reaction as being at best, mixed, and totally confused as most of the viewers were anticipating a traditional film about cars and car racing, with winners and losers, that included the relationships of the main characters. Most of the viewers seemed totally unprepared for such a dreamy existential exercise drifting on a river to nowhere." Gary Kurtz, who attended as well, agrees: "Many in the audience did not really understand the film. I think the preview was promoted as a hot rod film—a bad error."

But Danny Selznick recalls that the response was not all that bad. "In the world in which I grew up, sneak previews were essential," he says. "As I remember, the cards were mixed. They were not totally positive and they were certainly not negative, they were mixed. Some people loved it, some people were confused by it. But they were positive enough that the studio was prepared to go forward and try to create the most interesting poster campaign, and so forth, for it." After the preview, Hellman cut the film down to its final length of one hour and forty-two minutes. Unlike Selznick, Hellman did not put great stock in previews. "I don't pay much attention to preview cards. They were mostly bad, but I listened to the audience and saw where they shifted in their seats." Hellman said he didn't take out anything he didn't want to, and cut only because scenes didn't work or would make the film too long.

Lew Wasserman disliked the movie, but he had financed it and the previews were good enough to warrant an ad campaign. However, he had no optimism or enthusiasm for promoting it. "Lew Wasserman hated the film, no question," Danny Selznick recalls. "He chastised Tanen. He said, 'So you think this is hip? You think this is what the public wants to see?' Ned said, 'Oh Christ, yes. I mean, my God, with James Taylor and Dennis Wilson? Of course they're going to come see it.' And Lew said, 'Well, you know, this is what happens when you guys give filmmakers final cut. You're going to learn your lesson. I think this picture's going to go nowhere.'"

Wasserman, and many others, especially after the *Esquire* cover story touting the forthcoming *Two-Lane* as "the movie of the year," had expected it to be another *Easy Rider*. When it didn't turn out to be that sort of movie, they went forward with an ad campaign as if it were. Gary Kurtz remembers, "Universal really didn't like the film much, and Lew Wasserman hated it when he saw it, and they didn't put any time and energy into promoting it. One of the problems was they sold it like a hot rod movie, like some of the teenage hot rod films that were out in the early seventies or late sixties, and it wasn't that, it wasn't that at all. So that audience came, and it was disappointed, and the audience that would have been more interested in a more arty kind of existential road movie didn't understand that that's what it was, so it kind of missed on both counts."

One executive who actually liked the movie was Murray Weissman, who was then in charge of Universal's Motion Picture Publicity Department. "While I personally loved the film and always admired Monte's artistic talent, the studio did not. They didn't recognize what a gem it is and did little advertising to support its theatrical exhibition, much to my disappointment," Weissman says.

Michael Laughlin talked Universal into paying $10,000 to Stephen Frankfurt, then the highly regarded creative head at Young & Rubicam, to prepare an ad campaign for *Two-Lane*. Frankfurt had thought up the "Pray for Rosemary's Baby" poster and tagline in 1968 for Roman Polanski's now-classic film. Laughlin remembers, "He did research in schools and came up with the perfect ad for the generation: A California driver's license with the official photograph of James smoking a joint on the license. That was the ad—the California driver's license. Ned Tanen and I took it up to Lew Wasserman's office, and he and the Universal marketing people hated it. They wanted to capture the younger new market. But not really." The innovative poster conveyed that the film was cool and out of the ordinary; it was likely to have appealed to hip young people who would have enjoyed the movie. Danny Selznick also remembers the poster. "How foolish Lew was to reject it!"

*Two-Lane* also had a potential audience in car guys, who in later years would revere it for featuring a real race car instead of a cheap Hollywood imitation. But the studio didn't target car guys by placing ads in hot rod magazines, or booking theaters near streets where they liked to race in the San Fernando Valley and other locations in Southern California or elsewhere. The marketing campaign was mainly aimed at teenagers, and conveyed that it was an action movie about juvenile delinquents or daredevils who raced around in hot rods (even though this genre had gone out of fashion). Ned Tanen was savvy about car culture, Danny Selznick recalls, but the studio missed the boat. "Of course, it would have made great sense to promote this movie to car enthusiasts. Ned even suggested it to management. The idea was turned down out of a stupid fear that this would end up labeling the film as just a 'car movie.'"

Universal had some other posters made up that were ludicrous, failed attempts to convey the spirit of the movie and reach an audience that would appreciate it. One particularly outrageous and off-the-mark effort suggests a movie about fast cars, fast drivers, and fast women. On the top it shows an image of the Girl and her knapsack seen from the back; she looks stranded. Below, a row of pictures of the four lead actors foreshadows billboards advertising *Grand Theft Auto* video games with dangerous men and loose women. James Taylor frowns ominously, as though he's plotting revenge or illegal activities. Laurie Bird looks pretty, a little wide-eyed, and surprised, as if the hot rod gang had suggested tea and an orgy with their ladies auxiliary. Dennis Wilson looks downright thuggish, sneering as he chews on a fat cigar. Warren Oates seems unsettled by whatever dangerous and illegal proceedings are taking place. At the bottom of the poster is a scene of cars taking off in a drag race. Young men with a lot of facial hair wearing leather jackets are running; they resemble teenagers whooping it up or starting a riot. The poster suggests that these shady characters are brawling, screwing, and racing—and all at breakneck speed. The copy on the poster says: "Meet the Car Freaks . . . the Car Groupies . . . the Street Racers . . . the Spaced-out guys and girls who have speed to burn in life, in love!"

Danny Selznick would have liked to have objected to some of the inane, wildly misleading posters and ads the studio drummed up, but he knew better. "I was really quite frightened of Lew Wasserman," Selznick says. "I just found him really intimidating." When Selznick had seen the posters for *The Hired Hand*, he thought the image of Peter Fonda riding fast on a horse with two guns blazing gave a false impression of the movie and that it would have been a mistake to release them. One night when they were working late, Selznick went to Wasserman's office and told him the poster was misleading. He remembers explaining to Universal's chairman that people who liked the poster would be disappointed with the movie and create negative word of mouth. Meanwhile, people who might have liked the movie wouldn't go to see it. "So he said, 'So you want all these campaigns changed?' I said, 'I'm sorry, Lew, but you know I did grow up at my grandfather [Louis B.] Mayer's studio and I learned a few things, and you don't misrepresent what you're selling.' And he started to scream at me, with spit coming out of his mouth, and he said, 'Listen, Selznick, *you're* telling *me*, and Hy Martin, who's been here for twenty-three years, you're telling him how to run the advertising department? Get out of my office!' And I was shaking when I left, absolutely shaking when I left."

The final, lackluster poster that was released shows Laurie Bird sitting on the car and the other characters standing in front of her, with a country road in the background. Below is a close-up of James Taylor, presumably present to capitalize on his new popularity. While it is not misleading, it is vague; it doesn't suggest a teenagers-whooping-it-up movie, but it doesn't indicate what kind of movie it aims to evoke. Selznick remembers, "I would have preferred something that made it really look like a breakthrough movie, with very striking design or something. I mean, we all grew up loving Saul Bass and all those great titles and the posters he did, but Universal was still a big corporation and the decisions were handed down from on top." Hellman wasn't happy with the poster, either. "I preferred the driver's license poster," the director comments.

Monte Hellman had made a little film that, when it finally found its audience years later, would attract a committed following of cinephiles and car guys. Universal, unused to producing such movies, didn't have the understanding of the potential audiences, or the marketing apparatus needed, to reach them.

∞

*Two-Lane Blacktop* premiered at the Beekman Theatre in New York and the Pacific Theatre on Hollywood Boulevard in Los Angeles on July 7, 1971, the weekend after Independence Day, and the next week opened in Kansas City, Detroit, Atlanta, and other cities around the country. Hellman thought that Universal did a shoddy job advertising the film, and complained that the studio ran quarter-page ads for *Two-Lane* in the *New York Times* on opening day and on the following Sunday, while it paid for half-page ads on those days for its movie *They Might Be Giants*, starring George C. Scott, which had already been in release for a month.

Of the many studio films John Bailey would make, *Two-Lane* was the first, and he still remembers driving down Hollywood Boulevard and seeing it displayed on the marquee of the Pacific Theatre. "It was the first film that I did that I actually saw on a theater marquee," he says. "I remember the marquee, and I remember that *Esquire* magazine did something on the cover saying it was the movie of the year. Everybody was looking so forward to it, and I remember that when the movie was released the reviews were just so abusive I couldn't even read them. I read one and that was it. People openly mocked the movie because it was so unlike *Easy Rider*. I mean, it really was an American Bergman film in a way."

Some reviewers embraced the movie, others found it boring or pretentious. Jay Cocks, writing for *Time* magazine, gave it a rave review. "The film is immaculately crafted, funny and quite beautiful, resonant with a lingering mood of loss and loneliness.... Few film makers have dealt so well or so subtly with the American landscape.... Rock stars James Taylor and Dennis Wilson are fine as the Driver and the Mechanic: Taylor's gaunt face and haunted eyes and Wilson's strong, oblique presence suit Hellman's purposes perfectly. Best of all is Warren Oates as GTO.... It is a performance that places him among the finest American film actors ... one of the most ambitious and interesting American films of the year." *New York Times* critic Vincent Canby also liked it, calling it "a remarkably engaging movie."

But Roger Ebert in the *Chicago Sun-Times*, while recommending the film for Oates's performance, the road scenes, and its visual texture, objected to the characters' coldness. "It seems to come from a single vision of the road, the race and life, and paradoxically, the characters need to be impersonal so they don't interfere with this vision. They are all too impersonal, though, and that's bothersome. After half an hour or so, the fact that we're told so little about their inner workings becomes a distraction. There doesn't seem to be a good reason for making them so awesomely one-dimensional."

In the *New Yorker*, Penelope Gilliatt objected to the performances. "Apart from Warren Oates as GTO, nobody in this film acts. The members of the cast are simply photographed in leggy positions with varying species of scowl on their faces. They look zonked, and their minds have flown; typically uncharacterized symbols of the cracked-up nation that the cant of youth cinema makes America out to be."

And Joseph Gelmis, writing in *Newsday*, really slammed the unfortunate film. "The two young men who love, drive and care for the car are intellectual cretins. Their emotive impact is zero. They have as much personality as a crankshaft." *Newsweek*'s reviewer found the movie slow and lifeless. "Hellman turns the voltage so low that one is tempted to take the film's pulse to see whether the projector is still rolling."

Even *Esquire* turned against the movie; it retracted its earlier endorsement of *Two-Lane* as its pick for movie of the year. The Editor's Notes section announced a change of mind. "On the strength of the screenplay, which we read with avidity and delight, *Two-Lane Blacktop* was billed on April's cover as our nomination for movie of the year. Last week, preview screenings were held here in New York and some of us on the staff finally got to see a print. We now withdraw our nomination. The screenplay was wonderful—an account of a cross-country drag race in which a '55 Chevrolet serves as a metaphor for the human condition—but the film is vapid: the photography arch and tricky and naturally, therefore, poorly lit and unfocused; the acting (only one part is played by a professional) amateurish, disingenuous and wooden; the direction introverted to the degree that fundamental relationships become incidental to the film's purpose. The script has become a victim of the *auteur* principle." Beverly Walker was disappointed by *Esquire*'s aboutface. "They behaved very badly after the release. They disowned it and said, 'We made a mistake.' And they did that for years because the film was a flop. They were so embarrassed."

Hellman went so far as to write a letter to the editor of the *San Francisco Examiner* to point out that criticism in its review was unfair and based on a goof the writer made. In a letter dated August 24, 1971, on Michael B. Laughlin Enterprises, Inc., stationery, Hellman wrote: "In his review of *Two-Lane Blacktop*, Stanley Eickelbaum [Eichelbaum] demonstrates he can at least read, if he cannot watch and listen to movies. Following is Mr. Eickelbaum's quote:

"'I only talk when I'm uptight,' the Girl mutters, half unintelligibly. 'I'm not into words.'

"The dialogue he quoted from the film is not in the film at all, but in the screenplay published in *Esquire* magazine last April."

Like critics, audiences were split in their reaction, but not enough moviegoers went to see the film to make it even a modest hit; the overall response was lukewarm. The movie just didn't catch on; it played to dwindling audiences in a handful of theaters across the US for the next several months. Selznick remembers that the studio cut back theater bookings and the ad campaign "because the picture didn't open that well. It's classic, it happens every time a studio designates a certain budget for advertising. 'It shows if it has legs'—that was one of Lew's favorite terms. If the film has legs, they'll support it with more and more money and book it in more and more theaters, but if there doesn't seem to be an audience for it, they're not going to wait for some audience weeks later to discover it in Glendale. Or San Bernardino. So it was a very quirky film and *Two-Lane Blacktop* received mixed reviews. So Monte must have been very disappointed because up until then Monte had really been a cult figure and he really hoped, and I think we all hoped, this would establish him in the international film world."

*Two-Lane Blacktop* was shown at the Edinburgh International Film Festival, and it drew crowds in England when it opened there, but despite efforts by Universal and Gary Kurtz, it was not widely released with subtitles or dubbing overseas. In a letter to Kurtz, Arthur Abeles of Cinema International Corp. wrote that he had sent prints to various overseas territories for managers' assessments of the film's potential; "To our dismay, practically every manager rejected this picture on the grounds that it would cost more to release than we could possibly make back." He added that they had released the movie in one city, Auckland, New Zealand, where it had run for one week and had done "less than average business."

Similarly, a French representative for Cinema International Corp. wrote to Kurtz that he didn't think *Two-Lane* would make enough money to cover the costs of releasing it. In an ironic twist, the representative, Henri Michaud, informed Kurtz that the Universal chairman, who hadn't wanted to market the movie about street racing to car guys or hot-rodders, had told him *Two-Lane* was appealing to an automotive audience. "Mr. Wasserman," Michaud wrote in a letter dated September 23, 1971, "informed us of the surprising success it is enjoying in drive-ins throughout America."

Richard Ruth, who built the Chevys, heard that some audiences at drive-ins were fooled by the ending. "I know people back in Pennsylvania and Kentucky and Tennessee who went to the drive-in to watch it and they thought the movie was burning up. Everybody was honking their horns to try to tell the projector guy that it was burning up and then all of a sudden the credits came on."

The film's failure set off a flurry of finger-pointing. Some claimed that the movie was overhyped, that the *Esquire* cover story had set too high a bar and had raised expectations to a level that couldn't reasonably be met. Beverly Walker was blamed for doing too good a job: Hellman told her that the film had received excessive publicity and that that had harmed it. Hellman said that Wasserman had failed to support the movie because he disliked it; he said he thought the decision was personal, not professional. The studio blamed Hellman for insisting that his artistic integrity take precedence over commercial considerations and refusing to include a prominent, appealing musical score and a conventional ending.

Beverly Walker defends herself: "It is certainly true that very high-profile films do encourage an audience to expect certain things, and it's true the media campaign I orchestrated contributed to the *level* of disappointment. But the movie that Monte made would never have had great commercial success" because of the performances of the nonactors, the lack of a gripping musical score, and the pace, which was too slow to appeal to mainstream American audiences. For its part, the studio had demonstrated good faith by hiring top adman Stephen Frankfurt (although executives rejected his inspired ad of a driver's license showing James Taylor smoking a joint), and Wasserman had personally written to a foreign distributor to try to get the film released overseas after it bombed in the US.

The venture between the Hollywood studio and the auteur was doomed. Universal was not equipped to market a small artistic film to an audience of intellectuals and car guys, who years later discovered and championed the movie. But Michael Laughlin had chosen Hellman because he was a cutting-edge filmmaker, not because he was apt to produce a money-making movie, and he and Tanen believed in letting the director realize his vision without outside meddling. Hellman hoped and believed his film would be a financial success, but he stuck to his principles and refused to compromise to make the movie more appealing to a wider audience by capitalizing on James Taylor's fame and adding his music, or by changing the ending to resolve the storylines.

Not only was Hellman uncompromising (which was variously interpreted as nobly unwilling to sell out or foolishly intransigent), but his sensibility was less appealing to wide audiences than several other auteur directors of his time. Other young directors of groundbreaking studio films were more accommodating of audience expectations and desires. New Hollywood films such as *Easy Rider*, *The Graduate*, *The French Connection*, and *Bonnie and Clyde*, while inventive and innovative, were comparatively zippy, splashy, action-filled crowd-pleasers that observed established cinematic conventions. They had appealing, professional actors; engaging characters; stylish costumes; catchy tunes; emotionally manipulative soundtracks; witty, often humorous dialogue; dramatic or suspenseful storylines; and endings that resolved the story. If there was a race, somebody won; if there was a girl to be gotten, somebody got her. The heroine had good posture and wore makeup. By contrast, *Two-Lane* is a slow-paced car racing movie where nobody wins or even finishes the race, starring singers who don't sing, with near-mute, somewhat nasty protagonists, and a foul-mouthed, promiscuous leading lady. It has little dialogue, fairly drab costumes, and source music exclusively. *Two-Lane* is quiet, unhurried, and dreamy. The story, like the race, doesn't formally conclude. It just stops abruptly.

Rudy Wurlitzer notes that the movie's disregard for Hollywood conventions stumped audiences and hurt it at the box office. "I think what a lot of people were initially looking for in the film, they were looking for a film that had a beginning, middle and end, where you knew who won and who lost. And the same with the characters. You don't know whether these characters won or lost because they were outside that duality." Also, audiences expected a point of view, or guidance in what to feel about the story. But *Two-Lane* lacked good guys and bad guys, the music didn't tell the viewers which emotions they were supposed to feel, and the characters didn't triumph *or* get their comeuppance at the end. Some audiences felt cheated or confused. Wurlitzer continues, "That's part of the dreamlike quality of the film, that everybody comes at it with their own projections and fantasies, and that's what upset people when it first came out and they didn't know what to make of it."

Beverly Walker thought the performances hurt the movie. Although several reviewers praised the nonactors' work, in at least some scenes they are awkward, clunky, stiff, and self-conscious. In these years, directors often were put on a pedestal as the star of their movies; the director was the auteur while the collaborators were marginalized. "It's kind of insane when you consider Monte's background is in the theater," Walker says of Hellman's choice of nonactors to fill three of the four lead roles. "Was it just an ego trip—'I'm a genius who doesn't need trained actors?' It scared the shit out of me. I had just finished working on Antonioni's *Zabriskie Point* whose nonactors contributed mightily to the film's failure. Audiences laughed at their line readings. I feared Monte would suffer the same fate."

Not allowing the actors to see the script made matters even worse. *Two-Lane*, Walker continues, "has one actor who was so hostile and angry at Monte because of the way he was treated that he walked like a stone face. Imagine if he weren't James Taylor what people would think of *that* performance." In person, Walker found Taylor "warm, funny and sly" with the rare ability "to be completely himself at all times, not a scintilla of artifice." Peter Asher also was struck by the divide between his client and his onscreen persona. "I think James is kind of deadpan and that surprised me because he's such an excellent storyteller and so animated, and there was something a bit strangely kind of comatose about the whole thing and that surprised me. It wasn't good or bad, necessarily, maybe it's what Monte wanted, but knowing the funny, animated James that I knew, I was kind of going, 'Where's he gone?'" Asher adds that he thought the entire film had the same quality. "It is all a bit deadpan, the whole flavor of the movie. I mean, there are very few movies where there's a gigantic car chase and you actually don't really mind who won."

Selznick thought the studio should have insisted on additional music and a more traditional ending. "I felt we needed to support the filmmakers but also guide them to make the picture more acceptable to a wider audience. And there's something very heartbreaking to me about the fact that in order to give these filmmakers the freedom to make these films, we weren't permitted by Ned himself to coach them past a certain point."

A traditional ending and a musical score probably would have filled more seats. But they also would have destroyed the film's dreamlike quality and undercut its point. The three male characters establish a goal—a cross-county race for pink slips. However they allow this goal, which in a sense gives them identity as racers and gives their life meaning, to slip away and disappear. Instead of the finish line that will make them winners or losers, and will give their lives meaning, they are confronted with endless driving and meaningless racing on a never-ending road. Many viewers consider the movie a classic because of its quiet dreaminess, its philosophy, and its unconventional ending. Hellman's uncompromising fearlessness in crafting the movie his way made it unique and extraordinary.

On the other hand, some found it boring, elitist, or sexist. The deliberate, unhurried pace, while it appealed to some viewers, was not for everybody. The screenwriter, Rudy Wurlitzer, whose surname was a household name associated with jukeboxes, and the director, Monte Hellman, educated at the elite Stanford University, could have had many doors open to them. But they chose to, respectively, write cult novels and direct cult movies that could be interpreted as lamenting the meaninglessness of life. The two are highly regarded artists who were expressing themselves, but their art was outside of the mainstream and they were alienated from mass culture. Some find their work brilliant, but it also could be judged as self-indulgent whining—two privileged white guys estranged from the world because they cannot find purpose in the universe, complaining, "Oh, poor me."

And whereas GTO, the Driver, and the Mechanic are named for their possessions or their occupations, and although the film was written and made during the time of the women's liberation movement, the Girl is named for and defined in terms of her sex. Her name is more stereotypical than the others. Films don't always have a driver or a mechanic, and certainly don't have a guy named GTO (an exception is *Slacker*, in which the director Richard Linklater named a character in an homage to *Two-Lane Blacktop*). But most movies of those days and before did have a "girl" in her twenties or even thirties who was the love interest of the leading "man" (who generally wasn't much older than she was). While the Driver, the Mechanic, and GTO apply themselves to driving, racing, and picking up hitchhikers in their quest for meaning and identity, the Girl is a freeloader who hitchhikes rides from men, and only men, and she alone among the characters devotes herself to searching for a romantic partner. She's looking for her identity in romance. Although she picks up a few bucks panhandling in one scene, she is for the most part financially as well as emotionally dependent on men. While the character could be read as illustrating the futility of looking to others for self-fulfillment, it could also be considered a continuation of an unenlightened tradition of depicting women as wives or girlfriends whose chief interest is the man in their lives, to whom they play second banana.

∞

Hellman told friends he was chagrined that Universal and Lew Wasserman didn't market more aggressively a film that had been so eagerly awaited, that had had so many hopes riding on it, that Tanen and others anticipated would elevate the director's career. Martin Landau, a longtime friend of Hellman's, says, "I was in contact with Monte quite a bit at that time. It was heartbreaking."

# 8

# A Restoration

By the end of the summer of 1971, *Two-Lane Blacktop* had disappeared from all theaters except some drive-ins. As the years passed, colleges, revival theaters, and cinematheques would screen it from time to time, and later it started appearing on television. From 1972 to 1975, it played as part of a double bill at drive-in theaters that included the Starlite in Uniontown, Pennsylvania; the Cactus in Tucson, Arizona; the Lincoln in Buena Park, California; and the Grand in Paris, Texas. Starting in 1974, non-network channels started to broadcast it occasionally, and in 1991, A&E began showing it, followed a few years later by VH1 and Starz. Sometimes it was shown during prime time, sometimes at 9 a.m., sometimes at 3 a.m.

The experience of *Two-Lane* temporarily soured Michael Laughlin on Hollywood. After the film bombed, a disgusted Laughlin left Hollywood. He thought Universal had bungled the release. "Distribution is everything," Laughlin says. "Leslie and I were on our way to Sardinia. We both went into a meeting in New York with the executives, and they have seen it all before. They are the experts." Laughlin made no headway with the executives who had rejected the poster with James Taylor smoking a joint on a driver's license photo, and who wouldn't market the film to hot-rodders, and thus failed to target the hip crowd and the car guys who actually would have enjoyed the movie. "It was such a disappointment, Leslie and I got on the QE II and sailed for Paris and Sardinia and a grand, new summer house. I would have been happy never to return, and in fact, I took my time. And when we did return,

I put the house in Bel Air up for sale. The movie biz is very 'down market,' but when they really need to be, they're no good at it. Huge disappointment."

Laughlin next produced *Chandler* (1971), with Caron and Warren Oates. Laughlin and Caron were divorced in 1977, and he went on to write, direct, and produce several more films. Two that he directed, *Strange Behavior* (1981) and *Strange Invaders* (1983), received mostly favorable reviews but failed to catch fire at the box office. His last credit was as a writer of the 2001 flop *Town & Country*, starring Warren Beatty, but by all accounts he wrote a good script that was rewritten into a poor one. Laughlin became a golf enthusiast and wrote a book called *Radical Golf: How to Lower Your Score and Raise Your Enjoyment of the Game*, published in 1996.

Laughlin now lives on Oahu, in Hawaii, in a dandy house designed by the architect Cliff May. His full-time chauffeur drives a taxi, so as Laughlin escorts guests to fabulous bars and restaurants in Honolulu, the meter ticks away.

After *Two-Lane* was completed, Monte and Jaclyn Hellman ended their rocky marriage, and Laurie Bird moved into his house in the Hollywood Hills. They married, and he gave her a part as Harry Dean Stanton's wife in his film *Cockfighter*, released in 1974. She had a small role in one final movie, Woody Allen's *Annie Hall* (1977), as the girlfriend of a recording honcho played by Paul Simon. She then left Hellman and went back to New York, where she moved in with the singer Art Garfunkel. She was living with him in 1979 when she died from an overdose of Valium. She was twenty-six years old.

After the divorce, Jaclyn Hellman moved to Northern California. According to Martin Landau, "Jackie was an unusual person. She ended up being a guru of sorts and having a following."

Dennis Wilson never appeared in another movie. He continued as drummer and back-up vocalist for the Beach Boys, and in 1977 he released a critically acclaimed solo album, *Pacific Ocean Blue*. But his voice deteriorated, and he sank further into alcoholism and drug addiction. His natural playfulness and lack of self-control, combined with his frequently zonked-out condition, led to bizarre, anti-social behavior onstage, embarrassing his bandmates, who kicked him out of the group. In December 1983, he had just turned thirty-nine and was homeless when he spent a day drinking alcohol and then went diving in the ocean in Marina del Rey, California, where he drowned.

The beloved Warren Oates continued to work regularly in film and television. He appeared in two more movies directed by Monte Hellman, *Cockfighter* (1974) and *China 9, Liberty 37* (1978). In his later years, he was in ill health, and in the days leading up to his death, he complained of chest pains and troubled breathing, but he didn't see a doctor. He died of a heart attack in 1982 at the age of fifty-three.

With some ups and downs, James Taylor went on to have a mostly illustrious career and enjoy extraordinary longevity as a singer/songwriter, and became one of the most popular and honored American musicians. He kicked his heroin habit when he was in his mid-thirties. Despite the frustration and aggravation he felt during the making of *Two-Lane Blacktop*, he sat down with Monte Hellman for an interview for the Criterion Collection DVD released in 2007, during which he was gracious and pleasant. In 2015, he was awarded the Presidential Medal of Freedom, the country's highest civilian honor. Also that year, when he was sixty-seven years old, forty-five years after he filmed *Two-Lane Blacktop* and his initial hit song appeared on the Billboard charts, he had his first number 1 album, *Before This World*.

Taylor told a number of people that he would never make another movie after *Two-Lane*, and he never did. "That was enough for me," he comments. "In fact, I've never seen it. We looked at a little bit of footage when we needed to loop some sound to overdub dialogue on a couple of scenes and stuff, but aside from that I never went to it. I just have the sense always that it would be externalizing, in a way, to watch myself act, and since I didn't have any intention of doing any more of it there was nothing to gain by my seeing it and something to be lost, I thought. So I remember it as the experience of making it, but so far I haven't actually sat down and watched the thing."

In later years, the teamsters who worked on *Two-Lane* would succeed in various pursuits. The movie's transportation captain, Jim Thornsberry, hired smart drivers who, coincidentally, all wanted to go into business, and all of them did. Thornsberry owned businesses that rented portable dressing rooms, or honey wagons, for films, as well as a catering company and a limousine company. Thornsberry's son followed his father into the movie business, working as a location manager. One day he was scouting mansions in Louisiana when he found a particularly fine one and he knocked on the door. When the lady of the house heard his last name she asked if he was related to Jim Thornsberry; she was the wife of Rick Mercier, who had driven the car carrier on *Two-Lane*. In the 1970s, Mercier had gone into business catering and renting generators and other equipment for movies, making a fortune. The teamster Craig Pinkard also found success in the catering business. But he rued the day that he told his customers that he owned it. He says that although the business was lucrative, his customers drove him nuts calling him at erratic hours. He would be in Spokane and receive a call from a production assistant in Missouri complaining that the hairdresser didn't like the salad that Pinkard's catering truck had provided. Although his company made a pile of money, he says the phone calls were constant, and "it was awful." After four or five years, he quit the business. The driver Jim

Brubaker became a successful producer, and his credits include *The Right Stuff* (1983), *Liar Liar* (1997) and *Bruce Almighty* (2003).

Walter Coblenz later produced a movie that Michael Laughlin directed, *Strange Invaders*. Coblenz was nominated for an Oscar for producing *All the President's Men*, a Best Picture Nominee for 1976.

Rudy Wurlitzer gained considerable acclaim as a novelist and screenwriter. His screenplays include *Pat Garrett and Billy the Kid* and *Little Buddha*, and his novels include *Flats*, *Slow Fade*, *Quake*, and *The Drop Edge of Yonder*.

Michael Laughlin had no interest in the stacks and stacks of paper generated in the making of *Two-Lane Blacktop*, so Gary Kurtz scooped it all up, put it in boxes, and saved it, eventually donating it to his alma mater, the University of Southern California. His archive at the Cinema Arts Library, eight fat boxes full of papers, includes invoice upon invoice, budgets, the original contracts signed by Monte Hellman and the actors, deal memos leading up to the contracts, correspondence in the form of letters and telegraphs, all the requests for petty cash, records of each day's goings-on in daily production notes, and what the USC Cinema Arts librarian Edward Sykes Comstock calls "the Holy Grail"—the script supervisor's annotated screenplay.

After *Two-Lane* was finished, Kurtz did some work on another film for Michael Laughlin, *Chandler*. Next, Kurtz remembers, "I had already talked to George [Lucas] about *American Graffiti*, basically while I was working on *Two-Lane*, and a futuristic science fiction project which we were going to do later." When the director was ready to make *American Graffiti*, Lucas and Kurtz took it to the Tanen unit at Universal and set it up there for a budget of about $800,000. Kurtz thought that the '55 Chevy, not the real race car but the stunt car, would be perfect for Harrison Ford to drive, so he had it painted black for the film.

Kurtz found himself going beyond his job description as co-producer on *Graffiti* when the young actor Mackenzie Phillips, the daughter of John Phillips of the pop music group the Mamas and the Papas, presented herself for work at the office in San Francisco. "She was twelve years old, and she showed up and I said, 'Where is your chaperone?' and she said, 'Oh, my parents couldn't come, and it was supposed to be my aunt, and she couldn't come, and so I'm here on my own. I'm just going to stay at the hotel with everybody else.' And I said, 'No, you're not. I'm not going to allow that.' I had to go to Sacramento to a judge and have her declared my ward for the duration of the shoot. She stayed at my house with my wife and daughters."

Whereas Selznick was struck that Monte Hellman looked so skinny, he was taken aback that George Lucas looked so young. "I remember leaning over my desk. I said, 'George, I have a really personal question to ask and I hope you're not offended, but did you grow that beard so that you could get drinks at a bar?' He said, 'You know, I did actually.'"

When *American Graffiti* was finished, Tanen and Selznick gave a print to Lew Wasserman, who took it home and screened it over the weekend. Eager to hear Wasserman's opinion, Selznick approached him at the commissary the next week and asked how he had liked *American Graffiti*. Selznick remembers, "He said, 'Is it a comedy?' And I said, 'Of course it's a comedy.' He said, 'Well, nobody in my house laughed.' And I said, 'Is it rude for me to ask you what the age was of the people at your home?' And he said, 'Well, they were all my age.' And I said, 'Well, you set this unit up for young audiences, remember?'"

Wasserman told Selznick to preview the film and determine the reaction. Francis Ford Coppola, the movie's producer, set up a preview in Berkeley and the cards came back about 88 percent excellent. Tanen and Selznick told Wasserman, and he retorted, "Oh, for Christ's sake. Coppola stacked the house. Do you expect me to believe those cards?" So they previewed the movie in San Diego, where it received about 92 percent excellent ratings. Wasserman reluctantly agreed to release the picture. But the release was delayed until 1973, and in the interim, the studio fired Selznick because, he was told, the executives didn't think the Tanen/Selznick Unit had been successful.

Of the films the unit had released, *Two-Lane Blacktop* and *The Last Movie* stood out as the most unconventional; the former by using nonactors, discarding traditional genre and plot expectations, minimizing dialogue, omitting a soundtrack and slowing the pace of a car-racing movie. Unlike American studio films, *The Last Movie* blatantly called attention to itself and its director, and disregarded the expectation that a movie is supposed to make sense. Self-referential like some French New Wave films, *The Last Movie* broke the proscenium when Dennis Hopper mugged for the camera. Further signaling "this is a movie," he included a clapboard before a shot, and sometimes included several takes of the same scene. Hopper also failed to present a plot that cohered, and often cut from the story, such as it was, to unexplained scenes that left viewers scratching their heads. The other films the Tanen Unit had produced were more traditional. But none of them, until *American Graffiti*, had been the kind of crowd-pleaser, with potential mainstream appeal, that Universal executives knew how to market.

After Selznick was fired, Tanen stayed on, but it was really the end of the Tanen Unit, according to Selznick, because he started making bigger-budget movies (although Tanen did in later years return to backing some low-budget films with promising, emerging directors). The next movie Tanen put into production was *Ulzana's Raid* (1972), with Burt Lancaster, helmed by seasoned director Robert Aldrich. Selznick thought it was "a very violent picture." He recalls he called Tanen after the movie was released, and "I said, 'Are you proud of that picture?' He said, 'It's a business, Danny.'"

In 1976, Tanen was promoted to president of Universal's theatrical motion picture division, where he presided over *E.T. the Extra-Terrestrial* (1982), *Coal Miner's Daughter* (1981), and *Smokey and the Bandit II* (1980). Later, he independently produced some of John Hughes's movies and then went to Paramount, where he oversaw *Top Gun* (1986), *The Untouchables* (1987), and *Ferris Bueller's Day Off* (1986), among other films. Tanen died in 2009.

*Two-Lane Blacktop* was but one nail in the coffin of the Hollywood studios' experiment in empowering directors in these years. Inevitably, some directors let the power and adulation given to auteurs go to their heads. In realizing their vision, they would go over-budget and over-schedule, and sometimes turn in films that weren't even that good. The most notorious example of excess was Michael Cimino's *Heaven's Gate* (1980), which dealt a severe blow to United Artists, received excoriating reviews, and flopped at the box office. (However, like *Two-Lane Blacktop*, *Ishtar* [1987], and some other movies that were over-hyped yet underperformed, it has been rediscovered and reevaluated.) By 1975, *Jaws* had already started to usher New Hollywood films out the door; it had no arty intentions but it appealed to a huge audience that included young people.

∞

Jay Wheatley largely gave up racing and went to work for Dennis Wilson, driving him when he went on tour. He became a roadie who drove a truck, and went on to work for Eric Clapton and Kenny Rogers. He was working for Rogers when he died unexpectedly in 1989 at age forty after he was out boating with friends, fell off the boat, and drowned.

Richard Ruth moved to Merced, California, where he continued to make custom cars. As *Two-Lane Blacktop* gained a cult following among gearheads, Ruth acquired fans. Car guys called him to ask questions, as well as to hire him to replicate the '55 Chevy. He set up a website for his business, but he was inundated with so many emails that he shut it down.

Monte Hellman's next film was *Cockfighter*, released three years later, in 1974. Since then he has directed movies sporadically, with substantial hiatuses in between pictures. In the breaks between films, he developed projects and saw a lot of movies. His friend Dennis Bartok recounts, "I met Monte in the early 1990s when I first came to Los Angeles. I was working at the American Cinematheque. And I think he was already kind of a semi-fixture there, and he would come to various screenings and people would point him out and say, 'That's Monte Hellman. You should do a retrospective of his movies.'"

Hellman was the subject of several documentaries: Paul Joyce's *Plunging on Alone: Monte Hellman's Life in a Day* (1986), Romuald Karmakar's *Hellman Rider* (1988), and George Hickenlooper's *Monte Hellman: American Auteur* (1997). As the years passed, his stature as a director grew. Some considered him one of the greatest American directors, and he gained a substantial following in France. Retrospectives of his work were held in such cities as Rotterdam, Paris, Edinburgh, Montreal, San Francisco, and Hof, Germany, to name a few.

Bartok wrote and co-produced an anthology film released in 2006 for the purpose, he says, of giving Hellman an opportunity to direct. (The other directors were Sean S. Cunningham, Ken Russell, John Gaeta, and Joe Dante.) "One of the biggest motivating factors about getting our movie done, *Trapped Ashes*, even though he only directed one twenty-two-minute segment, was that I could see Monte getting his hopes up about a number of different projects that almost happened and then fell through, but happened with somebody else. And then I swore to myself that we were going to make this movie, and get the ball across the goal line for Monte so that he would get a chance to direct. And I fervently believed, and still believe, that he is one of the greatest filmmakers in the world."

Hellman's admirers consider *Two-Lane Blacktop* his masterpiece. This implies it shares much in common with his other works, since it is the culmination of them. Yet it is distinguished from them, at least in being superior, and therefore different in some respects. Hellman's films focus on outsiders and the moral choices they make to solve problems and to survive. The movies often begin with a criminal or nonconformist, or someone on the outskirts of society, who is in the country, jungle, or wilderness, or who inhabits a subculture, apart from the laws of society or civilization. They are cowboys, cockfighters, soldiers, paid assassins, thieves, a movie director, a deranged sailor, a mad doctor, and street racers. The protagonist is traveling, often because he's fleeing authorities, and several films feature more than one journey. Couples bicker and break up, and women are not monogamous. Wives betray husbands, friends betray one another. Most of the main characters confront a moral choice and they often choose badly, compromising their ethics and rationalizing their bad decisions. Somebody inevitably has a campfire.

As a cult film director, Hellman is an outsider on the fringes of mainstream society. Like the characters who must make moral choices in his movies, Hellman has often been confronted with moral choices by studios and producers who want to make money from his movies—and he has always chosen his artistic integrity and rejected pressure to make his work more commercial. He was initially involved with a number of movies that either fell by the wayside or were made by other directors. Had he compromised his principles, he could have made many more films, but they would not have been true to his vision or gained him the critical esteem he enjoys.

*Two-Lane Blacktop* addresses several of Hellman's common themes: outsiders as protagonists, a voyage, freedom, an unpopulated area on the outskirts of society, and death. As in the director's other films, the car-racing genre in *Two-Lane* provides a structure on which he hangs his story; he violates the genre's traditions at will. Hellman develops his themes most fully in *Iguana* and makes them most personal in *Road to Nowhere*, but that is not to say they are superior to *Two-Lane Blacktop*.

The director's earlier movies take place largely outdoors, often in uncivilized or lawless areas. *Beast from Haunted Cave* is set in snowy mountains in South Dakota, the Westerns unfold in the old West, *Flight to Fury* and *Back Door to Hell* were shot in the jungle in the Philippines, and *Iguana* takes place on a deserted island. (Hellman's later films, *Silent Night, Deadly Night III: Better Watch Out!*, *Stanley's Girlfriend*, and *Road to Nowhere*, have more interior shots than his earlier films.) *Two-Lane Blacktop* takes place mostly on back roads and small towns. Living largely in unstructured environments, characters make up their own rules and create their own codes of conduct.

Starting with *Beast from Haunted Cave*, Hellman presents prominent characters who are outlaws or inhabit subcultures. *Beast* features burglars, a gangster's moll, and a ski instructor who lives in the middle of nowhere. *Flight to Fury* is populated by a wanderer, jewel thieves, and bandits. The characters in *Back Door to Hell* are soldiers and guerillas, and the protagonist in *Iguana* is a disfigured sailor-turned-pirate and captor. Cowboys, a paid assassin and a bounty-hunter-turned-miner are the main characters in Hellman's Westerns. A mad doctor drives the action in *Silent Night, Deadly Night III*. The main characters in the *Stanley's Girlfriend* episode of *Trapped Ashes* and in *Road to Nowhere* are filmmakers of small movies who work outside mainstream Hollywood and nine-to-five society. The Driver and the Mechanic in *Two-Lane* are street racers who spend their days on country roads. Besides indulging in their illegal occupation, the *Two-Lane* characters ignore various other laws when it is convenient, such as the scene where the Mechanic steals a license plate.

Especially in the earlier films, Hellman's characters are always going somewhere. In *Beast from Haunted Cave*, they ski cross-country to a cabin. In *Flight to Fury*, they take a plane ride and then make their way through the jungle on foot. The soldiers in *Back Door to Hell* travel to free children held hostage and then go to a shortwave radio station. In the Westerns, the characters are pursuing or fleeing one another on horseback. In *The Shooting*, the female protagonist pursues a man to get revenge. Although the characters in *Two-Lane Blacktop* outrun the police a couple of times, their driving is usually less purposeful, and they change destinations mid-trip. They drive from race to race, but not to any particular one; any race will do.

Many of Hellman's characters are pursuing freedom, and often that means keeping one step ahead of the law so they don't land in jail. The crooks' flight from justice in *Beast from Haunted Cave* propels the story. In *Ride in the Whirlwind*, cowboys wrongly suspected of robbing a stagecoach run from pursuing vigilantes who want to lynch them. The protagonist in *Flight to Fury* is wrongly suspected of murder, and after his plane crashes in the jungle while he's fleeing the police, he and the surviving passengers then have to run from murderous bandits, in the film's second escape. The characters in *Silent Night, Deadly Night III* run from the psycho killer, who himself has escaped from the hospital. After his shipmates string him up and try to kill him, the protagonist in *Iguana* jumps ship, swims to an island, and sets up his own society, where he is free but nobody else is. In *Two-Lane*, freedom is portrayed as a myth. The characters have divested themselves of the trappings thought to tie people down and hinder freedom—they aren't physically or emotionally encumbered with possessions or relationships. But they will never be free from the limits of their minds and they are trapped in a life of pointless driving with no escape on the horizon.

Identity, mistaken identity, and masquerading or changing identity are themes in several of Hellman's films. The plot of *Ride in the Whirlwind* is set in motion when vigilantes think Jack Nicholson's character and his fellow cowboys are outlaws, and by the movie's end, Nicholson's character has actually become one. The vampire vixen in *Stanley's Girlfriend* passes herself off as a commonplace human temptress. In *Silent Night, Deadly Night III*, the doctor transfers the psychopath's experiences into the girl's brain, calling into question her identity. Velma in *Road to Nowhere* fakes her death and takes on a new identity to escape detection. In her new identity, she takes on her former identity for a role in a movie; essentially she plays herself. Rudy Wurlitzer says that his script for *Two-Lane Blacktop* is about the search for identity; all the characters are seeking to find themselves and their purpose. GTO changes his identity each time he picks up a hitchhiker, as he assumes a persona designed to impress his passenger.

Usually Hellman's characters are wrestling with moral choices, and they often regret their decisions. Ethical choices and their repercussions often drive the plots of Hellman's films. The wretched characters who make morally reprehensible choices pay dearly. In *Ride in the Whirlwind*, Jack Nicholson's character presumably will have to spend the remainder of his life plagued by a bad conscience because he killed an innocent man, and abandoned his partner to die, to save himself. The sailor-turned-tyrant in *Iguana* walks into the sea to escape his miserable fate. The gangsters in *Beast from Haunted Cave* suffer an ignominious death at the claws of a monster before the law has a chance to get them. The larcenous, murderous femme fatale is killed at the end in *Road to Nowhere*. The protagonist in *Stanley's Girlfriend* commits suicide when he finds out that his friend betrayed him by setting him up with a vampire. The doctor/mad scientist is killed by the psychopath on a killing spree whom he is trying to save in *Silent Night, Deadly Night III*. The characters in *Two-Lane Blacktop* do not concern themselves with moral choices; they exist in an insular universe where they don't take such matters into account.

Almost invariably, Hellman's protagonists betray someone or are betrayed. In *Stanley's Girlfriend*, Stanley deceives his unknowing friend by foisting off a vampire on him. In *China 9, Liberty 37*, the assassin double-crosses his employers, and the wife betrays her husband. In *Beast from Haunted Cave*, the gang boss plots to kill his loyal employee who is unnerved by the monster. The doctor in *Silent Night, Deadly Night III* abdicates his responsibility to his test subject by letting the sociopath mess with her brain. In *Iguana*, a captive sailor allows the tyrant/captor to manipulate him into betraying his friend by killing him. Warren Oates's character in *The Shooting* abandons the kid; he has promised to protect him but out of self-interest leaves him to fend for himself—although he knows the boy is impulsive, lacking in judgment, and not very smart.

In a minor scene, the Mechanic in *Two-Lane Blacktop* feels betrayed when the Driver sells their tools without consulting him. In another minor scene, the Driver lies to a cop who pulled over GTO and tells him that he was driving like a maniac. "Betrayal" is too strong a word for the Driver's neglect of the Girl. It presupposes a commitment or exchange of trust, but the two don't form a sufficiently strong bond so that breaking it would constitute betrayal. The Driver and the Girl are attracted to one another, but like the '55 Chevy in the scene where he tries, unsuccessfully, to teach her to drive, their romance sputters, stalls, goes nowhere, and dies. In *Two-Lane Blacktop*, betrayal receives less emphasis than in most of Hellman's other films.

Hellman acknowledges death in most of his movies through corpses, graveyards, or conversations. During the airplane ride in *Flight to Fury*, the characters played by Jack Nicholson and Jaclyn Hellman debate the ways that people avoid confronting death and the amount of attention they should pay to it. Nicholson's character is obsessed with death. He says he feels wonderful because he escaped death in the crash, and he projects that the reason the young Asian man is watching the older man is that he's waiting for him to die. In *Back Door to Hell*, when Nicholson's character asks his superior officer if the guerillas are friends or captors, the officer replies that it makes no difference since they're all going to die anyway. There is a gravestone at the homestead at the beginning of *The Shooting*, while the cowboys pass a lynched body hanging from a tree near the start of *Ride in the Whirlwind*. There are funerals in *China 9, Liberty 37* and in *Iguana*. A sequence about death from automobile crashes in *Two-Lane* begins when the Driver swerves to avoid a fatal accident in the middle of the road. To race cars is to tempt death, but the Driver and the Mechanic are oblivious to this danger, and only the Girl is shaken in this scene. Then, GTO picks up an old lady and an orphan going to visit the grave of her parents, who died when they were hit by a car, and he drops them off at a cemetery.

Hellman uses genre elements that help his story and that appeal to him, and discards the rest. In *Ride in the Whirlwind*, instead of riding into the sunset victorious, having beaten the bad guys, the cowboy disappears on horseback into the dusk in disgrace; he is a murderer who killed an innocent man to save his own life. Rather than heroically help the Filipino people they are trying to defend against the Japanese aggressors, the soldiers in *Flight to Fury* make their lives worse: they kill civilians, while locals die trying to save the American servicemen. The guerillas fighting for a righteous cause are not noble, either. They brag that they are not bound by the Geneva Conventions, and they abandon morality and kill Japanese soldiers after they have confessed. In *Two-Lane Blacktop*, nobody takes the race very seriously. There is no good guy to root for, there is no suspense about who will win, and there is no victor. The competitors help, as well as sabotage, one another; they switch cars, and once the Girl is gone and the true competition is over, they abandon the race without fanfare, and go their separate ways.

Hellman often ignores the genre framework entirely, or turns it on its head, because the genres often are incidental. *Beast from Haunted Cave* is about crooks who steal gold and try to evade the law, with the secondary plot of the disgruntled gangster's moll who decides to run away with the ski instructor. The titular beast plays a small, supporting role. If Hellman had left out the beast, you wouldn't miss him; the cops could have killed the bad guy just as easily and looked a lot less silly doing it.

In *Silent Night, Deadly Night III: Better Watch Out!*, Hellman strays far afield from the original, Christmas-oriented, 1984 film, *Silent Night, Deadly Night*, directed by Charles E. Sellier Jr. The first in the series, now a cult classic that is shown at revival theaters, is an inspired sendup of traditional, heartwarming holiday movies with adorable, wide-eyed tykes excited to see Santa and solemnly vowing they've been good, not naughty. In the original film, little Billy and his family journey on Christmas Eve to visit grandpa, a sneaky, sinister old psycho. On the way home, Billy witnesses a fiend in a Santa suit raping his mother and slaughtering his family. As a young adult,

Billy gets a job in a toy store. On Christmas Eve, the boss chooses Billy to play Santa, and once in the costume, Billy turns into a homicidal Saint Nick and kills people whom he considers naughty. Wielding an ax, he decapitates a bully and a snowman. At the home of a young woman who is about to have sex with her boyfriend, he garrotes the boyfriend with a string of Christmas lights before impaling the young woman on trophy reindeer antlers mounted on the wall. The film caused a brouhaha. On December 3, 1984, *People* magazine ran a story about the outcry under the headline, "Angry Moms Call a Movie Featuring Santa Claus as an Ax Murderer a Mean-Spirited Hatchet Job."

In Hellman's sequel to this Christmas satire/horror movie, he goes in a completely different direction. He briefly acknowledges the spirit of the original at the start of the film: a horny, foul-mouthed Santa makes a brief appearance, propositioning a little girl, belching, and guzzling booze. The movie does have a psychopathic, homicidal stalker, but he wears a helmet that is more comical than sinister. An upside-down bowl with metal trim and a boxy antenna, it brings to mind a beanie with a propeller. The movie is really about a blind young woman and a mad doctor (Richard Beymer, who played Tony in *West Side Story*) who pursues science with little regard to its potentially disastrous consequences, a theme also raised in regards to Hiroshima in *Stanley's Girlfriend*.

Hellman develops his themes to the extreme in *Iguana*. The protagonist is an outsider not only in his behavior but in his physical appearance because his face is hideously deformed. The wilderness he escapes to is even further removed from civilization than the West; he swims to an uninhabited island separated from society by an additional barrier—the ocean. Whereas characters in Hellman's other films make dubious or contemptible moral choices, this protagonist abandons morality altogether, rationalizing that he has been so sorely mistreated that he is entitled to do as he wishes. He chops off his captives' fingers and hands when he's displeased, and in an unspeakable act, he successfully persuades one captive to cut off his friend's head. While characters in other films try to escape—from a bad marriage, from the law, or from vigilantes—this protagonist makes the ultimate escape: he drowns himself.

Hellman's characters rationalize questionable decisions and practice self-deception for moral justification. Warren Oates's character justifies leaving the kid behind in *The Shooting* by maintaining the boy is safer where he is. The tyrant in *Iguana* justifies his behavior because he has endured cruelty. The doctor in *Silent Night, Deadly Night III* thinks he is furthering science by experimenting with the human brain, and Jack Nicholson's character makes excuses for stealing a horse, and presumably killing its owner, in *Ride in the Whirlwind* because vigilantes are trying to lynch him for a crime he didn't commit. In *Road to Nowhere*, where the familiar themes apply to a film director, the protagonist says he is interested in the leading lady only because of the film.

*Road to Nowhere* is self-referential and autobiographical. The producer/director in the film-within-the-film share producer/director Monte Hellman's initials, and the fictional producer shares real-life producer Melissa Hellman's initials. Steven Gaydos, who wrote the screenplay for *Road to Nowhere* and co-wrote *Iguana*, says of the latter, "When the script was first written, the characters were named Monte Hellman and Steve Gaydos." The movie depicts situations that occurred during the making of *Two-Lane Blacktop*. The leading lady in both *Two-Lane*, and in the film-within-a-film in *Road to Nowhere*, plays herself; Hellman has said many times that the Girl was based on Laurie Bird, and Thelma plays herself in the movie being filmed in *Road*. Just as Monte Hellman fell for Laurie Bird before shooting began on *Two-Lane*, the director in *Road to Nowhere* becomes smitten with his leading lady before he begins filming his movie. Both Laurie Bird and the fictional Thelma are nonactors thrust into leading roles. Both titles bring to mind a highway, and *Road to Nowhere* would also have made an apt title for the film called *Two-Lane Blacktop*.

While *Two-Lane* takes up some of Hellman's common themes—outsiders, a journey, and death—it also, like his other movies, exhibits his consistent visual style. He had a background as an editor, and his films have a rhythm. Also, he often sets up scenes like the oft-cited gas station sequence in *Two-Lane* where the camera focuses on a location where characters carry out their parts and leave before new characters come on the scene. Often in these multi-episodic scenes there is action simultaneously in the background and foreground. Hellman used this type of choreography in one of the first scenes in the first film he directed, *Beast from Haunted Cave*. Characters talk in front of a ski lift as we see people periodically passing by in gondolas in the background. A skier joins the group. Next, two other skiers get off a gondola and join the group. They take off skiing down an incline. Finally, two more characters leave the group and take off in a gondola. In his later films, these types of scenes are much longer and more elaborate, such as one prolonged and complicated scene in *China 9, Liberty 37* in which a group eats al fresco in front of a cabin while the camera, without moving a great deal, captures much activity as people come and go.

Years after its release, a new audience came to appreciate *Two-Lane* not only for its visual style but also for its similarity to European films of the 1960s. Hellman has said he was influenced by Michelangelo Antonioni, and *Two-Lane* has much in common with *Red Desert* (1964), a movie ahead of its time in bringing to the forefront humans degrading and polluting their environment. The heroine of *Red Desert*, Giuliana, is alienated and distressed by all the garbage and junk that surrounds her and that ruins the beauty of nature. To emphasize his theme of humans destroying their environment, in one scene Antonioni shows his characters literally destroying their environment: they take apart the wooden walls of the shack where they are having a party and chuck the boards in a fireplace.

Like *Red Desert*, *Two-Lane* is characterized by slow-moving action, sequences that focus on landscapes, and characters who don't talk much, if at all. Neither film sets up conflict or drama from the beginning, and neither immediately lets the audience know what the movie is about. Both have meandering storylines, and lack Hollywood-style suspense, action, sentimentality, and emotional manipulation of the audience. Both present characters who are largely alienated from others. And, in *Red Desert*, Richard Harris's character says that he's been traveling for six years but that he ends up in the same place, bringing to mind the Driver and the Mechanic.

Hellman also said he was influenced by Francois Truffaut's *Shoot the Piano Player* (1960). In both films, the protagonist (played by the singer Charles Aznavour in *Piano Player* and the singer James Taylor in *Two-Lane*) loses a woman he loves because he is so consumed with his occupation. Antonioni and other European and New Wave directors of the time have long had cachet, and some of that rubbed off on *Two-Lane*.

In the ghoulish manner that tragedy enhances the fame of actors who die young, the premature deaths of Bird and Wilson, both of whom were extremely attractive, and Oates, an exceptionally accomplished actor, conferred mystique on *Two-Lane Blacktop*. Its rarity also added to its appeal. In a review of a week-long run at Cinema Village in New York, Michael Atkinson wrote in the *Village Voice*, "No road movie is as in touch with its own road-movie-ness as Monte Hellman's long-unseen, long-martyred *Two-Lane Blacktop*. Never released on video (a hostage to soundtrack rights and studio indifference) it is now 25 years old and has become an unofficial I-saw-it-first Rediscovered '70s cult wonder."

One aspect of the film that was first considered a drawback eventually became an asset. Initially some viewers were baffled; the movie didn't lead audiences by the nose and was unusually open to interpretation due to the lack of a soundtrack to steer viewers' emotions and the minimal character development. Yet the sparse dialogue allows viewers to project their own ideas and thoughts onto the characters and overall movie. Viewers interpret the film differently and sometimes like it for diametrically opposed reasons. So, another audience came to appreciate and champion *Two-Lane*—car guys.

To cinephiles who admire Monte Hellman's work, *Two-Lane Blacktop* is an auteur film. But to hot-rodders, *Two-Lane* is a car movie, and an exceptionally realistic one. They note that much care was taken to build a real race car, that the plot is ostensibly about a car race, that the cars are in many of the shots, that the main characters are a driver and a mechanic, and that much of the dialogue—and virtually all of the dialogue between the Driver and the Mechanic—concerns cars.

Car guys appreciate realistic movies about automobiles because relatively few such films have been made. Oscars are handed out for makeup and hairstyling, costume design, and production design, but not for cars, so automobiles usually don't get as much attention. Cars are the province of production designers who concentrate on (and win awards for) interiors and exteriors of buildings and for set decoration. They often hire companies in the business of providing automobiles—sometimes custom-made, but often ready-made—for movies.

Dennis McCarthy, owner of Vehicle Effects by Dennis McCarthy, is a former hot-rodder who has made the cars for the last five *The Fast and the Furious* movies. He says he likes *Two-Lane* because it's a "cool movie, with no crazy special effects, just the real old-school, hot rod stuff." In his work, he doesn't have the budget to make each car realistic because so many of them go kablooey. "If all goes as planned," he notes, "The car that gets blown up is a car that we've specifically built to get blown up, so we don't put the same effort in the car that gets blown up as we would into the car that's doing the beauty shots or the sliding or the burning rubber and all of that stuff. If there's a primary vehicle, there's usually a minimum of five cars that represent one car on screen, and we've had as many as twelve and thirteen cars to represent one vehicle on screen."

But once these movies are released, car guys sit in theaters and try to spot inaccuracies, inconsistencies, and fakery. Hot-rodders bring up *American Graffiti* as a film that got the cars wrong. Jim Aust, a hot rod historian and car builder, complains that in most car movies, "The continuity is very bad. The cars don't match scene to scene, and in movies where they're chasing, they'll have cars that are wrecked, then they're not wrecked, then they're wrecked again. As a matter of fact, probably one of the continuity glitches that upsets most hot-rodders involves the same car, but when it was in *American Graffiti*, the '55 Chevy. At the very end of the movie they had two cars—they had the picture car, which was the beauty car, then they had another car and they flipped it over and lit it on fire at the very final drag race scene and it didn't match, and that bothers a lot of the *American Graffiti* fans." The original car had chrome wheels on it, Aust explains, and the one that was wrecked had painted steel wheels, "and it was just obviously not the same car." Gary Kurtz says that since they had a low budget and many cars on *Graffiti*, they couldn't afford to make them all authentic.

Richard Ruth, who built the '55 Chevy, also takes issue with *American Graffiti*. He points out that the inside of the coupe is missing a window frame, and that the interior of the Mercury is not upholstered; the fabric is merely glued in. Ruth says, "Guys who really watch the movie look at that kind of stuff. They might have a friend who has a Mercury or they're building a Mercury and they look at it and they go, 'Aw, that's terrible.' They pick the car movies apart big time because of that."

The author and hot rod authority Pat Ganahl says the cars in *Two-Lane* are outstanding for movie cars. "*Two-Lane Blacktop* was the most realistic car-racing film that's probably ever been done, in terms of hot rod/drag racing." Since the cars are realistic, Aust notes, viewers are not distracted by phony-looking substitutes. "In *Two-Lane Blacktop* the details always were matching. The car didn't change back and forth into two different cars, and that can happen in movies. They'll have the good cars and then they'll have the beat-up car and that really can take you out of the moment of the movie and what's going on."

Although Richard Ruth was disgusted when the filmmakers covered with primer the powder-blue Chevy that he turned in to them, some car guys say the exterior looks right. First of all, a hot-rodder would want to fake out opponents and make them believe he was driving a junky old car that wouldn't go very fast. Second, hot-rodders generally didn't have a lot of extra cash to make their cars ornamental. According to Dennis McCarthy, "You see primered cars all the time. Usually, if you're a street racer trying to make money winning a race, you're going to put your money into mechanical parts to make the car go faster and not parts that would just be cosmetic enhancements."

Not only are the cars in *Two-Lane* realistic; they are prominent. Since most of the characters don't draw attention to themselves by talking a lot, hot-rodders who watch the film focus on the cars. Ted Moser, founder and owner of Picture Car Warehouse, says, "To me, it was fascinating because there was so little dialogue that it was more about the cars than it was the characters." McCarthy agrees, saying, "What hot-rodders look for in a car movie is having the cars featured more than anything else." But they also appreciate that all of the Driver and the Mechanic's conversations concern automotive matters. McCarthy adds, "The slicks in the trunk, the floor jack, jacking it up, talking about carburetor jetting, it gets really technical, which is great. I love to hear that technical talk." Car guys also approve of pairing the GTO, the first "factory hot rod," with the old Chevy. Ted Moser offers an unusual interpretation of the then-new car and the character named for it: "I think Warren Oates stole that car, didn't he? He told so many lies that you didn't know which one was right."

The characters in *Two-Lane Blacktop* also ring true. With their raggedy, down-at-the-heels look—shaggy hair, old T-shirts, and worn-out jeans—the Driver and the Mechanic look like real hot-rodders. One faction of hot-rodders were fancy, well-dressed guys with day jobs who didn't race but just cruised around and tried to look cool and pick up girls. The other faction of serious hot-rodders is perfectly represented in *Two-Lane*, Aust says, "the dirtbag guys with the car with no interior and the crappy paint."

However, the premise of those two cars racing across the country for pink slips is preposterous, according to Ganahl. The '55 Chevy was modified to make it a race car that would go fast from a standing start to the end of a quarter mile. It was not built to race across the country. Ganahl explains, "If you're only going to race a quarter mile, you put a gear ratio in your rear axle so that the engine revs up to a high rpm very quickly, and it runs from zero to 8,000 rpms, that's 8,000 revolutions per minute. That gets it to the end of the quarter mile very quickly. But it can't go much further than a quarter mile or it would blow up. It's not made to stay at a high rpm. It would have to run at a very high rpm to go fast on the freeway, and it would blow itself up, it would wear out. The GTO is a highway car. It has a much lower gear ratio, so the engine's running much slower when the car's going a lot faster, so it could go 100 miles an hour all day long." Knowing all this, the Driver and the Mechanic would never have agreed to a race across the country that they were doomed to lose, especially with their prized possession on the line.

The realism of the division of labor into driving and repairing is debatable, too. Most hot-rodders could drive as well as fix their own cars, so if they won a race they didn't have to divide the winnings. "It did seem a little strange to me that all James Taylor did was drive," says Ted Moser. "Normally, guys in that era, they weren't specialists yet." But Aust has a more animistic interpretation of the relationship between the two men and the car: "There are some people who feel the car is a means to an end, and the car isn't respected. And that's why he has the Mechanic, who I consider more like the animal trainer/tamer, the one who's caring for the car and at the end of the day pets it and feeds it and makes sure everything's right with it. And that's the two of them. The one is beating it to get through the circus performance while the other one is more in tune with caring for it. To me, it's just like the circus."

The authenticity of the impolite, hostile dialogue also is arguable. Some drag racers are civil and polite when they challenge one another, but others bring arrogant machismo to their dares. Challenging an opponent in combative, foul-mouthed language "is what you're supposed to do," says Ganahl. "The same as in dueling, it's mano a mano. If you're going to chew somebody out, you can't be polite about it. That's part of street racing."

An extremely realistic depiction of street racers, according to Ganahl, is the scene early in the film where the Driver and the Mechanic stop in Needles to change the tires before they come into town to look for a race. The Mechanic takes off the regular tires that have tread and puts on the slicks in preparation for racing. Slicks are tires with the tread worn off so they have more traction on a dry road because more of the surface of the tire comes in contact with the pavement. Drag racers do a burnout, as in the beginning sequence of *Two-Lane*, before racing, to heat up the tires, which makes them stickier (and also generates smoke). Slicks are run with very low air pressure, and are only used for drag racing. They are unsuitable for driving around town or on the highway because they would wear out very quickly and, if the car ran into oil or water on the road, it would wiggle and slide around.

The filmmakers took authenticity so far as to feature a real-life legend in the movie, Big Willie Robinson, "probably one of the most famous street racers of all time," according to Moser. Ganahl says, "Starting the movie with Big Willie and the LA Street racers was very realistic, because Big Willie *was* LA street racing. It was totally underground, it was totally illegal. Later on, that movie helped him legitimize it and actually get a track to race on."

Most of all, the '55 Chevy was the right car. "The 427 would definitely be the hot motor at the time that movie was made," says McCarthy. "The movie is cool, but I mean the '55 Chevy is really what I like about it. It's just a really cool car. I like everything about it—the fact that it's a four-speed, the fact that it does have the 427 big block in it. It has that old-school hot-rodder look—the straight axle and the radius rear wheels. It has the plexiglass side windows for light weight, just a cool car, definitely what street racing was about at that time." Jim Aust agrees: "The '55 Chevy was *the car* that a young guy would get fixed up, and put the effort into making it fast."

The '55 looked different from earlier Chevys, and it became iconic because it was the first one with a V8 engine that was lightweight and that middle-class Americans could afford. Aust explains, "It was the first quick or fast car that had a style that Americans liked and that was marketed and priced right" for people working in a mine or a mill or on a drilling rig. It was the "everyman's car," according to Aust, and it was easy to modify to make it speedier. When it came out, manufacturers of spare parts started making parts to make it go faster, whereas it was much harder to get parts to modify Pontiacs or Oldsmobiles. Aust continues, "It's great that that's the car in that movie because if it had been another car, if it were for some reason a '55 Ford or Oldsmobile, that movie wouldn't have the impact it does, and the longevity and the attraction. They got the car right. Even if you're not a Chevy guy—there are guys who hate Chevys—but I don't think a guy who loves cars can hate that movie because it's done right."

While hot-rodders praise the Chevy's authenticity, muscle-car guys quibble with Warren Oates's inaccurate description of the GTO Judge's innards. GTO expert Scott Tiemann admits, "I haven't watched that movie in years, and I forget all the details of it," but he accurately remembers Oates "talking about this 455 Mark IV Ram Air. That's just not possible." (This error was also in the script. Rudy Wurlitzer was not a car guy, and Billy Kincheloe, who helped him with automotive terminology, was a hot-rodder, not a muscle-car guy.) The standard engine in the 1970 Judge was a 400 cubic-inch Ram Air III with 366 horsepower. An option for the car was a 400 cubic-inch Ram Air IV with 370-horsepower. In 1970, Tiemann says, "to throw a little monkey wrench into it, because all the companies were coming out with bigger and bigger engines, Pontiac built some with a 455 cubic-inch engine," but without as many high-performance components in the engine. "So the question has always been, in the GTO world, 'Was it a 455 cubic-inch Judge? Or was it a 400 cubic-inch Ram Air IV Judge?' Either one is quite rare, but a Ram Air IV Judge is very, very desirable, worth a lot more money in today's world—I mean, a huge difference. So, again, just talking about that movie, they kind of goofed up in typical Hollywood fashion. So which engine did the car really have? Did it have the big cubic-inch 455 that was such a big engine it just made the car a nice cruiser? The internal components of it made it idle smoothly and it was just a nice cruising engine, where the 400 Ram Air IV was more for the guys that were into drag racing, it had a lot more high performance components inside the engine." Whereas a 400 Ram Air IV meticulously restored could fetch $200,000, a 455 in mint condition would struggle to sell for $100,000, Tiemann says. "That's just one of the weird things about the movie that people have discussed for forty years."

∞

*Two-Lane Blacktop* documents the end of an era. *American Graffiti* tells the same story, according to Aust. "Hot-rodding didn't die, but it changed, and those two movies represent the change where the older cars start to become old battle-scarred warriors and they're making brand-new cars at the factory that go just as fast, where you can just walk in and buy one. Those guys are trying to squeak out every last gasp of speed out of this old car, and Warren Oates goes and just buys a new car and a sweater and he's going just as fast as them. So it would change—where like my dad's era of guys fixed up their cars, and then just a few years later, the muscle cars came out, '67, '66 with Mustangs and Camaros and you'd just go buy a fast car. It didn't die, but it changed, and the people changed with it. The hardcore wrencher guys like the guys in the Chevy would fade out a little more and everybody would just have a fast car."

Floyd Mutrux—whom Laughlin proposed, and Hellman rejected, to rewrite Corry's script—was an unofficial adviser on *Two-Lane*. He also wrote and directed *The Hollywood Knights* (1980), another film that car guys cite as exceptionally realistic. Mutrux says that *Two-Lane* "was romanticized. It was the end of an era. In that particular car culture, they did it in the back yard." Afterwards, Detroit caught up and co-opted or commercialized the car culture, Ralph Nader cast a shadow over cars made in the US, and kids began driving Volkswagens.

# 9

# Picking Up Speed

Scarecrow Video in Seattle, which sent a petition signed by fans of *Two-Lane Blacktop* to Universal, has often been credited with spurring *Two-Lane Blacktop*'s belated release on video. Notes on the film on the Turner Classic Movies website maintain that "the petition gained publicity that inspired Anchor Bay Entertainment to license the film from Universal and convince the surviving members of the rock band the Doors to allow their song 'Moonlight Drive' to remain in the soundtrack, clearing the way for video release." In an article published in *BBC News Magazine* in May 2010, Ian Haigh writes that *Two-Lane* "is the archetypal cult film. Hardcore fans forced its release on video in the 1990s, goading a studio that had let it spend years in obscurity." But that's not exactly what happened.

∞

In 1988, newly married George and Rebecca Latsios left Pennsylvania with his collection of approximately 200 videotaped movies, drove across the country, and settled in Seattle. George Latsios, who had studied computer sciences at Penn State, managed restaurants while he continued to build his video collection. Then one day, when he had accumulated about 500 tapes, "George just came to me and said, 'I quit my job and I'm opening a video store and I need your help,'" Rebecca (now Rebecca Soriano) recalls. "I was *shocked* he quit his job, and was just going to open a video store, and had already signed a lease, and I had nothing to say about it." Not knowing what else to do, she agreed with the plan. She worked two jobs, and George worked as a cook at a restaurant early in the mornings before he opened the store, in the Latona neighborhood of Seattle, at 11 a.m. The store lacked shelves, so Rebecca, who had studied photography in college, built some, painted them outside on the street, and carted them inside. Sometimes the couple was too tired to go home, so they slept on the floor of the store, which they called Scarecrow Video. The store grew quickly, Rebecca thought, because Seattle was a magnet for creative young people in that era of Sub Pop Records, Nirvana, and the grunge scene. "People were looking for things that were different, and we had that. We had videos that nobody else had."

Latona was a residential neighborhood of old houses, many of them Craftsman style, and a lot of bands practiced in the garages. In January 1992, shortly after the band first appeared on *Saturday Night Live* and their album *Nevermind* reached number 1 on the Billboard charts, Nirvana's front man, Kurt Cobain, came into Scarecrow. George, who was concentrating on filling out papers to set up an account for this new customer, didn't recognize the musician. Rebecca and other employees frantically tried to get George's attention, whispering, "Oh my God! It's Kurt Cobain! Oh my God, he was just on *Saturday Night Live*!" When Cobain gave George his gold American Express card to set up an account to rent movies, the merchant asked his new customer what he did for a living. "I play music," Cobain told him. "Oh, you're one of those grunge bands, aren't you?" George Latsios asked.

As Scarecrow's video collection and its reputation grew, other celebrities visited the store. Roger Ebert, at that time the *Chicago Sun-Times* film critic and the co-host, with Gene Siskel, of the TV show *At the Movies*, came into the store with his wife. Ebert, the first movie critic to win a Pulitzer Prize for criticism, helped some customers find videos. Rebecca got phone calls from customers who could barely believe that Roger Ebert, the famous film critic, had effectively waited on them in the store. The acclaimed French director Bertrand Tavernier (*'Round Midnight*) came in and asked Scarecrow's buyer, Mark Steiner, to show him around. Tavernier, who championed blacklisted directors, berated Steiner for not having a section devoted to these filmmakers. But Steiner remembers getting an education as the French director went through the film noir section, taking out videos to inspect and declaring, "This is great!" or "This is aowfool."

In 1993, Scarecrow joined the Seven Gables Theatre and Cinema Books at Roosevelt Way Northeast and Fiftieth Street, near the University of Washington, on what's been described as one of the great movie corners in the world. The 8,300-square-foot building, which had housed a Radio Shack and a clothing store, had a huge atrium. Videos filled the floor level and five small upstairs rooms. A sixth upstairs room became Seattle's smallest theater, the nineteen-seat Sanctuary, where Scarecrow screened 16 mm movies on weekends. The growing staff imported many videos and sought out rare titles from obscure sources. George and Rebecca Latsios lived frugally, reinvested their income in more videos, and amassed a huge inventory. An employee suggested they organize their videos by director and buy all the works of those directors. George embraced the idea. "Enthusiasm was probably his greatest trait. It was contagious," recalls Sean Axmaker, the assistant manager in the store's buying department at the time. University students and cinephiles shopped at Scarecrow, as did the general public. "This was the era when stopping at the video store was part of your weekly routine," notes Axmaker, so the store was often filled with customers who rented or bought tapes. Rebecca attributed the store's success to serendipity—settling in the right Seattle neighborhood at the right time—since neither she nor George were businesspeople. "That was the funny thing," says Steiner, Scarecrow's buyer. "They wanted a store full of movies."

George, who was born in Greece, retained a strong accent, and, according to Axmaker, "He would always, without fail, call everyone 'my friend' in conversation." Hospitable and garrulous, George stood by the door like a maître d', greeting customers. Rebecca remembers that "he knew pretty much everybody's name who walked in the store at that time." When a customer left, he unfailingly bid them farewell by saying, "Thank you very much, my friend." Rebecca worked behind the scenes designing ads, setting up displays and making signs.

One day, a visitor to Seattle from out of town telephoned to get directions to Scarecrow from downtown. The staff suggested that he take a cab or a bus, but the man said he wanted to walk. They warned him that the five-mile route meandered and went across a bridge, but he still insisted he wanted to come by foot, so they gave him walking directions. About two hours later, Steiner recalls, "I was standing on the street in front of the store and talking to this longtime customer who is quite a tall fellow, and I see Quentin Tarantino over his shoulder, walking up the street. And I just had to stop and say to the guy I was talking to, 'Quentin Tarantino just walked in.' And we realized later that this was the person who had called for walking directions. And one side of his face was sunburned" from his long walk, which actually was a pilgrimage. Tarantino asked not to be disturbed while he perused seemingly every title in the store, then came up to the counter, talked to the staff and customers, and signed anything that anybody put in front of him.

Bernardo Bertolucci was Steiner's favorite director, and when he was shooting *Little Buddha* (screenplay by Rudy Wurlitzer) in Seattle, the film's star, Bridget Fonda, and cinematographer, Vittorio Storaro, came into the store. Storaro told the staff that Tower Records in downtown Seattle wouldn't rent movies to Bertolucci, who had won the Best Director Oscar for *The Last Emperor* in 1988 and also had directed *The Conformist* (1970) and *Last Tango in Paris* (1973) among other films, because he didn't have an American driver's license. "I kept waiting for Bertolucci to come in, because he was my guy," Steiner says. Finally, on Valentine's Day, Bertolucci came in, walked up to Steiner, and asked him for Busby Berkeley's *The Gang's All Here*, which was in stock, and Alfred Hitchcock's *Murder!*, which was not.

Steiner later tracked down *Murder!*, and when Bertolucci returned to town for the premiere of *Little Buddha* at the Seattle International Film Festival, Steiner and Rebecca sneaked into the director's hotel room and put the video on his pillow. That night, Rebecca remembers, she and Steiner attended the opening of the film festival. Bertolucci "got up on stage—and the place was packed, the mayor was there and everything—and in front of everybody, he said, 'I'm so happy to come back to Seattle. I'm so happy to come back to my friends at Scarecrow Video because they have the best video store in the whole world.' And Mark and I, we just couldn't believe it, we were just astounded."

As Scarecrow continued to expand, George and Rebecca Latsios began to work with the Seattle International Film Festival, and then decided to invite directors who hadn't attended the festival, just because they wanted to meet them and show their movies. They brought Nicolas Roeg, John Woo, Werner Herzog, Monte Hellman, and other directors to Seattle for weekend retrospectives of their work. The directors would introduce the films and answer questions afterwards. Rebecca designed programs for these events, and advertising helped pay for them. But, unbeknownst to Scarecrow's employees, George had a brain tumor that evidently impaired his judgment, because he stopped paying taxes. Steiner recalls that they would invite directors to come to Seattle, and offer to do whatever was necessary to put on a retrospective. Scarecrow would pay for their plane tickets, put them up at a swanky hotel, take them out to dinner, give them a sightseeing tour (which included the building where Bruce Lee had lived in the attic while he worked as a waiter in the restaurant downstairs), and rent a theater at the Seattle Art Museum, the University of Washington, or the Landmark chain. "We had the money because we weren't paying taxes," Steiner learned in hindsight.

The director Werner Herzog memorably answered questions about his erratic and demanding behavior on film shoots. He admitted that he had put a pistol to Klaus Kinski's head and threatened to shoot the actor if he walked off the set of *Aguirre, the Wrath of God*. They filmed the movie on rafts on Amazon tributaries in Peru, and at one point a flood inundated the set. Herzog related that he'd told his friend Kinski that if he, the director, was crazy enough to finish the troubled film, he expected the actor to do the same. "Talk about dry humor," Steiner recalls, "He'll say something completely—'Did he just *say* that?'—in the same tone he's talking about what lens he used in a particular shot." Rebecca also observed this trait. "He always cracked me up, because I never knew if he was being totally serious or totally crazy."

Wim Wenders (*Wings of Desire, Paris, Texas*) particularly impressed Scarecrow's staff when he came for a retrospective. Steiner admired Wenders's response to a question after a showing of *The End of Violence*, starring Bill Pullman. "So a snotty kid says, '*Oohh*, so Bill *Pull*man. Did you see *Independence Day*?'" (No favorite of the art-house crowd, that 1996 blockbuster directed by Roland Emmerich won kudos for its special effects but scorn for its one-dimensional characters and stilted dialogue.) "And he looked out and he said, 'Actually, I thought he was very good in *Independence Day* and that's why I cast him.'"

Scarecrow sponsored a Monte Hellman retrospective at the Seattle Art Museum one weekend in early March 1995. At the time, none of Hellman's films had been released on video. "The people that ran Scarecrow at that time were very cool because they wanted to see movies, and if they weren't available on video, they would decide, 'OK, fine, if they're not available on video then we'll just bring the director in and bring a print and we'll show it,'" Rebecca says, and that's the reason they brought Hellman to Seattle. Scarecrow was able to assemble and show most of his films; they screened *Ride in the Whirlwind, Flight to Fury, Back Door to Hell, Cockfighter, Two-Lane Blacktop*, and *China 9, Liberty 7*. *Two-Lane* drew the biggest crowd; all 300 seats of the theater were sold out for the show. Hellman spoke before and after every screening, and "was really, really informative and gracious and very, very dry, but not in a standoffish way," Steiner recalls. "He seemed like all business, just very, very dry and direct, and like his movies; they're very spare." The retrospective left a lingering impression on Steiner. "I remember coming out of that weekend just feeling like his voice was ringing in my head and it was impossible to separate him from his films."

Rebecca also found Hellman less grandiose and egotistical than most other directors they brought to Seattle. "You get a lot of personalities in the film business, and some people are crazy and some people are high-strung and some people are wound up. And Monte was just generally a nice guy," she says, who was happy somebody wanted to show his films. She thought he projected a Zen-like attitude, accepting whatever befell him.

Steiner was interested in directors, such as John Frankenheimer, who worked during the Golden Age of Television in the 1950s. Hellman had directed part of an episode of the 1970s award-winning TV series *Baretta*, starring Robert Blake. Hellman and Blake did not get along, and after three days, Hellman was replaced. Nevertheless, Steiner was curious about Hellman's experience on a critically acclaimed television show. "I asked him about *Baretta* and he just looked at me dead-eyed and said, 'It was like working at a gas station,' and I felt like crawling under my seat." Steiner says the answer surprised him, since Hellman had done other uncredited work on movies such as *The Greatest*, a 1977 film starring Muhammad Ali, for which he supervised editing after the film's director, Tom Gries, died. "He did a lot of work for hire and seemed happy to do it for the paycheck, but I don't think he got anything out of the freedom of TV whatsoever," Steiner comments.

Hellman told his Scarecrow sponsors that Universal had not released his most famous movie, *Two-Lane Blacktop*, on video because the studio could only release a limited number of films each year, and didn't think the film's following was large enough to warrant its inclusion on the slate. (That year, 1995, in addition to releasing *Jaws*, Universal Home Video put out VHS editions of *Radioland Murders* [1994], which has a 19 percent fresh rating on the website Rotten Tomatoes, and *Street Fighter* [1987], which has a 12 percent fresh rating. *Two-Lane Blacktop* has a 94 percent fresh rating.) Also, the studio didn't want to pay to license the rights to fragments of songs used in the movie. Rebecca and Norman Hill, who was the video store's promotions director, remember that Hellman suggested that his Scarecrow sponsors draw up a petition to Universal to release *Two-Lane* on video, and encourage customers at the store to sign it. Rebecca felt sad that not everyone in Seattle who wanted to see *Two-Lane Blacktop* had been able to attend the screening, and they couldn't watch it on video. As the Scarecrow staff discussed the dilemma, they agreed that arguing over music rights was silly, and embraced the idea of drawing up a petition to Universal to release the film for home viewing. Steiner credits Rebecca with spearheading the project, describing her as a pipe dreamer with a can-do attitude. "She was a beautiful, warm person who loves film and really didn't think that there was anything we couldn't do." They decided to gather 2,000 signatures, and named their effort "2,000 for Two-Lane."

An employee printed up the petition and they put it on the counter near the checkout space with a small sign saying that Scarecrow wanted *Two-Lane Blacktop* made available for home viewing and asking customers to please sign the petition to Universal. The staff was not pushy about gathering signatures, but they would mention the petition, and most customers knew of the movie, even if they hadn't seen it, and were happy to cooperate. After about a year, 2,375 people had signed the petition, including the directors Werner Herzog, whom Scarecrow had brought to Seattle in September 1995, Todd Haynes, and Kelly Reichardt. Reflecting the chameleon-like nature of the film, the petition states, in part, "Though made in the seventies, *Two-Lane* is the ultimate 'slacker' movie—well ahead of its time in expressing currently fashionable themes of alienation and aimlessness." Scarecrow sent the petition to Universal. The video store's proprietors and staff didn't celebrate, but they were proud of their accomplishment and anticipated results.

The petition was accompanied by a letter signed by Scarecrow's owners and other key employees. They wrote that Monte Hellman had been their guest at a sold-out screening of *Two-Lane Blacktop*, and that he had told them that Universal was not releasing the film on video because executives thought there was no audience for it. They wrote that college professors, video distributors, and magazine editors had signed the petition, and that their cause had received national coverage in the press. They sent the letter and petition to Louis Feola, then President of MCA Home Video, on April 19, 1996.

The petition never reached his desk. Twenty years later, Feola, now a self-employed consultant, says that when he was in charge of home video for Universal he received many letters from people asking him to put their favorite movies out on video. But he doesn't recall the Scarecrow petition, and he is certain he would have remembered it. He was running an international department and overseeing 1,500 employees, he says, and probably a secretary opened Scarecrow's correspondence and forwarded it to the marketing department.

Feola now lives in Calabasas, California, and tourists from New Zealand ask him for directions to the home of the Kardashians, who live nearby. He, in turn, asks them if they don't have something better to do. He can talk corporate-speak with the most buttoned-down bean counters, but he reveals the heart of a film lover. He laments that only a limited number of films can be released on video, that many very good ones simply aren't preserved, and that young people aren't familiar with stars of the Golden Age of Hollywood such as Edward G. Robinson.

Even if he had received it, Feola says, the petition by itself it wouldn't have convinced Universal that a video of *Two-Lane* would have a large market, that they would make money on it, and that they ought to release the film for home viewing. The studio took many factors into account (including the cost of licensing music) when it made decisions about "multiple revenue streams," according to Feola. "It's a complicated process of the studios deciding what gets released in ancillary markets," Feola says, wearing his bean-counter hat. Decisions "at all the studios come down to a financial analysis of what makes economic sense."

∞

Although George Latsios had kept his brain cancer secret from his employees, they found out in 1997. Steiner learned he didn't have a W-2 form on file with the IRS because Latsios didn't withhold payroll taxes. "It was crazy. I remember a day when George went out and bought the whole *Highlander* set on videotape when the state income-tax people were going to start coming after us, because everything was C.O.D. in those days—well, most things were—so if an assistant manager signed a check for a C.O.D. they were essentially spending the money we owed the income-tax people. So the income-tax people were going to start coming after individuals here. It got pretty ugly."

George and Rebecca Latsios declared bankruptcy, and in 1999 they sold Scarecrow to two Microsoft programmers, Carl Tostevin and John Dauphiny, who continued to operate the store at the same location. The couple divorced, and George moved back to his hometown, Kozani, Greece, where he died in 2003 at age forty-four. Rebecca remarried and lives in Seattle, where she is an art docent and teacher.

∞

While *Esquire* magazine had raised expectations to unreasonable levels when the film hit theaters, Scarecrow's campaign, which had been covered in *People* magazine, generated great anticipation. Just as audiences in 1971 had expected another *Easy Rider*, so did Scarecrow's customers. Although the store sold many copies of *Two-Lane* tapes, discs, and special editions in tin cases, Steiner remembers that some customers were disappointed: "Everybody thought that this was going to be this awesome, hip, counterculture, entertaining thrill ride, and it was a Monte Hellman film." His wife, who had been a Scarecrow customer and had signed the petition, was nonplussed when she finally saw it, and she and some others wondered, "What's the big deal?"

∞

While *Two-Lane Blacktop* foundered when it was first released in 1971, by 1999 word of mouth had finally spread, and pent-up demand for the movie made it a small hit when Anchor Bay released it on video in 1999. It bombed initially because it wasn't made for a mainstream audience, and it failed to reach niche audiences that would have appreciated it. *Two-Lane* was ballyhooed as the Second Coming of *Easy Rider*, and moviegoers expected a more conventional, exciting film. Universal aimed its marketing campaign at the wrong audiences and pulled the movie from theaters before word of mouth had a chance to spread among people who actually would have liked the movie. But by the turn of the century, years and years of acclaim had worked in the film's favor. Most viewers knew what to expect, and hardcore fans launched their own marketing campaign.

The "New Hollywood" films of the late sixties and early seventies gained cachet in the nineties, and cinephiles looked back at that time with nostalgia.

Magazines and film journals printed articles that paid tribute to the era when directors could make experimental, personal films without studio interference. In an article in the *New York Times* about *Two-Lane Blacktop*'s release on video, Peter M. Nichols noted that by 1999 studios would usually make movies only if they featured well-known actors. Directors of studio films in the earlier era had had more freedom to make choices based on what would make a movie good rather than what would make it a hit. In 1991, McFarland & Company published the author James Bernardoni's book *The New Hollywood: What the Movies Did with the New Freedoms of the Seventies*, which discussed films by Martin Scorsese and Francis Ford Coppola, among others. *Easy Riders, Raging Bulls: How the Sex-Drugs-and-Rock 'n' Roll Generation Saved Hollywood*, Peter Biskind's gossipy, hard-to-put-down nonfiction chronicle of New Hollywood directors, their films, and their exploits, came out in 1998 to both acclaim and, especially from Biskind's subjects, outrage. Although Biskind mentions Monte Hellman and *Two-Lane Blacktop*, he doesn't go into enough detail to warrant dishing any dirt.

In addition to gaining prestige as a New Hollywood film, *Two-Lane* became coveted due to its unavailability on video. Fans could only see it occasionally, at drive-in theaters, screenings at colleges and cinematheques, and on television. In 1996, the American Cinematheque in Los Angeles included it in a tribute to the director, "3-Card Monte: The Films of Monte Hellman," and it was part of other Hellman retrospectives held in the United States, Canada, and Europe. When the video finally came out, a reviewer for *Hot Rod* magazine remarked that *Two-Lane* had previously been available on video solely from "underground" sources—that is, from people who taped it illegally and sold the bootlegged copies.

In reviews and articles marking its release on video, writers remarked on its popularity. The *Los Angeles Times* described it as "long-sought" and "one of home video's most wanted," and *Combustible Celluloid* said it "had long been a coveted cult movie, little seen" but favorably compared to *Easy Rider* by its fans. Dennis Bartok, who was the programmer for the American Cinematheque when the video came out, recalls that "it was near the top of film buffs' want lists for years and years, and people were constantly saying, 'When can you get *Two-Lane Blacktop*?'" Jay Douglas, who was vice president of Anchor Bay at the time and spearheaded the video's release, said *Two-Lane* was a movie that most film buffs had heard of but had not necessarily seen.

In addition to its status as a New Hollywood film, and its scarcity, its timelessness added to its appeal. Unlike the two lead characters in *Easy Rider*, the Driver and the Mechanic don't dress like hippies. The cinematography is in the classical style. The movie's look and themes had not dated by 1999. Nothing about *Two-Lane Blacktop* was trendy. Jay Douglas of Anchor Bay comments,

"Maybe it's because the film was done on back roads in small-town America, but it looks like it could have been made two weeks ago. You could put two other actors in there who are current actors, and they would fit in perfectly."

Conventional wisdom credits Scarecrow Video's petition to Universal for *Two-Lane*'s release on video. But Douglas says he doesn't remember the petition. He says he had wanted to release the film for home viewing for years previously, and the petition, sent to Universal in 1996, didn't prod him to put out the video three years later. Douglas had long been a fan of *Two-Lane Blacktop*. He liked the movie because he was a Beach Boys fan, and Dennis Wilson was one of his heroes when he was growing up because he admired Warren Oates and because he found the photography exceptionally beautiful. "I know it's not considered a 'feel-good' film, but that said, there was something uplifting about the film." As vice president of acquisitions at Anchor Bay, he had long before put the film at the top of his list of favorite movies that he wanted to release on video. The company's mission at the time, he explains, was "to release really cool films" for home viewing "that hipsters would like." Many were well-made films that had failed at the box office. "We always felt like we were raising the bar," Douglas recalls. "It didn't always work. We didn't always raise the bar; sometimes we lowered the bar. At the same time, we just felt like we were sort of trying to act like we were a different kind of video company." Other movies on his list that Anchor Bay released were Werner Herzog's *Nosferatu the Vampyre* (1979) and *They Might Be Giants* (1971); the latter made the list because of George C. Scott's performance, out of character with his persona, as a widower who believes he is Sherlock Holmes, Douglas says. "It was a George C. Scott that most people don't associate him with. In other words, it was a George C. Scott that wasn't angry, it was a George C. Scott that wasn't yelling at people, and he was fantastic in the movie."

Anchor Bay had a licensing agreement with Universal Studios to issue video releases of movies in the studio's catalog of films it had produced in the past. Universal had never brought out *Two-Lane Blacktop* through its home video division because it had been a commercial failure and because obtaining the rights to the music for video would be prohibitively expensive. But the studio agreed to license the film to Anchor Bay. Douglas had lunch with Hellman in Los Angeles, and remembers the director's reaction to the first video release of any movie he had directed. "He was really happy about it, really happy about it. I mean, for obvious reasons. Here's a guy who made one of the great films of the 1970s or late sixties and it had been heralded as sort of the new *Easy Rider* and then the film just sort of fell off the face of the earth."

To transfer the film to video and to record audio commentary and extras, Douglas hired William Lustig, director of the cult classic slasher movies *Maniac*

(1980) and *Maniac Cop* (1983), and Norman Hill, who had met Monte Hellman when he worked for Scarecrow Video in Seattle. When Hill was a little boy growing up in Northern California, his mother wouldn't let him see *Star Wars* or almost any other movies until she had seen and vetted them. But his babysitter's little brother got the first copy of *Fangoria* (a horror movie magazine for fans of gore) and the sitter told Hill she'd like to take him to some of the movies it covered. He recalls, "I said, 'But, I'm not allowed,' and she said, 'Oh, don't worry about it, we'll tell your mom we're going to see a Disney film.'" She took Hill, when he was about nine or ten years old, to see *Maniac*, *The Evil Dead*, *Halloween*, and other scary movies. As for Hill's reaction, "I was horrified. There was a double feature on Halloween night of *Dawn of the Dead* and *Night of the Living Dead* when *Dawn of the Dead* came out, when I wasn't even supposed to be allowed in the theater, because I believe that that was rated the equivalent of 'NC-17,' and I thought I was going to be arrested. I thought I was watching a movie where people were really being murdered. Still to this day—I watched *Dawn of the Dead* not too long ago, and obviously now I can see that it's people in makeup and blah, blah, blah—but I still have that sort of feeling in the pit of my stomach that I'm watching something I shouldn't be watching." Hill, along with Lustig, went on in later years to work on video releases of many of the films that had scared the living daylights out of him.

Hill worked with Hellman in transferring *Two-Lane Blacktop* to video; Hellman wanted to correct some of the color timing, which adjusts the film's color. Lustig recorded an audio commentary with Hellman and the movie's associate producer, Gary Kurtz. Kurtz starts out by mentioning that Universal was upset that the sounds of car engines revving ran over its logo at the film's start. Hellman talks about never getting a straight answer from Universal about why the movie wasn't put out on video, difficulties in casting, and other studios turning down the film after Cinema Center dropped it. Kurtz says that Oates's wardrobe of white shirts, wool slacks, and cashmere sweaters was inspired by the film's producer, Michael Laughlin's, outfits when he visited the production offices.

As an extra on the release, Hellman told the Anchor Bay crew about a short documentary that filmmaker George Hickenlooper had recently made, and they tracked it down and included it. A fourteen-minute short, *Monte Hellman: American Auteur* consists of interviews with Harry Dean Stanton, Dennis Bartok, and then-reviewers Kevin Thomas of the *Los Angeles Times* and David Kipen of *Variety*. Hickenlooper interviewed Bartok at the offices the American Cinematheque was renting at the historic Roosevelt Hotel across the street from Grauman's (later TCL) Chinese Theater on Hollywood Boulevard. The "offices" being hotel rooms, each staff member had a bathroom with a shower. The documentary was "George's valentine to Monte and his movies," Bartok says. In the short documentary, Bartok presciently predicts that *Two-Lane Blacktop* will gain increasing esteem in the future.

But the video project stalled as lawyers negotiated for music rights to use fragments of three songs that are heard in the movie: "Hit the Road Jack" by Ray Charles, "Satisfaction" by the Rolling Stones and "Moonlight Drive" by the Doors. Prices fluctuate with the whims of the musicians. Jay Douglas remembers the headaches caused by a triple whammy: Charles's decision to raise the fees for his songs because he felt he'd been taken advantage of previously; the Doors' members' falling-out, making it difficult to get them to agree to license a song or to do anything else; and the high fees charged by Allen Klein, who had finagled the publishing rights to songs the Rolling Stones had recorded up to 1971. "I don't know this for a fact, but I did hear that for years Ray Charles was very easy to work with. In fact, maybe too easy to work with as far as licensing his songs, so when it became our turn to get clearance from him he was being incredibly hard because he had been too easy in the past," Douglas says. Lawyers negotiating for the rights didn't haggle over prices: they paid what was asked.

To avoid paying sometimes exorbitant fees, broadcasters that air movies on network television often substitute songs that sound exactly like the originals, but aren't. Douglas explains: "Most of the songs you hear in movies on network television are sound-alike bands. They have bands that sound like the real band, but they're not the real band, so they get away without having to pay a performance royalty." Douglas said that although Anchor Bay had left music out of some previous films it had brought out on video, he did not consider omitting songs from *Two-Lane Blacktop*. "You just couldn't do that," he says. "You had to put your Monte Hellman hat on and say, 'How do we want this film to come out?'"

"Moonlight Drive," which briefly plays on outside speakers at a drive-in restaurant, took the longest time to clear, Lustig recalls, "because of the infighting of the Doors." Jay Douglas remembers that "the Doors weren't necessarily speaking" at the time, and so it wasn't easy to get the three surviving members to come to an agreement on licensing their song. Lustig adds, "They weren't interested in the money, they weren't interested in anything." According to Douglas, the situation was even more complicated. "I worked with [former member of the rock band the Monkees] Michael Nesmith on a couple of projects, and he said something very interesting to me, and I really hadn't thought about this before, but when bands get to a certain stature, each of the members of the band has their own manager. So now you have to get not only the four members, or the three members, actually, of the Doors to agree, but each of those members has their own business manager, and it just gets a lot uglier than it needs to be."

But Hellman stepped in and persuaded the Doors, telling them that Jim Morrison had told him he wanted the music used in the film. Lustig continues, "The lawyers and everything sort of hit a brick wall with the Doors, and after Monte interceded, they agreed and got paid a really enormous amount of money for just that little, brief moment of that song on screen." The Doors received $45,000, which was $11,250 per Door or their estate, for the snippet of song. For the rights to all the music combined, Anchor Bay paid $75,000, so the Doors received well more than half of that total. Most of that sum went to the rights to three songs, and, Douglas notes, "between the three songs, there wasn't really even a minute's worth of music."

The movie didn't even use the Rolling Stones' version of the third song that caused Anchor Bay such grief, "Satisfaction"; the Girl sings it, off-key, in a coffee shop. She doesn't even sing that much of it. But she sang enough of the tune so that they had to clear the music rights. Lustig remembers that they had to deal with Allen Klein, who had swindled the Rolling Stones, tricking them into signing over the rights to their songs to him, when he had briefly been their manager. A notorious crook, Klein was jailed in 1979 for embezzling money due to UNICEF for a Concert for Bangladesh album. "Allen Klein, as I recall, I don't know if he was more difficult or just time-consuming, but that was the one that also took time to clear," Lustig says. Anchor Bay ended up paying as much for the fragments of the three songs as it did for licensing the entire movie from Universal.

When the music was finally cleared, the VHS version was ready for release; it came out first, followed by the DVD version. Anchor Bay also put out a collector's edition in a tin box, with a postcard, a key chain with a miniature '55 Chevy, and a booklet of stills from the movie. This deluxe packaging was unusual at the time for a film that had not been a hit. Universal supplied so many captivating photos that Douglas and his team had trouble deciding which ones to use. Universal provided "literally hundreds and hundreds of stills" that had never been used for any purpose, Douglas says, and he compares it to opening a time capsule. Wilson and Taylor not only had on-screen charisma, Douglas remarks, but "those guys didn't take a bad picture. The camera was their friend, that's for sure."

The video was received "rapturously," Bartok observes. It sold "incredibly well," Douglas adds, and the tens of thousands of copies sold were numbers he would have expected for a much more popular movie. The VHS cost about $16 and the DVD edition about $30. Although he anticipated that film buffs would buy it, Douglas was surprised that the GTO Association of America ordered hundreds of copies for its members. It had never occurred to him, he said, that "gearheads" would be fans of the movie. Bartok said one measure of a film's popularity is its online price: "Everybody's got their own opinion, but eBay doesn't lie. I do know that after the film went out of print with Anchor Bay that the DVD I think was selling up to $125-plus a copy before it got reissued through Criterion."

Anchor Bay didn't need to mount a big promotional campaign; the fans took that task upon themselves. The level of awareness of the movie had surprised Hellman and Norman Hill when Scarecrow Video screened *Two-Lane* in Seattle. Hill says the people who filled the theater at the Seattle Art Museum "were not museum-type people. They weren't the regulars who would come to the screenings at the museum. They were like car kids, and Monte flat out didn't know how they knew about the film." The audience had included women as well as men, and they had laughed at the right places, and applauded at the end, and many had stayed for the question-and-answer session afterwards.

Fans launched a grassroots marketing campaign. They not only bought the video, they talked about it and promoted it online; they were evangelical in their mission to publicize the movie. Douglas describes them as not just "passive fans. They were active fans, and they sort of felt obligated to go out and convert everyone into being a fan of *Two-Lane Blacktop*."

Reviewers were more enthusiastic this time around. "One of the essential movies of the Seventies, Monte Hellman's scandalously unavailable 1971 masterpiece *Two-Lane Blacktop* is available at last," wrote Gavin Smith in *Film Comment*. Smith goes on to call it the "ne plus ultra of the road film," and writes, "While a whole generation of cineastes will finally be able to see for themselves, let's not forget that Hellman's existential road movie, co-written by novelist Rudolf Wurlitzer, was dismissed in its day and dumped by Universal, who've done an admirable job of keeping it down ever since." Automotive magazines praised it, too. The reviewer (who didn't receive a well-deserved byline) for *Car Craft* wrote: "About the only movie ever made about street racers, director Monte Hellman's *Two-Lane Blacktop* is now available as a collector's edition on VHS or DVD. This is the first time the '71 film has been available on home video, and both the DVD and tape feature a truly sweet, color-corrected digital transfer so good it's astounding. That GTO now seems to be the same color throughout the movie and the '55 Chevy never looked nastier. If you've only seen *Two-Lane* on television, it's like looking at a completely different and completely better movie. And even when it looked crappy, it was still one of the best car movies ever made."

Bartok maintains that *Two-Lane* is "*the* great American road movie" because it goes beyond films like *Easy Rider* in exploring the concept of freedom: "Here are the Driver and the Mechanic, and they seem to be completely free. All they have to do is tool around the United States in their '55 Chevy, drag racing for a living, and yet they don't seem incredibly happy. They're completely emotionless. And by the end you realize that this kind of false promise of ultimate freedom means nothing but emptiness and one more race, which Monte expresses at the end by the slowed-down drag race and then the film catching fire and burning. Freedom in *Two-Lane Blacktop*—even the title of the film—freedom becomes kind of a Mobius strip that leads nowhere and constantly cycles back on itself, and you can imagine these guys are still out there somewhere on the horizon."

The accolades showed promise of reigniting Hellman's languishing career. He had not directed a movie since *Silent Night, Deadly Night III: Better Watch Out!*—which was released in 1989. Directing the third movie in a franchise that was, even for slasher films, considered in poor taste by people who sentimentalize Christmas and Santa (but considered a brilliant sendup of Christmas by Scrooges) seemed an out-of-character choice to such Hellman admirers as Norman Hill. But he'd made it his own. Hill, who had avoided seeing Hellman's sequel on its initial release because of the franchise's notoriety, says, "When I finally got to see the film, it was so quirky and off-the-wall that I could see why he decided to go for it as a director. I mean, obviously the financial considerations aside, he was able to craft it into just a completely bizarre movie, totally out of whack with the other direction that those films had gone in." Although Hellman discussed projects with producers, few came to fruition at this time, and he didn't direct another feature until *Road to Nowhere*, which was released eleven years later, in 2010.

The *Two-Lane Blacktop* video still disappointed some viewers, just as the film had on its initial release; the movie is polarizing, and some find it compelling while others find it deadly dull. For example, Jay Douglas told his friends about the video, but most of them are not cinephiles. "They actually didn't really quite know what to think about the film because there was so little dialogue, and most of it, at least between the Driver and the Mechanic, had to do with the automobile," Douglas says. Even some of his friends who love movies didn't appreciate *Two-Lane Blacktop* when they finally saw it on video. "Most of my friends are not car buffs either, so the language between the Mechanic and the Driver was something they really didn't understand. And then they would ask questions like, 'What was the ending? What was happening at the end?'"

# 10

# The Finish Line: The Film Catches Fire

*Two-Lane Blacktop* has made the leap from a movie that flopped to a highly lauded cult classic, released on video by the prestigious Criterion Collection and preserved for posterity in the National Film Registry, with its own T-shirts, toy cars, and Rob Zombie song. Rudy Wurlitzer, recalling the preview in San Diego where many in the audience expected a more traditional movie and were disappointed and confused, observes that "now, of course, the reaction to the film is the opposite, and the times that I've screened it, as well as Monte Hellman, viewers have been enthusiastic, with many people having seen the film several times." Upon its release on DVD in 2007, Dave Kehr wrote in the *New York Times* that the movie had come full circle, from its pre-release hype by *Esquire*, to its disastrous theatrical release, to its subsequent acquisition of an underground reputation with requisite bootleg copies, to its achievement of cult status, and finally to its elevation to rarefied stature in December of that year. Kehr wrote: "This month it was released on DVD by the Criterion Collection, which puts it as close as any movie can come to the official canon." Had Hellman caved in to pressure from Universal executives to make his movie more conventional and commercial, the film might have appealed initially to a larger audience, but it would have been a less committed one. *Two-Lane* would not have been unique, would have received fewer accolades and would not have stood up as well.

When Criterion released the movie on DVD and later Blu-ray, and when it played at revival theaters, cinematheques, colleges, and retrospectives, reviewers often commented that it had aged well. An article in *Sight and Sound* in February 2012 called *Two-Lane* "one icon of post-60s counterculture that hasn't dated, but now seems darker, sadder and more beautiful than ever." Writing for the *Chicago Reader* in February 2001, Jonathan Rosenbaum opined, "This exciting existentialist road movie by Monte Hellman, with a swell script by Rudolph Wurlitzer and Will Corry and my favorite Warren Oates performance, looks even better now than it did in 1971, although it was pretty interesting back then as well." In an article in the *New Republic* from 2011, David Thomson compared *Two-Lane* favorably with *Easy Rider*. "It is so much more worthwhile as a film," he wrote, adding "*Two-Lane Blacktop* never stoops to the hippy v. redneck politics of *Easy Rider*." Instead, *Two-Lane* addresses themes that continue to resonate: alienation, the futile quest for freedom, the longing for intimacy, and the hollowness of consumerism and conspicuous consumption.

In 2012, *Two-Lane Blacktop* was honored by inclusion in the National Film Registry, which was established to preserve and promote the nation's film heritage. Movies are chosen for their cultural, historical, or artistic significance. In announcing its selection of *Two-Lane*, the Library of Congress explained its importance: "During a short-lived period following the success of such youth-oriented films as *Bonnie and Clyde*, *The Graduate* and especially *Easy Rider* in the late 1960s, Hollywood executives financed—with minimal oversight—a spate of low-budget, innovative films by young 'New Hollywood' filmmakers. With influences ranging from playwright Samuel Beckett to European filmmakers Robert Bresson, Jacques Rivette and Michelangelo Antonioni, one such film was the minimalist classic *Two-Lane Blacktop*.... Director Monte Hellman and screenwriter Rudolph Wurlitzer allow audiences time to absorb the film's spare landscapes, car-culture rituals and existential encounters, and to reflect on the myth of freedom that life on the road traditionally has embodied."

*Two-Lane* also was honored with placement on "favorite" or "best" lists. In its February 21, 2013, issue, *Rolling Stone* chose the scene in the drive-in where the Doors'"Moonlight Drive" briefly plays as number 25 of the greatest rock'n' roll movie moments. The British Film Institute picked *Two-Lane* as one of the ten great American road trip movies. And *Film Comment*, in its "Trivial Top 20" list of the best road movies, chose *Two-Lane* as number one.

Of course, the film has its detractors. It is too slow. Nothing much happens. The acting is terrible. But such viewers are not nearly as vocal as the film's fans— cinephiles and gearheads alike.

Automotive magazines and websites also celebrated the movie. On its undoubtedly hyperbolic list of 100 hot rods that changed the world, Hotrod.

com picked the '55 Chevy from *Two-Lane* as number 10. Edmunds.com, a prominent automotive site, designated *Two-Lane*'s Chevy as number 11 and the GTO as number 55 of "the Top 100 Movie Cars of All Time." Hot Rod Network chose *Two-Lane* second on its list of "the Top 10 Car Movies Ever." Despite a threat of rain, the venerable *Hemmings Motor News* screened *Two-Lane* for a few dozen motorists at a drive-in theater in July 2011. Toy-car manufacturers have produced miniature *Two-Lane Blacktop* '55 Chevys and GTOs. A large assortment of T-shirts feature images of the movie's cars and actors.

The Glendale Speed Center T-shirt that Richard Ruth wears at the gas station scene in Needles features the sixties cartoon character Fred Flintstone. A "vintage" one with a small hole was offered on eBay for $1,000, but new ones sell for about $20. Ruth moved to Merced, California, and set up a business, Ruth Industries, where he still builds cars. Although he gave up his email address because the task of replying to all the questions he received about the *Two-Lane* car was onerous, fans of the Chevy and the movie still find him. "I had some guys show up here, there were three of them actually, and they came here from North Carolina and drove a '55 Chevrolet on a road trip" that was actually an automotive pilgrimage to see Ruth. "They showed up and they knew every single word of that movie, all three of them. And it just blew me away. They think I'm some kind of guru. It's flattering, but that's not really me. They just wanted to meet Richard Ruth. All my friends crack up. I'm just a normal guy." He receives several phone calls a week from people with questions about the '55 Chevy, and customers regularly ask him to make clones of it. He restored the picture car used in the film for a customer, who had it auctioned at Barrett-Jackson in Scottsdale in 2015, where it fetched $159,000. Like a modern blockbuster, *Two-Lane* has spun off tie-in products that generate ancillary revenue, although not always for the studio.

Just as car guys put Richard Ruth on a pedestal, some aspiring and established directors, as well as film lovers, look up to Monte Hellman and his most famous movie. Dennis Bartok, who wrote and produced *Trapped Ashes*, compares *Two-Lane Blacktop* to the Velvet Underground's first album. In a 1982 interview with the *Los Angeles Times*, the musician and record producer Brian Eno said that although *The Velvet Underground and Nico* sold only 30,000 copies in the initial five years after its release, he thought that everyone who bought one of those albums started a band. The unit publicist Eileen Peterson, who had a long career in Hollywood, also observes that Hellman inspired some young people. "It's like Bob Downey Sr. I went to a film festival for his films and there were all kinds of people like Louis C. K. and Alan Arkin who were saying that his early films were what got them interested in the indie film scene. Monte has made that mark, has had that influence."

The director Richard Linklater (*Slacker* [1991], *Boyhood* [2014]) agrees that Hellman and *Two-Lane Blacktop* have motivated young filmmakers. Linklater says he thinks Hellman has had a broad influence in the sense that personal films encourage young people to make movies of their own. He knows from experience that Hellman is especially encouraging to directors who are starting out—Linklater sent Hellman the first film he made. "He's a very generous guy. He's very sweet and supportive, and he helps out people," Linklater concludes. "I think he's encouraged a generation" of filmmakers.

Directors who say they've been influenced by Monte Hellman and *Two-Lane Blacktop* include Allison Anders (*Gas, Food Lodging* [1992]), Quentin Tarantino (*Pulp Fiction* [1994]), Wim Wenders (*Wings of Desire* [1987]), and Kelly Reichardt (*Wendy and Lucy* [2008], *Certain Women* [2016]).

Reichardt teaches at Bard College and sometimes includes *Two-Lane Blacktop* in her curriculum. She shows *Two-Lane* to her students, she says, because "the camera's never doing anything for the sake of anything besides keeping you in the movie, keeping you in the car, and/or keeping you looking at the road where the car's going." Also, the acting isn't stagey. "That style of performance that's inside this really well-constructed framework is really what appeals to me about the movie, and just the texture of the sound design and the dirtiness of it all, that you feel the dust of the road, and you feel all these things that people feel, and the way the sound mixes, like I guess the way Altman was doing before this, just putting their voices in the mix of everyone else's that's standing around, all the other drivers, and not putting them out front."

In her films, Reichardt spotlights outsiders, and she admires the way Hellman focuses on characters on the fringes of society. "I guess that was the idea originally of the B movie, that there were people on the screen that were outside the sort of winners of the world, that were more relatable, as far as class, and everyone wasn't a model," even though the actors in *Two-Lane* are exceptionally attractive.

What she admires most about the movie, Reichardt says, is its construction—how it is stylized without being showy, and the relationship between form and subject. "It fits in with the people who are working on their engines and building their cars. The film is built like that. The big scene at the gas station where they talk about pink slips, it's such a well-constructed scene and fits together really like a puzzle, probably because Monte Hellman is an editor and is thinking about how things go together." Also, the film doesn't include extraneous material that calls attention to the director or the cameraman, or that is thrown in just because it looks pretty. Reichardt continues, "There's no shot in the whole movie that's a landscape shot that you could say is for the sake of beauty. There's no beauty shot, everything is working all the time. There's nothing for the sake of sentiment, or for beauty. There's a real rigor to it."

On the other hand, the film's openness appeals to her. In recent years, Reichardt has driven across the country frequently, and she says she appreciates the depiction of roads and a way of life that don't exist any longer. "Twenty-year-olds don't have lost years rambling around the highways anymore. You start your career." Also, many small motels and diners and local radio stations have disappeared. "A film about alienation and disconnection, that are things other than plot and story, and just the lack of direction as far as what the film is, is much like the open road. Those things are lost things that are hard to come by now," and are no longer portrayed in studio films. Reichardt adds that the movie not only conveys the atmosphere of mom-and-pop businesses and a way of life that have passed, it transmits sensory experiences such as the weather and the dust in the road. "That scene in the rain where they steal the license plates, you can smell that scene, you know that now they're in the South and that morning rain, you know exactly what that feels like."

Finally, speaking as a teacher and admirer, Reichardt says she appreciates that Hellman doesn't lead the viewer by the nose. "There's no one ever telling you what the movie's about, so it's just such a lived-in experience."

As for the ways that *Two-Lane Blacktop* has influenced her filmmaking, she says, "There's something about the scale of this movie, which I think has to do with the level of intimacy, an unsentimental kind of intimacy, but real intimacy with just what's happening in the frame. It's something that's easy to want to aspire to. Just the sort of low-fi-ness of it, but not in any kind of messy way. It's a really well-crafted film." Also, she says the process of going out on the road and shooting a film transfers some grit, fatigue, and realism to the screen. "I'm not trying to romanticize this, because *Two-Lane* and the making of it have been well romanticized, and I'm sure it was as much of a pain in the ass as every other film is, but there is something about making a film somewhere where you're a little bit off the grid and you're traveling with this sort of carnival of people that you're making the film with, and the hours you put in in a day in the cold, in the incredible heat or whatever it is, and then what happens in the evenings" partially translates to the screen. "All of those things influence me. The way it's cast. Just finding people who are up for the experience." For instance, when she made *Wendy and Lucy*, she says, Michelle Williams "could come make that film and sit on a curb all day." Other actors, such as Jesse Eisenberg and Dakota Fanning in *Night Moves* (2013), had to adapt to Reichardt's low-budget procedure for making a movie, which resembles *Two-Lane*'s production in its pared-down crew with everybody pitching in to do what needs to be done. "Making films with us is pretty different than what they're used to," Reichardt explains. "Instead of hanging out in a trailer, they really have to help push the car out of the mud, and the crew and the actors are all sort of in it together. And I think that's like a relief for the actors, and you get the sense of that, probably."

Hellman makes a complex process look simple, Reichardt says. "It's deceiving how open and doable it all looks." Yet the frames are not flat, and often there is action in both the foreground and background. She concludes, "It's rare to find films that are so well crafted, and at the same time are not about the filmmaking, that you can really live in, and so it's just a little gem."

A director who is an especially vocal champion of *Two-Lane Blacktop* is Richard Linklater. He remembers that the first time he saw the film "was back in, I want to say '83, '84, long before it was available. I'd read about it for years, and just couldn't find it. It never played much, and it certainly wasn't on video. It was listed in a book called *Cult Movies*. I'd read about it there, and read about it other places, and I'd seen a couple of other Monte Hellman films, so I was just curious to see it. I remember I'd driven to Houston, I was staying at my sister's place. I had a doctor's appointment or something. I was living in Austin, a little film freak. I turned on her TV and flipped through a few stations and saw, it was probably like one, two in the morning and saw an interesting image and the sound, and I looked. And it was the opening credits of *Two-Lane Blacktop*. And I was like, 'Holy shit!' I was like, 'It's on TV. *OK!*' and so I planted myself and watched it, just glued to a little crappy TV, but it didn't matter. I was just soaking it up. So it was great. The end, it was just a revelation. I just loved it. I loved it even more than I thought I would going into it."

A few years later, he says, he found a 16 mm print and started screening it. Then, in 2001, he recalls, he and a friend convinced Universal to strike a brand-new 35 mm print. He took it to the Toronto International Film Festival, where a couple of his films were premiering, and showed it there two days before September 11, 2001. "I had two films there, I remember, and so that was really wonderful to go from seeing it on TV and bad 16 prints to actually get to finally see it in a beautiful 35 print."

To introduce a screening at the South by Southwest Festival in Austin in 2000, he came up with ten reasons, which ballooned to sixteen reasons, why he loves *Two-Lane Blacktop*. Criterion printed the reasons in a booklet that accompanies its DVD release. *Two-Lane* appeals to him, Linklater explains, because "the film defies so many expectations. It was probably never destined to be a big hit, even in its day. James Taylor fans—if you go for that, you're a little disappointed he doesn't sing a song, doesn't whip out a guitar. And Dennis Wilson. They don't make music, they don't talk that much, they're not that interesting, all the things that would compel you. That's what's so *great* about it. I think that's what I got most out of it at that first screening. Knowing it's a studio film, but just having the *absolute* conviction to go all the way with that idea. It takes guts." Linklater says he admires Hellman's courage in refusing to bend to studio pressure to give the film a conventional ending. He praises the film for being "pure" in the sense that "in its intentions, it's not trying to be anything more than it is. It's just kind of uncorrupted."

Although the tones of Hellman's and Linklater's movies are quite different, both directors have an unadorned, naturalistic style, and both focus on outsiders. Movie reviewers often write that Linklater pays homage to *Two-Lane Blacktop* by featuring GTOs in some of his films, and he even has a character named "GTO" in *Slacker*. But, Linklater says, "anytime you have a GTO" in a movie it's interpreted as an homage to *Two-Lane Blacktop*. Linklater points out, "There's an homage, and then there's a sensibility," and his films probably would not be a lot different had he never seen Hellman's. However, he says, he does think he was influenced by road movies, and "you're influenced by everything you love," and he loves *Two-Lane Blacktop*. He mentions his car, a '68 GTO Judge, which he put in *Dazed and Confused* and *Boyhood*. "Would I have bought that car had I never seen *Two-Lane Blacktop*? Maybe not."

∞

When the director Wes Anderson (*The Royal Tenenbaums* [2001], *Moonrise Kingdom* [2012], *The Grand Budapest Hotel* [2014]), a native Texan, first came to Hollywood, the director he most wanted to meet was Monte Hellman. A critically acclaimed maker of highly stylized movies, Anderson nevertheless appreciates Hellman's naturalistic films. Anderson explains, "I loved *Two-Lane Blacktop*, and I had read a little article, maybe around 1992 or so, which Quentin Tarantino had written for *Sight and Sound* about *The Shooting* and *Ride in the Whirlwind*, and I watched them on VHS and I loved them both, too." After Anderson met Hellman, they became friends. "I watched *China 9, Liberty 37* (which Monte seemed to have the only tape of on the planet at that time) with Monte at his house up in Laurel Canyon," Anderson recalls. He adds, "I remember Monte telling me how he used to take cabins in cargo ships to get to and from Europe," a habit that Michael Laughlin recalls, since Hellman and Laurie Bird traveled on one to visit Laughlin and Leslie Caron at their house in Sardinia after *Two-Lane Blacktop* was finished.

Although their styles differ radically, Anderson says Hellman and *Two-Lane* made a mark on him. "I am sure the first movie Owen Wilson and I did together, *Bottle Rocket*, takes some real inspiration from *Two-Lane Blacktop*. And I would love, one day, anyway, to do a Monte Hellman Western." Anderson says he admires *Two-Lane* because "I like very much how he takes what ought to be a genre picture and kind of erases the genre out of it. It's sort of much more Beckett than AIP, if that makes any sense. He casts these two musicians, both very interesting to watch, and there is something vaguely documentary about them. Like we are aware of watching the actual people playing scenes together in some strange way that pulls you into their presence."

Anderson says he thinks the influence of *Two-Lane* lies in its availability and the kudos it has received. "I think it's better known than ever. It had sort of dropped below the radar for a few years, and now it is back to stay. It is now canonized."

∞

Since *Two-Lane Blacktop* didn't have a soundtrack composed for it, the film has invited musical tributes from several musicians drawn to the movie—but not because they like James Taylor or Dennis Wilson.

Musicians of various ages and styles have honored *Two-Lane Blacktop*. The singer Ladyhawke, aka Phillipa "Pip" Brown, formerly had a band called Two-Lane Blacktop. In 2003, Rob Zombie released a song called "Two-Lane Blacktop" that was loosely based on the movie. And Bruce Springsteen has brought up and plugged the movie at some concerts he's given. Introducing "Racing in the Street," he has told audiences how much he likes the film, called it a masterpiece, and pointed out its similarities with his song, which he wrote before he saw the movie.

In 2013, the Nashville guitarist William Tyler released a seven-and-a-half-minute video remake of *Two-Lane Blacktop* for his song "A Portrait of Sarah" on his album *Impossible Truth*. Made for an ultra-low budget, the video homage meticulously recreates several scenes from the film. Tyler shot the video in Nashville, and the settings and the cars are different. But, to an uncanny extent, the director, Michael Carter, duplicates the original's staging and its camera angles and movements. The actors wear close replicas of the costumes in the film—GTO's sweater, the Driver's blue shirt, the Girl's green duffel bag, the Mechanic's jean jacket. The actors also faithfully mimic the original actors' facial expressions, positions, and movements; the young woman who plays the Girl, a Nashville model named Ashley Fisher, even copies Laurie Bird's self-conscious gait and gestures. Using some locations that are quite similar to those in *Two-Lane*, plus some that are jarringly different, the video copies the shot where the Driver and the Mechanic eat at a café while through the window we see the Girl move her stuff from her last ride into the Chevy. Another scene carefully replicates the Girl and Mechanic's impassive, businesslike preparation for sex in a motel room. The video also recreates the scene where the Girl and the Driver sit on a fence, the drag strip sequence where the Girl wanders around by herself, and the scene where the Girl leaves the Driver, the Mechanic, and GTO at a café, dumps her duffel bag on the ground, and takes off with the motorcyclist.

The idea for the video, according to Tyler, who was thirty-four when he made it, grew out of his fascination with 1970s cinema. "There's a lot of romanticism about the era of the seventies amongst musicians my age and a little bit younger. I think it is a recent development, and there are a lot of levels to it. There's a certain kind of nostalgia for that era of what would have been our parents' youth that is very appealing, I think, to people now because there's a certain sense of space and lyricism and meditative wandering to the music and the cinema of that era that just is missing from a lot of stuff now." *Two-Lane*, in particular, he says, is like a portrait of part of the United States at that time. He also appreciates the movie's naturalism, which reminds him of a documentary. "I'm just fascinated with the vibe of that film." He praises it because it seems spontaneous and improvised, and because Warren Oates is so good. "Every scene he's in he sort of carries, and James Taylor and Dennis Wilson aren't really actors, and there's not much dialogue, and it's just a great fucking film, really."

Tyler says he thinks of his music as good traveling music, so it lent itself to a road-movie theme for a video. He considers *Two-Lane* "the ultimate road movie of the seventies." The song in the video is from Tyler's album *Impossible Truth*, which was the guitarist/songwriter's homage to seventies singer/songwriter records, so he thought of James Taylor being a character in his video. Tyler says he also is a big fan of Rudy Wurlitzer. "Growing up watching a lot of movies, I was really fascinated with two of his other films, the Pat Garrett one [*Pat Garrett and Billy the Kid*] and *Walker*, that Alex Cox directed. Those were all like huge failures. He seems like a very well-historically informed person who writes movies that no one actually ends up going to see." Finally, Tyler speaks highly of Dennis Wilson, saying he thinks the musician was unfairly pigeonholed as middle-of-the-road because of his association with the Beach Boys. "Dennis Wilson's an interesting figure because he was kind of like the guy in the Beach Boys who was the bad one, and he was the one who died young and hung out with Charles Manson. And he did make a very interesting solo record." Tyler says he is not a big fan of James Taylor, but gives him credit for writing songs with dark themes, especially early in his career.

Tyler says like-minded friends agreed to collaborate with him. "There was a shared fascination with that film amongst a group of my friends, and that's kind of how we came up with the idea of doing the video." Tyler suggested adding an homage to the British television show of the seventies and eighties *The Old Grey Whistle Test*, which featured performances by talented yet lesser-known rock 'n' roll bands. In a nod to the show, in scenes in the motel room and the café Tyler is seen on a television set playing his guitar. The video's director and editor, Michael Carter, was enthusiastic. Carter, says Tyler, "was also similarly fascinated with *Two-Lane Blacktop*. He had an almost shot-by-shot knowledge of that movie," as is evidenced in the video.

They found an old car, which was the same color but a different shape, and a drag strip. "It wasn't really feasible to do. We literally didn't have the kind of equipment that was really necessary to do the kind of car stuff" that was seen in *Two-Lane*, Tyler says. "I think we had about $2,000 to spend on that video. That basically went toward the camera. I think everybody basically did it for free, and you don't want to make a habit out of that." Tyler, like Taylor, a guitarist, plays the Driver in the video and Jamin Orrall, like Wilson, a drummer, plays the Mechanic.

Tyler thinks that young fans of *Two-Lane* like the movie partly because it was a box-office flop. "I think if it had been a big success it wouldn't be considered as cool." He appreciates the movie's minimal music and its subtlety, compared to *Easy Rider*, which he says is more popular with his parents' generation than with his own. "The way they end that movie—the guys get shot by rednecks—and I'm sure that's supposed to be symbolic, but it's so leaden. And as somebody who grew up in the Deep South—all my family is from Mississippi—it's like, oh, yeah, so obviously they make it all the way across the country and they die in Mississippi, because that's easy, that's where all the really scary rednecks are." Tyler thinks *Two-Lane*'s ending is superior because it is vague, and says he prefers movies with "unsatisfying" endings.

Tyler also says that road movies in general appeal to musicians because it reminds them of going out on a tour. "I think the movement inherent in a road film is easy to relate to as a musician because it's very similar to touring. There's not any sort of static reality there, there's this constant shift in scenery and outside personnel with the protagonist remaining the same." And he finds that joining music and cinema can produce powerful results. For example, he says, people who hear a song for the first time in a movie will often think of the film whenever they hear the song. When he thinks of the folk music group Holy Modal Rounders, he associates them with *Easy Rider* because the group got the most exposure of their career when their song "If You Want to Be a Bird" was heard in the movie.

∞

Late one night at the end of the seventies or in the early eighties, when Filippo Salvadori was still living in his hometown, Arezzo, Italy, he turned on public television and watched a movie that had started a few minutes previously.

"For years, I had no idea what that movie was, but I always thought it was great." Finally, he described the mystery movie to a film-buff friend, who told Salvadori, "Oh, that's Monte Hellman's *Two-Lane Blacktop*."

Salvadori later moved to Berkeley, California, and started some record companies. Finally, in the mid-nineties, he saw *Two-Lane* in a theater. "It was pretty amazing to see it on the big screen and finally hear every little thing," he remembers. Also at that time, a number of tribute albums to bands and artists were being released, but Salvadori didn't notice any that honored movies. So he made a tribute album to *Blow-Up* and then decided to dedicate one to *Two-Lane Blacktop*. Salvadori approached musicians whom he admired and whose songs seemed to fit with the feeling he got from *Two-Lane*. "Most of the people, if not all, loved the movie, and they kind of said, 'Oh, yeah, that's a curious project, I want to be part of it.'" Will Oldham, Alvarius B. (aka Alan Bishop), and Roy Montgomery in particular told Salvadori they were big fans of the movie and were eager to contribute a song. Some of the musicians hadn't seen the film but agreed to participate after he sent them a DVD, and a few just weren't interested.

Musicians and groups that agreed to contribute a tune to the CD, called *You Can Never Go Fast Enough* after a line from the film, were Will Oldham and Alan Licht, Alvarius B., Calexico, Wilco, Steffen Basho-Junghans, Mark Eitzel and Marc Cappelle, Suntanama, Giant Sand, Charalambides, Sonic Youth, and Roy Montgomery. Salvadori also licensed songs previously recorded by Sandy Bull, Roscoe Holcomb, Leadbelly, and Cat Power. He says he didn't think much of "Moonlight Drive" and "Me and Bobby McGee," songs used in the movie. "I'm not a fan of those. I mean, they are kind of famous songs. I don't think they add anything to the movie. So, probably unconsciously, I was maybe trying to say maybe they could have done a better job. It probably cost them a lot of money, but I feel like the Sandy Bull track is better chosen."

It took Salvadori about a year and a half to put the album together before it was released by his company, Plain Recordings, in 2003. The artist Savage Pencil made an ink collage for the cover that depicts the '55 Chevy, with the Driver and the Mechanic standing near the front, the Girl in the backseat looking out the window, and GTO outside the car, looking at the Girl. Salvadori says, "Compilations are kind of hard, per se, because there are ten or fifteen artists that have to send in tapes. First you have to get in touch with them, then they have to tell you, 'Yes, I can do it, maybe next month or several weeks down the line,' so it kind of takes time to collect things." So long, in fact, particularly when he had to go through a manager or when an artist procrastinated, or was touring or recording something else, that it was the last such project he put together. "It took me too long. I was happy that it came out and came out nicely and had some good press, but I've never done a project like that since."

∞

One song on the *You Can Never Go Fast Enough* album, "Don't Cry for Me, Driver," was contributed by Will Oldham and Alan Licht. Oldham played the kid in *Matewan* (1987), directed by John Sayles, and the young man trying in vain to rekindle a lost friendship in *Old Joy* (2006), directed by Kelly Reichardt. He delivers moving performances in both films. He also is an accomplished musician who has been profiled in the *New Yorker*, and a list of the names of singers who have covered his songs extends for pages and includes Johnny Cash, who recorded a version of "I See a Darkness." Instead of trying to appear hip or handsome, Oldham looks hirsute. He'll perform in sweatpants and a hoody, and he has a long, shaggy blond beard and a mustache. In a video for "I See a Darkness," as well as some others, Oldham plasters white makeup on his face, which gives him an eerie, ghostly appearance. Oldham writes some beautiful songs, but, like Monte Hellman, he gives his vision and self-expression priority over commercial considerations.

Licht is a musician and a conceptual artist. For instance, at one performance, Oldham recalls, Licht composed some music for the guitar to add to a rapid recording of a hog-calling contest. Another time, Licht was invited to play a solo with a band in New York. Oldham recalls, "So he just came up and for the length of the solo he dribbled a basketball. It was great because it was really exciting, it wasn't just like a 'fuck you' thing, the audience actually got excited by it because it was truly exciting."

When Salvadori approached Oldham, the actor/musician had admired *Two-Lane Blacktop* for years. Serendipitously, he and Licht had just put together a benefit performance for Anthology Film Archives in New York. For part of the performance they played "Don't Cry for Me, Argentina," while Licht spoke all of the Driver's lines from *Two-Lane Blacktop*. "We had done it literally a month or two before the invitation came, so the kismet was too intense to ignore," Oldham says.

The duo was not attracted by Madonna's well-known version of the song, but by Sinead O'Connor's recording. That version, they thought, "was a beautiful and strange and ironic performance from her in the way she sort of inserted herself as a pop music voice into this political/Broadway narrative in a way that could be compared, I guess, to James Taylor and Dennis Wilson inserting themselves into a completely different context for their talents," Oldham says.

Like other avant-garde musicians who have paid tribute to *Two-Lane*, Oldham says that the traditional Wilson and Taylor were not what drew him to the film. "I'm not a huge James Taylor fan, and I'm one of the only people I know who really just doesn't care for the Beach Boys," Oldham says. But, he adds, they have some appeal to even innovative young musicians. "James Taylor was super middle-of-the-road, and remains so, but Dennis Wilson had access to some fringe aspects, and I think his Charlie Manson dalliance or just being sort of the force that was stepping away from the Beach Boys with his own vision and his own creativity" gives him an edge and makes him more interesting than his bandmates. And, despite his own opinion, "Some musicians," he says, "think James Taylor was cool because he had a heroin addiction."

Oldham, who was born in Louisville, Kentucky, and still lives there, was originally taken with *Two-Lane* because of Warren Oates, a native Kentuckian who spent time in that city. When he first saw the movie what struck him most was its resemblance to Robert Bresson's films, Oldham says. "And it was so amazing that it was American, and so cool that the actors weren't actors, because that was very Bressonian—he hated actors. And potentially Hellman hired these two guys for the same reason, not for the reason that somebody would make a movie with Mariah Carey or Whitney Houston, but just the opposite. And it's like they could get somebody who can't act. It's like, 'I don't want actors in this. I want to be able to tell this story and have people view something more.' You have to look at other things beyond the acting performances, and yet you do respect these two people, you know that they are accomplished and intelligent and talented people."

Nevertheless, he continues, "It was apparent that they couldn't act, and they didn't try, so you were watching something else. And it was a great movie, so what were you watching? You were watching the interplay, you were listening to the dialogue, you were watching America. It was kind of a little freeing kind of religious experience to watch that movie. There was no spontaneity, those were two of the worst performances ever in any movie because they were so wooden and not spontaneous, and at a certain point he had to realize that was happening and he continued to go with it. I don't know if he just didn't have any options. Coming from the Roger Corman school of filmmaking, you probably just get what you can get and then move along."

To critics of the movie who say it would have been better with professional actors, Oldham retorts, "There are enough movies of that time that tell the road story with great actors, so you don't need another one, necessarily, and this is just its own beast, altogether unlike anything else." Oldham particularly admires the movie's deadpan aspects—the actors' lack of affect, and Hellman's restrained style and refusal to manipulate viewers' emotions.

Years after it was made, the drawbacks that caused the movie to bomb were reinterpreted and seen as merits that helped make it a classic. Had the characters finished the race, it would have undercut the timeless themes of alienation and quest for identity and purpose. The film melting in flames at the end, which initially alarmed or confused some viewers, became a provocative and celebrated feature of the movie. If Universal had had the ability and inclination to market the movie to cinephiles and car guys, and waited for word of mouth to spread until the film gained an audience, then if the studio had released it on video, *Two-Lane Blacktop* would not have built up cachet in the seventies, eighties, and early nineties as an abandoned, sought-after, hard-to-find film. Had Dennis Wilson not befriended Charles Manson, and had James Taylor not been addicted to heroin for a time, younger musicians would now regard them as more traditional and square, and less daring and cool. Had it been a hit with their grandparents, instead of a colossal failure, *Two-Lane* would have had less appeal to young people who feel they have discovered a little gem that their elders failed to appreciate. Its minimal dialogue and music, unpolished acting, and ambiguous ending have left room for interpretation and allowed it to appeal to a range of movie lovers with different tastes and preferences, from Jay Douglas at Anchor Bay, a businessman/cinephile whose job is releasing overlooked movies on video; to Wes Anderson, a director of formal, studied films; to the mainstream rock star Bruce Springsteen; to the experimental guitarist/noise-rock musician Alan Licht. Had the film been more conventionally pleasing and fun to watch, it would not have eventually become hip and cool.

# Appendix

## *Two-Lane Blacktop* Location Personnel List

Associate Producer: Gary Kurtz
Director: Monte Hellman
Production Manager: Walter Coblenz
Location Manager: Steve Henschel
Location Auditor: Reg Bisgrove
Technical Advisor: Jay Wheatley
Production Secretary: Sue Myers
Unit Publicist: Beverly Walker
Script Supervisor: Bonnie Prendergast
Photo Advisor: Gregory Sandor
Cameraman: Jack Deerson
Camera Operator: Hugh Gagnier
Assistant Camera: John Bailey
Still Photographer: Jack Albin
Sound Mixer: Charles Knight
Boom Operator: James Contreras
Gaffer: George Holmes
Best Boy: Larry Howard
Generator Operator: Arley Waters
Key Grip: Chuck Record
Best Boy: Ronnie Stafford
Crane Operator: Verlin Matthews
Props: Gene Booth

Wardrobe: Dick Bruno
Driver Captain: Jim Thornsberry
Equipment Driver: Dick Austin
Utility Driver: Craig Pinkard
Bus Driver: John Brumby
Insert Car Driver: Gene Clinesmith
Driver: James Taylor
Mechanic: Dennis Wilson
Girl: Laurie Bird
GTO: Warren Oates

# Notes

### Chapter One: Starting Line

3    "The new people": Leslie Caron, author interview (AI) 1/16/15
4    "Robbie Wald": Michael Laughlin, AI 7/20/12
4    "gave them to their literary": Michael Laughlin, AI 3/17/16
5    "Poetic. Not long-haired." Michael Laughlin, email to author 6/2/17
5    "If that script" and following: Michael Laughlin, AI 7/20/12
6    "Monte asked me to": Martin Landau, AI 7/14/16
7    "wonderfully innovative": Leslie Caron, email to author 12/29/14
8    "was the most adorable": Michael Laughlin, AI 7/20/12
8    "I couldn't talk them into Steven": Michael Laughlin, AI 3/17/16
8    "Michael was really" and following: Leslie Caron, AI 1/16/15
8    "For Monte to bring": Michael Laughlin, AI 7/20/12
9    "He was a director": Martin Landau, AI 7/14/16
9    "I just assumed": Michael Laughlin, AI 3/17/16
9    "Floyd was very": Michael Laughlin, AI 9/12/15
9    "Rudy [Wurlitzer] wrote a really" and following: Floyd Mutrux, AI 9/5/15
9    "She'd be home": Billy Kincheloe, AI 1/27/15
10    "Monte and I": Floyd Mutrux, AI 9/11/15
10    "Floyd knew much more" and following: Michael Laughlin, AI 9/12/15
10    "was kind of a hip": Mutrux, AI 2/18/17
10    "and I really needed" and following: Rudy Wurlitzer, AI 3/20/15
10    "The Writers Guild": Michael Laughlin, email to author 2/11/17
10    "55 Chevy two-door": Will Corry, *Two-Lane Blacktop* screenplay, collection of Billy Kincheloe

## Notes

10 "55 Chevy two-door": Rudy Wurlitzer, *Two-Lane Blacktop* screenplay, January 5, 1970
11 "Call him a": Will Corry, *Two-Lane Blacktop* screenplay, collection of Billy Kincheloe
11 "Make it $300": Ibid.
11 "A yard and a half": Rudy Wurlitzer, *Two-Lane Blacktop* screenplay, January 5, 1970
11 "Do you need": Will Corry, *Two-Lane Blacktop* screenplay, collection of Billy Kincheloe
11 "You need me as": Rudy Wurlitzer, *Two-Lane Blacktop* screenplay, January 5, 1970
11 "Stick to the": Will Corry, *Two-Lane Blacktop* screenplay, collection of Billy Kincheloe
11 "Stick to the": Rudy Wurlitzer, *Two-Lane Blacktop* screenplay, January 5, 1970
11 "General Delivery": Will Corry, *Two-Lane Blacktop* screenplay, collection of Billy Kincheloe
11 "General Delivery": Rudy Wurlitzer, *Two-Lane Blacktop* screenplay, January 5, 1970
11 "no studio pressure": Michael Laughlin, email to author 2/14/17
11 "I was given total freedom": Rudy Wurlitzer, AI 3/20/15
12 "She was a street": John Bailey, AI 1/15/15
12 "Once she got into": Eileen Peterson, AI 4/16/15
12 "Monte was from Day 1": Floyd Mutrux, AI 9/5/15
12 "She was almost the first": Monte Hellman, American Film Institute (AFI) Harold Lloyd Master Seminar 7/7/71
12 "I think she was very excited" and following: Rudy Wurlitzer, AI 3/20/15
12 "I don't think": Rudy Wurlitzer, email to author 1/29/17
14 "lots of chicks": Rudy Wurlitzer, *Two-Lane Blacktop* screenplay, 1/5/70
16 "*Two-Lane* represents": Rudy Wurlitzer, email to author 8/8/15
17 "Every motorcycle guy": Jim Aust, AI 6/16/17
19 "I explored this new": Rudy Wurlitzer, AI 3/20/15
19 "a terrific script": Billy Kincheloe, AI 1/27/15
19 "As soon as you got": Gary Kurtz, AI 11/19/15
19 "how male egos can get": Richard Ruth, AI 5/19/15
20 "You took an engine": Richard Ruth, AI 1/28/16
20 "He ran this organization": Billy Kincheloe, AI 1/27/15
20 "That's what killed": Pat Ganahl, AI 5/27/15
21 "There are lots of people" and following: Scott Tiemann, AI 9/14/16
22 "Well, what they found out" and following: Pat Ganahl, AI 5/27/15
22 "They became prop builders": Richard Ruth, AI 2/15/16
22 "He didn't know": Pat Ganahl, AI 5/27/15
22 "They really didn't know": Richard Ruth, AI 5/19/15
23 "I do remember": Leslie Caron, email to author 9/13/15
23 "because it was very fast": Gary Kurtz, AI 11/19/15
23 "GM's big race engine" and following: Richard Ruth, AI 5/19/15
23 "The race car was": Billy Kincheloe, AI 1/27/15
24 "Monte thought that": Gary Kurtz, AI 11/19/15
24 "didn't understand the street": Richard Ruth, AI 4/25/16
24 "Because drag racers": Richard Ruth, AI 8/26/15
24 "So we spent" and following: Gary Kurtz AI 11/19/15
24 "They had a guy" and following: Billy Kincheloe, AI 1/27/15
25 "took this beautiful car": Pat Ganahl, AI 5/27/15
25 "I'm a Levis and T-shirt" and following: Richard Ruth 5/19/15
25 "You wanted to make": Pat Ganahl, AI 5/27/15

| | |
|---|---|
| 25 | "We went drag racing": Richard Ruth, AI 5/19/15 |
| 26 | "For the car that": Gary Kurtz, AI 11/19/15 |
| 26 | "A 366-horsepower" and following: Scott Tiemann, AI 9/14/16 |
| 26 | "That's what's so great about" and following: Richard Linklater, AI 9/12/16 |

## Chapter Two: Stalled

| | |
|---|---|
| 28 | "has got an ocean": Buck Wheatley, AI 5/20/15 |
| 29 | "We were country" and following: Buck Wheatley, AI 5/14/15 |
| 29 | "was really playing" and following: Michael Laughlin, AI 7/20/12 |
| 29 | "They didn't know anything" and following: Buck Wheatley, AI 5/14/15 |
| 29 | "lo and behold" and following: Buck Wheatley, AI 5/14/15 |
| 30 | "I'd just gotten" and following: John Bailey, AI 1/15/15 |
| 31 | "one actor sort of" and following: John Bailey, AI 1/27/15 |
| 31 | "he wasn't a schmoozer": Monte Hellman, AI 8/6/16 |
| 31 | "He always ate" and following: John Bailey, AI 1/15/15 |
| 32 | "didn't actually do": Gary Kurtz, AI 2/24/15 |
| 32 | "to do a hand-held" and following: John Bailey, AI 1/15/15 |
| 32 | "It saves money": Monte Hellman, email to author 6/30/15 |
| 32 | "Somebody would have a cigarette": John Bailey, AI 1/15/15 |
| 33 | "Monte always got" and following: Michael Laughlin, AI 3/17/16 |
| 33 | "saw lots of actors" and following: Michael Laughlin, AI 9/12/15 |
| 33 | "he doesn't fly": Monte Hellman, email to author 9/17/16 |
| 33 | "It became apparent": Monte Hellman, AFI Harold Lloyd Master Seminar 7/7/71 |
| 34 | "It was still basically": Fred Roos, AI 12/15/14 |
| 34 | "Singer/songwriters can be": Michael Laughlin, AI 3/17/16 |
| 35 | "His stage presence": Gary Kurtz, AI 2/24/15 |
| 35 | "bright red hair": Michael Laughlin, AI 12/1/14 |
| 35 | "My feeling was" and following: Peter Asher, AI 2/8/16 |
| 36 | "James Taylor will write": Mike Medavoy, memo, USC Cinematic Arts Library, Gary Kurtz Collection, Box 89: Folder 12 |
| 36 | "The big creative decision": Michael Laughlin, AI 3/17/16 |
| 36 | "I was not for" and following: Fred Roos, AI 11/20/12 |
| 36 | "The circle was": Fred Roos, AI 12/15/14 |
| 37 | "We knew each other": Harry Dean Stanton, AI 12/16/15 |
| 37 | "would get furious" and following: Fred Roos, AI 12/15/14 |
| 37 | "a terrific guy": Leslie Caron, AI 1/6/15 |
| 37 | "There was a problem" Monte Hellman, AFI Harold Lloyd Master Seminar 7/7/71 |
| 37 | "She was a very troubled": Beverly Walker, AI 2/24/15 |
| 38 | "She was very" and following: Eileen Peterson, AI 4/6/15 |
| 38 | "I thought she was very naïve": Martin Landau, AI 7/14/16 |
| 38 | "she was very aware of": Eileen Peterson, AI 4/6/15 |
| 38 | "very difficult, disturbed" and following: Leslie Caron, AI 1/6/15 |
| 38 | "we would really have": Monte Hellman, AFI Harold Lloyd Master Seminar 7/7/71 |
| 38 | "I was not for" and following: Fred Roos, AI 11/20/12 |
| 38 | "She was kind of": Fred Roos, AI 12/15/14 |

39 "People thought that they" and following: Fred Vail, AI 4/7/16
41 "He said, 'Why'" and following: Fred Vail, AI 4/7/16
41 "It was very colorful" and following: Gary Kurtz, AI 2/24/15
42 "We had gone on": Monte Hellman, AFI Harold Lloyd Master Seminar 7/7/71
42 "I think it broke" and following: Floyd Mutrux, AI 9/11/15
42 "Gordon Stulberg": Floyd Mutrux, AI 9/5/15
42 "I was very happy": Monte Hellman, AFI Harold Lloyd Master Seminar 7/7/71
42 "Nobody liked it": Billy Kincheloe, AI 1/27/15

## Chapter Three: A Jump Start

45 "I think people": Daniel Selznick, AI 8/15/15
45 "When I took over" and following: John Calley, AI 11/3/04
47 "built a huge, black tower": Daniel Selznick, AI 12/18/14
47 "The Black Tower" and following: Daniel Selznick, AI 5/5/15
48 "where the music tracks" and following: Daniel Selznick, AI 8/15/15
49 "Ned kept saying" and following: Daniel Selznick, AI 8/15/15
49 "The guy Ned chose": Reg Bisgrove, AI 5/12/16
49 "So you're thinking" and following: Daniel Selznick, AI 12/18/14
51 "I was made an honorary": Reg Bisgrove, AI 5/12/16
51 "Monte Hellman comes in" and following: Daniel Selznick, AI 12/18/14
51 "By the time I met": Michael Laughlin, email to author 1/17/17
51 "Monte was a health-food": Beverly Walker, email to author 2/3/17
51 "He is much too": Beverly Walker, AI 2/3/17
51 "I didn't perceive any" and following: Daniel Selznick, AI 12/18/14
53 "We had decided before" and following: Gary Kurtz, AI 8/16/16
54 "There are always idiots": Craig Pinkard, AI 2/13/15
54 "was just barely adequate": Gary Kurtz, AI 11/19/15
56 "I dressed, as I do": Michael Laughlin, AI 7/20/12
56 "we never had to use them": Gary Kurtz, AI 11/19/15
57 "I was the youngest": Lawrence Jacobson, AI 9/2/16
58 "I had to say" and following: Carrie Fisher, AI 2/7/05
58 "We agree to supply": USC Cinematic Arts Library, Gary Kurtz Collection, Box 89: Folder 14
58 "Monte's wife worked" and following: Michael Laughlin, AI 12/1/14
59 "I believe that Monte": Bonnie Prendergast Freeman, email to author 10/29/15
59 "Even though I didn't" and following: Walter Coblenz, AI 3/18/16
59 "were a little sort of": Michael Laughlin, AI 12/1/14
60 "But they said, 'No'": Walter Coblenz, AI 12/10/14
60 "He was a boob": John Bailey, AI 1/15/15
60 "We had to get": Walter Coblenz, AI 12/10/14
61 "If I had gone" and following: Michael Laughlin, AI 12/1/14

## Chapter Four: On the Road

62 "These things were clandestine": Billy Kincheloe, AI 1/27/15
63 "I knew about the LA": Gary Kurtz, AI 11/19/15

## Notes

63 "we were very": Walter Coblenz, AI 3/18/16
63 "He walked to the beat": Buck Wheatley, AI 5/14/15
63 "What a neat": Bonnie Prendergast Freeman, email to author 10/29/15
63 "It didn't want to": Richard Ruth, AI 5/19/15
64 "He was a good": Richard Ruth, AI 4/29/16
64 "character" and following: Jim Thornsberry, AI 2/19/15
64 "had pretty good control" and following: Walter Coblenz, AI 12/10/14
64 "I fell asleep": Chuck Record, AI 3/3/15
65 "The cars were overheating" and following: Richard Ruth, AI 4/25/15
65 "good until garage mechanic's": USC Cinematic Arts Library, Gary Kurtz Collection, Box 86
65 "Louie, Louie" and following: Richard Ruth, AI 1/28/16
67 "and we couldn't have": Gary Kurtz, AI 8/8/16
67 "insisted on riding" and following: John Bailey, AI 1/15/15
69 "Some actors are not": Rick Mercier, AI 2/19/15
69 "a regular guy": Craig Pinkard, AI 2/13/15
69 "bridged the above-the-line": Bonnie Prendergast Freeman, email to author 10/29/15
69 "there wasn't a whole lot": John Bailey, AI 1/15/15
69 "To my memory" and following: Bonnie Prendergast Freeman, email to author 10/29/15
69 "They really didn't have much": Jim Thornsberry, AI 8/31/16
69 "the shooting crew" and following: Gary Kurtz, AI 2/24/15
70 "He always did seem": Peter Asher, AI 2/8/16
70 "When we were in between": Rick Mercier, AI 2/19/15
70 "were really amateurs": Jim Brubaker, AI 2/10/15
70 "After working with": Bonnie Prendergast, email to author 10/29/15
70 "He was a very quiet" and following: Jim Thornsberry, AI 2/11/15
70 "It felt like he was from" and following: Gary Kurtz, AI 11/19/15
71 "He's just not a chitchatty" and following: Beverly Walker, AI 6/24/16
71 "Universal asked me" and following: Reg Bisgrove, AI 5/12/16
71 "normally weren't supposed to": Gary Kurtz, AI 2/24/15
71 "What was happening was": Walter Coblenz, AI 12/10/14
71 "was almost ready to rebel" and following: Jim Thornsberry, AI 2/11/15
72 "I did a few": Walter Coblenz, AI 12/10/14
72 "Everybody helped the electricians": Jim Brubaker, AI 2/10/15
72 "I gave him the assistant": Walter Coblenz, AI 12/10/14
72 "I had a hairy experience": Beverly Walker, email to author 8/31/16
73 "stayed to themselves" and following: Jim Thornsberry, AI 8/31/16
73 "We were working very short": Walter Coblenz, AI 12/10/14
73 "corralling Dennis Wilson": Bonnie Prendergast, email to author 10/29/15
73 "absolutely brilliant": Walter Coblenz, AI 12/10/14
73 "It seemed to be kind" and following: Gary Kurtz, AI 11/19/15
74 "I must have worked": Gary Kurtz, AI 11/19/15
74 "was always asking": Billy Kincheloe, AI 1/27/15
75 "I did look very much": Gary Kurtz, AI 2/24/15
75 "Meredith, who was quite": Beverly Walker, email to author 10/2/16
75 "She did look very, very": Gary Kurtz, AI 8/8/16
75 "Warren had his own" and following: James Taylor, AI 12/14/15
77 "worked with my ex-wife": Monte Hellman, AFI Harold Lloyd Master Seminar 7/7/71
77 "At one point, he": Bonnie Prendergast Freeman, email to author 10/29/15

| | |
|---|---|
| 77 | "I think that rather": James Taylor, AI 12/14/15 |
| 77 | "James was, as far": Gary Kurtz, AI 11/19/15 |
| 78 | "everybody wanted to get" and following: Craig Pinkard, AI 2/13/15 |
| 78 | "It was still kind of": John Bailey, AI 1/15/15 |
| 78 | "we got the police": Walter Coblenz, AI 12/10/14 |
| 79 | "buy off nuisance" and following: USC Cinematic Arts Library, Gary Kurtz Collection, Box 87: Folder 3 |
| 79 | "When we stopped": Rick Mercier, AI 2/19/15 |
| 79 | "Some of the local": John Bailey, AI 1/15/15 |
| 80 | "Laurie was petrified": Gary Kurtz, AI 2/24/15 |
| 80 | "Monte liked to talk": Gary Kurtz, AI 8/8/16 |
| 80 | "They'd go somewhere" and following: Pat Ganahl, AI 5/27/15 |
| 81 | "It's really an argument": Monte Hellman, AFI Harold Lloyd Master Seminar 7/7/71 |
| 81 | "I always encourage actors": Monte Hellman, email to author 6/30/16 |
| 81 | "I was very nervous": Rudy Wurlitzer, AI 3/20/15 |
| 81 | "From the beginning": Bonnie Prendergast Freeman, email to author 10/29/15 |
| 81 | "never one of the guys" and following: Michael Laughlin, AI 3/17/16 |
| 81 | "I never have been": Gary Kurtz, AI 2/24/15 |
| 81 | "Nice guy": Jim Thornsberry, 2/11/15 |
| 82 | "Monte was not always": Gary Kurtz, AI 2/24/15 |
| 82 | "we would usually run": Gary Kurtz, AI 11/19/15 |
| 82 | "That's what Warren": Pat Ganahl, AI 5/27/15 |
| 82 | "That was a gruesome": Warren Oates, AFI Harold Lloyd Master Seminar 7/7/71 |
| 82 | "He complained to me": Bonnie Prendergast Freeman, AI 10/29/15 |
| 83 | "Warren Oates was": Walter Coblenz, AI 12/10/14 |
| 83 | "Whereas when you're working": Gary Kurtz, AI 2/24/15 |
| 83 | "Because Laurie and James": John Bailey, AI 1/27/15 |

## Chapter Five: The Fast Lane: Sex, Drugs, and Rock 'n' Roll Stars

| | |
|---|---|
| 84 | "a motel that had": Beverly Walker, AI 2/24/15 |
| 84 | "He was such a kid" and following: Jennifer Oates, AI 3/31/15 |
| 84 | "James got a little": Gary Kurtz, AI 2/24/15 |
| 85 | "We [the crew]": Bonnie Prendergast Freeman, email to author 10/29/15 |
| 85 | "these two hippies": Sheila Thornsberry, AI 2/11/15 |
| 85 | "On the road": John Bailey, AI 1/27/15 |
| 85 | "And he said, 'John'" and following: John Bailey, AI 1/27/15 |
| 86 | "I think there were": Robert Stradling, AI 2/13/15 |
| 86 | "I had anticipated": Michael Laughlin, AI 2/11/16 |
| 86 | "She was really sweet": Jim Thornsberry, AI 2/11/15 |
| 87 | "Laurie was younger": Craig Pinkard, AI 2/13/15 |
| 87 | "I think that, in Laurie's": Gary Kurtz, AI 11/19/15 |
| 87 | "These acting exercises": Peter Asher, AI 2/8/16 |
| 87 | "The line was crossed": James Taylor, AI 12/14/15 |
| 87 | "She did not know": Bonnie Prendergast Freeman, email to author 10/29/15 |
| 88 | "He did keep her" and following: Beverly Walker, email to author 2/3/17 |

| | |
|---|---|
| 88 | "Hamilton is, in fact" and following: Beverly Walker, email to author 7/20/16 |
| 88 | "Laurie was very nervous" and following: Gary Kurtz, AI 11/19/15 |
| 89 | "Well, if things got": Eileen Peterson, AI 4/6/15 |
| 89 | "The reports I was getting": Peter Asher, AI 2/8/16 |
| 89 | "was screwing everything": Beverly Walker, AI 2/24/15 |
| 89 | "really had a kind of": Beverly Walker, email to author 9/1/16 |
| 90 | "He was a druggie": Craig Pinkard, AI 2/13/15 |
| 90 | "Everybody was talking": Chuck Record, AI 5/30/16 |
| 90 | "Everybody was really uncomfortable": Gary Kurtz, AI 2/24/15 |
| 90 | "idiot": Jim Thornsberry, AI 2/11/15 |
| 90 | "We used to do" and following: Craig Pinkard, AI 2/13/15 |
| 90 | "amusing when he was": Bonnie Prendergast Freeman, email to author 10/29/15 |
| 91 | "lots of times when" and following: John Bailey, AI 1/27/15 |
| 91 | "I never discuss" and following: Monte Hellman, email to author 6/30/16 |
| 91 | "There were times when": John Bailey, AI 1/27/15 |
| 91 | "I recognized the style": Bonnie Prendergast Freeman, email to author 10/29/15 |
| 91 | "Monte set the tone": Walter Coblenz, AI 12/10/14 |
| 91 | "From the point of view": James Taylor, AI 12/14/15 |
| 91 | "Monte would sit on": Warren Oates, AFI Harold Lloyd Master Seminar 7/7/71 |
| 92 | "He was stoned": Buck Wheatley, AI 5/14/15 |
| 92 | "seemed stoned": Bonnie Prendergast Freeman, email to author 10/29/15 |
| 92 | "did a little bit": Rick Mercier, AI 2/19/15 |
| 92 | "When we were leaving": Jennifer Oates, AI 3/31/15 |
| 92 | "They all thought I": Reg Bisgrove, AI 5/12/16 |
| 92 | "there was some drinking" and following: James Taylor, AI 12/14/15 |
| 92 | "I know they were taking": Peter Asher, AI 2/8/16 |
| 93 | "We were from": Buck Wheatley, AI 5/14/15 |
| 93 | "what affected that show": Reg Bisgrove, AI 5/12/16 |
| 93 | "We'd have to wait": Gary Kurtz, AI 8/8/16 |
| 94 | "Greg was really good": Gary Kurtz, AI 8/8/16 |
| 94 | "A faggot cowpuncher": Jay Cocks, "Cinema: Wheels: Hi Test," *Time*, July 12, 1971 |
| 94 | "They didn't tell me" and following: Harry Dean Stanton, AI 12/16/15 |
| 95 | "was flirting shamelessly": Jarod Hellman, AI 8/6/16 |
| 95 | "If he likes it": Warren Oates, AFI Harold Lloyd Master Seminar 7/7/71 |

## Chapter Six: Potholes

| | |
|---|---|
| 97 | "and just heavy": Dick Austin, AI 2/18/15 |
| 97 | "On any show" and following: Reg Bisgrove, AI 5/12/16 |
| 97 | "There was a man" and following: Buck Wheatley, AI 5/14/15 |
| 97 | "had no concept": Reg Bisgrove, AI 5/12/16 |
| 97 | "I just did a lot": Walter Coblenz, AI 12/10/14 |
| 98 | "It was just a little" and following: Craig Pinkard, AI 2/13/15 |
| 98 | "The people were kind of": Jim Thornsberry, AI 2/11/15 |
| 99 | "A bunch of the": Walter Coblenz, AI 12/10/14 |
| 99 | "We left and" and following: Craig Pinkard, AI 2/13/15 |

| | |
|---|---|
| 99 | "My wife was born": John Bailey, AI 1/27/15 |
| 99 | "The people were very": Gary Kurtz, AI 2/24/15 |
| 100 | "He was just becoming": Gary Kurtz, AI 11/19/15 |
| 100 | "a song, and I've": James Taylor, AI 12/14/15 |
| 100 | "There was nonstop": Beverly Walker, AI 2/24/15 |
| 100 | "Nobody bothered": Monte Hellman, AFI Harold Lloyd Master Seminar 7/7/71 |
| 100 | "He came back" and following: Danny Selznick, AI 12/18/14 |
| 101 | "The executives at both" and following: Michael Laughlin, AI 3/17/16 |
| 101 | "We tried to fold" and following: Gary Kurtz, AI 2/24/15 |
| 102 | "Jay Wheatley was our": Gary Kurtz, AI 2/24/14 |
| 102 | "Jay definitely did": James Taylor, AI 12/14/15 |
| 102 | "We were doing": James Taylor, AI 12/14/15 |
| 103 | "broke everything": Buck Wheatley, AI 12/23/15 |
| 103 | "Afterwards, he said": Peter Asher, AI 2/8/16 |
| 103 | "It was enjoyable": James Taylor, AI 12/14/15 |
| 104 | "I rented a medium-size": Bonnie Prendergast Freeman, email to author 10/29/15 |
| 104 | "I came back": Gary Kurtz, AI 2/24/15 |
| 104 | "The last day": Jim Thornsberry, AI 2/11/15 |
| 104 | "I remember going": Gary Kurtz, email to author 2/8/17 |

## Chapter Seven: The Wreck

| | |
|---|---|
| 105 | "Monte wanted to edit": Gary Kurtz, AI 11/19/15 |
| 105 | "had many discussions": Dorothy Alsup, AI 9/8/16 |
| 105 | "We edited near": Monte Hellman, email to author 6/30/16 |
| 105 | "I felt Monte was": Michael Laughlin, AI 3/17/16 |
| 106 | "crams a lot" and following: Monte Hellman, AFI Harold Lloyd Master Seminar 7/7/71 |
| 106 | "Monte had a routine" and following: Gary Kurtz, AI 11/19/15 |
| 106 | "I had spent": Gary Kurtz, AI 11/19/15 |
| 107 | "I am sort of" and following: Billy James, AI 4/29/15 |
| 108 | "dozens and dozens" and following: Billy James, AI 4/29/15 |
| 108 | "Read it first!": *Esquire*, April 1971 |
| 108 | "I was a hot publicist" and following: Beverly Walker, AI 2/24/15 |
| 109 | "Filmmakers are just so" and following: Danny Selznick, AI 12/18/14 |
| 110 | "They were expecting": Michael Laughlin, AI 7/20/12 |
| 110 | "They didn't like" and following: Gary Kurtz, AI 11/19/15 |
| 110 | "The agreement we had": Michael Laughlin, AI 3/17/16 |
| 111 | "They suggested that maybe": Gary Kurtz, AI 11/19/15 |
| 111 | "The issue of music": Beverly Walker, email to author 2/5/16 |
| 111 | "was a guy" and following: Danny Selznick, AI 5/15/15 |
| 111 | "People were furious": Beverly Walker, AI 2/24/15 |
| 111 | "I must say that": Monte Hellman, AFI Harold Lloyd Master Seminar 7/7/71 |
| 112 | "my hands tied": Monte Hellman, AI 8/6/16 |
| 112 | "I remember the reaction": Rudy Wurlitzer, email to author 2/11/16 |
| 112 | "Many in the audience": Gary Kurtz, AI 11/19/15 |
| 112 | "In the world in which": Danny Selznick, AI 5/5/15 |

| | |
|---|---|
| 113 | "Universal really didn't like": Gary Kurtz, AI 11/19/15 |
| 113 | "While I personally": Murray Weissman, email to author 3/28/15 |
| 113 | "He did research in": Michael Laughlin, email to author 11/14/15 |
| 113 | "How foolish Lew was": Danny Selznick, email to author 1/25/16 |
| 113 | "Of course, it would": Danny Selznick, email to author 3/20/16 |
| 114 | "Meet the Car Freaks": USC Cinematic Arts Library, Gary Kurtz Collection, Box 87: Folder 6 |
| 114 | "I was really quite frightened" and following: Danny Selznick, AI 12/18/14 |
| 115 | "I preferred the driver's": Monte Hellman, email to author 6/30/16 |
| 115 | "I remember the marquee": John Bailey, AI 1/27/15 |
| 115 | "The film is immaculately": Jay Cocks, "Wheels: Hi Test," *Time*, July 12, 1971 |
| 116 | "a remarkably engaging": Vincent Canby, review of *Two-Lane Blacktop*, *New York Times*, July 8, 1971 |
| 116 | "It seems to come": Roger Ebert, review of *Two-Lane Blacktop*, *Chicago Sun-Times* July 8, 1971 |
| 116 | "Apart from Warren Oates": Penelope Gilliatt, review of *Two-Lane Blacktop*, *New Yorker*, July 10, 1971 |
| 116 | "The two young men": Joseph Gelmis, review of *Two-Lane Blacktop*, *Newsday*, July 8, 1971 |
| 116 | "Hellman turns the voltage": Paul D. Zimmerman, "Three for the Road," *Newsweek*, July 5, 1971 |
| 116 | "On the strength": Editor's Notes, *Esquire*, July 1971 |
| 116 | "They behaved very badly": Beverly Walker, AI 2/24/15 |
| 117 | "In his review": Monte Hellman, letter, 8/24/71, USC Cinematic Arts Library, Gary Kurtz Collection, Box 89: Folder 24 |
| 117 | "because the picture didn't open": Danny Selznick, AI 5/15/15 |
| 117 | "To our dismay": Arthur Abeles letter to Gary Kurtz, 3/6/72, USC Cinematic Arts Library, Gary Kurtz Collection, Box 89: Folder 24 |
| 118 | "Mr. Wasserman" and following: Henri Michaud and Arthur Abeles letter to Gary Kurtz, 9/23/71, USC Cinematic Arts Library, Gary Kurtz Collection, Box 89: Folder 24 |
| 118 | "I know people back": Richard Ruth, AI 5/19/15 |
| 118 | "It is certainly true": Beverly Walker, AI 2/24/15 |
| 119 | "I think what a lot" and following: Rudy Wurlitzer, AI 3/20/15 |
| 119 | "It's kind of insane": Beverly Walker, AI 2/24/15 |
| 119 | "Was it just an ego": Beverly Walker, email to author 9/7/16 |
| 120 | "has one actor who": Beverly Walker, AI 2/24/15 |
| 120 | "I think James": Peter Asher, AI 2/8/16 |
| 120 | "I felt we needed": Danny Selznick, AI 8/15/15 |
| 121 | "I was in contact": Martin Landau, AI 7/14/16 |

## Chapter Eight: A Restoration

| | |
|---|---|
| 122 | "Distribution is everything" and following: Michael Laughlin, email to author 11/14/15 |
| 123 | "Jackie was an unusual": Martin Landau, AI 7/14/16 |
| 124 | "That was enough": James Tayor, AI 12/14/15 |
| 124 | "It was awful": Craig Pinkard, AI 2/13/15 |

125  "the Holy Grail": Edward Sykes Comstock, AI 2/9/16
125  "I had already talked" and following: Gary Kurtz, AI 8/8/16
125  "I remember leaning" and following: Danny Selznick, AI 5/5/15
126  "a very violent": Danny Selznick, AI 8/15/15
127  "I met Monte" and following: Dennis Bartok, AI 3/2/14
128  "one of the biggest": Ibid.
133  "Angry Moms": Kristen McMurran, *People*, December 3, 1984
134  "When the script was first": Steven Gaydos, AI 9/3/16
135  "No road movie is as": Michael Atkinson, "On the Road Again," *Village Voice*, July 9, 1996
136  "cool movie, with no crazy" and following: Dennis McCarthy, AI 7/13/15
136  "the continuity is very": Jim Aust, AI 5/31/15
137  "Guys who really watch": Richard Ruth, AI 2/15/16
137  "*Two-Lane Blacktop* was": Pat Ganahl, AI 5/27/15
137  "In *Two-Lane Blacktop*": Jim Aust, AI 5/31/15
137  "You see primered": Dennis McCarthy, AI 7/13/15
137  "To me, it was": Ted Moser, AI 9/8/15
137  "What hot-rodders": Dennis McCarty, AI 7/13/15
137  "The slicks in the": Dennis McCarthy, AI 7/13/15
137  "I think Warren Oates": Ted Moser, AI 9/8/15
138  "the dirtbag guys": Jim Aust, AI 5/31/15
138  "If you're only going to race": Pat Ganahl, AI 5/27/15
138  "It did seem a little": Ted Moser, AI 9/8/15
138  "There are some people": Jim Aust, AI 5/31/15
138  "is what you're supposed": Pat Ganahl, AI 5/27/15
139  "probably one of the": Ted Moser, AI 9/8/15
139  "Starting the movie": Pat Ganahl, AI 5/27/15
139  "The 427 would definitely": Dennis McCarthy, AI 7/13/15
139  "The '55 Chevy was" and following: Jim Aust, AI 5/13/15
139  "I haven't watched that" and following: Scott Tiemann, AI 9/14/16
140  "was romanticized": Floyd Mutrux, AI 9/5/15

## Chapter Nine: Picking Up Speed

142  "George just came to" and following: Rebecca Soriano, AI 12/5/12
143  "This is great": Mark Steiner, AI 12/5/13
144  "Enthusiasm was probably" and following: Sean Axmaker, AI 12/10/12
144  "That was the funny": Mark Steiner, AI 12/5/13
144  "he would always": Sean Axmaker, AI 12/10/12
144  "he knew pretty much": Rebecca Soriano, AI 12/5/12
144  "I was standing": Mark Steiner, AI 12/5/13
145  "I kept waiting": Ibid.
145  "got up on stage": Rebecca Soriano, AI 12/5/12
145  "We had the money": Mark Steiner, AI 12/4/12
145  "Talk about dry": Ibid.
146  "He always cracked": Rebecca Soriano, AI 12/10/13
146  "So a snotty": Ibid.

## Notes

146 "The people that ran": Rebecca Soriano, AI 12/5/12
146 "was really, really" and following: Mark Steiner, AI 12/4/12
146 "You get a lot": Rebecca Soriano, AI 12/10/13
147 "I asked him about" and following: Mark Steiner, 12/5/13
147 "She was a beautiful": Ibid.
147 "Though made in the": Scarecrow Video's petition to Universal Studios, 4/19/96, courtesy of Scarecrow Video
148 "multiple revenue sources" and following: Louis Feola, AI 9/21/16
148 "It was crazy": Mark Steiner, AI 12/14/12
149 "Everybody thought that this": Ibid.
150 "underground": Jeff Koch, "Two-Lane Blacktop on DVD," *Hot Rod*, March 2000
150 "long-sought": Donald Liebenson, "Classic 'Two-Lane Blacktop' Takes the Long Road to Video," *Los Angeles Times*, November 3, 1999
150 "had long been a coveted": Jeffrey M. Anderson, "Race for Your Life," Combustible Celluloid.com, 2000
150 "it was near the top": Dennis Bartok, AI 3/2/14
151 "Maybe it's because" and following: Jay Douglas, AI 3/25/14
151 "He was really happy": Jay Douglas, AI 7/29/16
152 "I said, 'But": Norm Hill, AI 3/29/14
152 "George's valentine": Dennis Bartok, AI 3/2/14
153 "I don't know this": Jay Douglas, AI 11/7/15
153 "Most of the songs" and following: Jay Douglas, AI 7/29/16
153 "because of the infighting": Bill Lustig, AI 3/26/14
153 "the Doors weren't necessarily": Jay Douglas, AI 7/29/16
153 "They weren't interested": Bill Lustig, AI 3/26/14
153 "I worked with": Jay Douglas, AI 3/25/14
154 "The lawyers and": Bill Lustig, AI 3/26/14
154 "between the three": Jay Douglas, AI 11/7/15
154 "Allen Klein, as I" Bill Lustig, AI 3/26/14
154 "literally hundreds and hundreds": Jay Douglas, AI 3/25/14
154 "rapturously": Dennis Bartok, AI 3/2/14
154 "incredibly well": Jay Douglas, AI 3/25/14
155 "Everybody's got their own": Dennis Bartok, AI 3/2/14
155 "were not museum-type": Norm Hill, AI 3/29/14
155 "passive fans": Jay Douglas, AI 3/25/14
155 "One of the essential": Gavin Smith, "Vidi vidi vidi," *Film Comment*, May/June 1999
155 "About the only movie": "Car Craft Video Library Two-Lane Blacktop Collector's Edition," *Car Craft*, March 2000
155 "*the* great American": Dennis Bartok, AI 3/2/14
156 "When I finally got": Norm Hill, AI 3/29/14
156 "They actually didn't" and following: Jay Douglas, AI 3/25/14

### Chapter Ten: The Finish Line: The Film Catches Fire

157 "now, of course, the reaction": Rudy Wurlitzer, email to author 2/11/16
157 "This month it was": Dave Kehr, Critic's Choice, New DVDs, *Two-Lane Blacktop*, *New York Times*, December 8, 2007

158 "one icon of post-60s" Ian Penman, "Los Highway," *Sight and Sound*, February 2012
158 "This exciting existentialist": Jonathan Rosenbaum, *Chicago Reader*, February 22, 2001
158 "It is so much": David Thomson, "David Thomson on Films: A Road Film that Transcends Hippy v. Redneck Politics," *New Republic*, October 17, 2011
158 "During a short-lived": "Cinematic Firsts Enshrined in 2012 Film Registry," Library of Congress News Release, www.loc.gov/film/ 12/20/12
159 "I had some guys": Richard Ruth, AI 2/15/16
159 "It's like Bob Downey Sr.": Eileen Peterson, AI 4/6/15
160 "He's a very generous": Richard Linklater, AI 9/12/16
160 "the camera's never" and following: Kelly Reichardt, AI 9/18/15
162 "was back in" and following: Richard Linklater, AI 9/12/16
163 "I loved *Two-Lane*" and following: Wes Anderson, AI 10/7/16
165 "There's a lot of" and following: William Tyler, AI 7/8/15
167 "For years, I had" and following: Filippo Salvadori, AI 7/3/15
168 "So he just came up" and following: Will Oldham, AI 6/15/15

# Index

Abeles, Arthur, 117
above the line/below the line, divide between, 68
Alsup, Dorothy, 74, 99, 105
*American Graffiti*, 22, 26, 33, 108, 125–26, 136, 140
Anchor Bay Entertainment, 142, 149–56
Anderson, Wes, 163–64
Antonioni, Michelangelo, 58–59, 134
Asher, Peter, 35–36, 70, 87, 89, 92, 120
Aust, Jim, 17–18, 136–37, 138, 140
Austin, Dick, 96

*Back Door to Hell*, 7, 32, 129, 131
Bailey, John: on being overworked, 85–86; on disappointment over release of film, 115; on film company's wives, 85; on filming at races, 101; on friendliness of townspeople, 78; on Gregory Sandor, 30–32, 68, 94; on Hugh Gagnier, 67–68; on improvisation on the shoot, 79; on Jack Deerson, 60; on lack of contact between cast and crew, 69; on Laurie Bird, 12, 91; on Monte Hellman, 91; on Techniscope, 32; on Warren Oates, 83

Bartok, Dennis, 127, 128, 150, 152–56, 159
BBS Productions, 45
Beach Boys, 22
*Beast from Haunted Cave*, 7, 129–32, 134
Beckett, Samuel, 14–15
Bertolucci, Bernardo, 144–45
Bird, Laurie: age of, 89; and audition, 12; contract, 58; death from overdose, 123; early life, 12; on illness during shoot, 88–89; insecurity, 87–88; and Monte Hellman, 12, 86–87, 123; nude swimming scene, 57, 88; panhandling scene, 79; and performance in gas station scene, 94; in role of the Girl, 37; subsequent roles, 123; youth and immaturity of, 75, 91
Bisgrove, Reg: on budgets, 96–97; as driver for James Taylor, 71; on drug use, 92–93; and *The Hired Hand*, 50–51; in South America after *The Last Movie*, 49
Biskind, Peter, 150
*Bonnie and Clyde*, 17, 44
Boswell, Oklahoma, 97–99
*Boyhood*, 26–27
Brubaker, Jim, 70, 72

Brumby, John, 72, 73
*Bullitt*, 17–18

Calley, John, 45–46
Caron, Leslie: career of, 3; on Laurie Bird, 38; and Michael Laughlin, 3, 7, 8; on street racing, 23; on Warren Oates, 37
*Chandler*, 123, 125
Charren, Barbara, 90
*China 9, Liberty 37*, 131–32
*Christian Licorice Store, The*, 4, 5, 8, 28–29
Cinema Center Films, 4, 42
Cobain, Kurt, 143
Coblenz, Walter: on caterer, 71; complaints about Jaclyn Hellman, 86; on decision to shoot in rain, 97–98; on Gary Kurtz, 73, 74–75; on Jack Deerson, 60; on John Bailey, 85–86; on Ken Swor, 72; on Laurie Bird in hospital, 89; as Michael Laughlin's proxy on film, 61; on Monte Hellman, 91; on Ned Tanen, 100; on police and firefighters' help, 78–79; as production manager and assistant director, 58–59; on rigging of cars and Chuck Record, 64; on small crew, 73; on street racers in opening scenes, 63; on Warren Oates, 83
*Cockfighter*, 123, 127
Comstock, Edward Sykes, 125
Condon, Bill, 7–8
Coppola, Francis Ford, 126
Corman, Roger, 7, 73, 74
Corry, Will, 4, 5; on Chevy in original script, 25; on contributions to film script, 9
Criterion Collection, 157, 158

*David and Lisa*, 49
*Dazed and Confused*, 27
Deerson, Jack, 31–32, 60
*Detour*, 16
*Diary of a Mad Housewife*, 49
Dogme, 53, 95
"Don't Cry for Me, Driver," 168
Doors, 107, 153
Douglas, Jay, 150–51, 153–56

*Easy Rider*, 16, 29, 44–45, 49, 50, 109, 158, 166
*Easy Riders, Raging Bulls: How the Sex-Drugs-and-Rock 'n' Roll Generation Saved Hollywood*, 150
Ebert, Roger, 116, 143
*Esquire* magazine, 108–9, 116

Feola, Louis, 148
'55 Chevy: in *American Graffiti*, 26, 125; on distressed look, 24–25; and Jay Wheatley, 102; pairing with GTO, 137; on suitability for racing, 23–24; in Will Corry's script, 9, 10, 25
"Fire and Rain," 99
Fisher, Carrie, 57–58
*Flight to Fury*, 7, 32, 130–32
Fonda, Peter, 50–51
Freeman, Bonnie Prendergast: on Dennis Wilson, 73, 92; on Jaclyn Hellman's exercises with actors, 77; on James Taylor and Joni Mitchell, 85; on lack of socializing between cast and crew, 69; on Laurie Bird's insecurity, 88; and Michelangelo Antonioni, 58–59; on Monte Hellman, 91; on nonactors in leading roles, 70; on Rudy Wurlitzer, 81; on Walter Coblenz, 73; on Warren Oates, 83
Frankfurt, Stephen, 113
Frawley, James, 5, 8, 29

Gagnier, Hugh, 67–68, 82
Ganahl, Pat, 20, 22, 25, 80, 82, 137, 138–39
Gaydos, Steve, 134
Glendale Speed Center T-shirt, 66, 159
*Grapes of Wrath, The*, 16–17
GTO (car), 140; as "factory hot rod," 9; history of, 20; "the Judge" model, 26; pairing with '55 Chevy, 137; in Richard Linklater's films, 26–27; in Will Corry's script, 10

Hamilton, Jack, 88
Hellman, Jaclyn Ravell, 58; behavior of, 86–87; on calling for extra takes, 86; as dialogue coach, 58; guru, 123; on

husband's affair with Laurie Bird, 87; as location scout, 41–42; on Richard Ruth and Dennis Wilson in gas station scene, 66; and sense memory exercises, 6, 76, 87; and sympathy of crew, 86

Hellman, Jarod, 90, 95

Hellman, Monte: on actor improvisation, 81, 90; on *Baretta*, 146–47; on casting, 33–38; on Cinema Center Films, 42; on directing film, 8; documentaries about, 128; early films, 7; early life, 5–6; ethereal quality, 51; family, 75; films of, 128–34; focus on set, 70; on Gregory Sandor, 31; influence on younger filmmakers, 159; on Jaclyn Hellman's work with actors, 76–77; on lack of direction, 91; letter to *San Francisco Examiner*, 117; liaison with Laurie Bird, 12, 86–87; and Los Angeles theater, 6–7; movies of, 128–34; on multiple takes, 86; on poster, 115; refusal to compromise on film, 120; retrospective at Seattle Art Museum, 146–47; on scene in Santa Fe bar, 81; on source music in film, 110–11; on studio pressure to change film, 110; on Techniscope, 32; on tendency to cut films, 112; on Universal, 100, 111; on video release, 151; and Warren Oates's performance, 91–92; on withholding script from actors, 76, 91

Henshaw, Jere, 4, 42

Herzog, Werner, 145–46

"Hey Mister, That's Me up on the Jukebox," 95, 100

Hickenlooper, George, 152–53

Hill, Norman, 147, 152, 155, 156

*Hired Hand, The*, 50–51

"Hit the Road Jack," 153

Hopper, Dennis, 49–51

hot rodding, 18–20, 21

*Iguana*, 129, 130, 133

*It Happened One Night*, 16

Jacobson, Lawrence, 56–57

James, Billy, 107–8

Kincheloe, Billy: on "Big Willie" Robinson, 20; on Chevy's weathered appearance, 24–25; on Cinema Center Films, 42–43; and '55 Chevy, 23–24; on Gary Kurtz, 74; on Leslie Caron, 9; on street racing in Los Angeles, 62

Klein, Allen, 154

Kristofferson, Kris, 34, 107–8

Kurtz, Gary: on budget, 54; casting James Taylor, 35; on Chevys, 23, 24; on crew, 69, 71; on crew and "Fire and Rain," 100; debate over color of Chevys, 24; on driving VW van, 75; efforts to socialize with crew, 69, 81–82; extreme intelligence, curiosity, and competence, 73–75; family, 75, 78; on '55 Chevy in *American Graffiti*, 26; on film school, 79; on film's opening titles, 106; on gas station scene, 93; on Gregory Sandor, 94; on hot rodding in Los Angeles, 19; on Jack Deerson, 32; on James Taylor, 77, 85, 111; on Jay Wheatley, 102; on Laurie Bird, 80; location scouting, 41–42; method of rigging cars, 60; on Monte Hellman, 70, 80, 106; on panhandling scene in Santa Fe, 79–80; on shooting on roads, 67, 82; on shot of film catching fire, 106–7; similarity of film to Dogme 95 films, 53; on skinny-dipping scene, 88; on Universal, 53–54, 110, 112, 113; on USC, 73–74; USC Cinema Arts Library collection, 125; on Warren Oates, 83; on work on Roger Corman movies, 7, 74

Lakeland International Raceway, 101–2

Landau, Martin: on Jaclyn Hellman, 123; on Laurie Bird, 38; on Monte Hellman, 9, 121; on sense memory exercises, 6, 76

*Last Movie, The*, 49–50, 126

Latsios, George, 142–45, 148–49

Latsios-Soriano, Rebecca, 142–47

Laughlin, Michael: on attempt to hire Steven Spielberg, 8; on California driver's license ad, 113; on casting, 33–35;

and Cinema Center Films, 4–5; decision not to go with film company, 61; on editing of film, 105; innovative ideas, 7, 8; on Jaclyn Hellman's instability, 58; marriage to Leslie Caron, 3; on Monte Hellman, 51; on Peter Asher, 35; on purchase of film screenplay, 4; sociability, 81; on soundtrack for film, 36, 110; and studio pressure to change script, 11; on Universal, 110; on Walter Coblenz, 59, 61, 86

Licht, Alan, 168–69

Linklater, Richard, 162; on appeal of GTOs and muscle cars, 26, 27; on Monte Hellman's influence, 160; praise for film, 163

*Little Buddha*, 144–45

Lucas, George, 125–26

Lustig, William, 151–54

Manson, Charles, 39–40

Martin, Hy, 111

McCarthy, Dennis, 136, 137, 139

"Me and Bobby McGee," 107–8

Medavoy, Mike, 36, 58, 110

Melcher, Terry, 107

Mercier, Rick, 69, 70, 73, 79, 92

Mitchell, Joni, 76, 84–85, 92

*Monkees, The*, 5, 8, 29

*Monte Hellman: American Auteur*, 152–53

"Moonlight Drive," 107, 153, 158

Morrison, Jim, 154

Moser, Ted, 137

muscle cars, 20–21

Mutrux, Floyd: and *The Christian Licorice Store*, 4; on *Two-Lane Blacktop*, 140–41; on Gordon Stulberg, 42; on Jay Wheatley, 28–29; knowledge of cars and street racing, 9; on rewriting film, 10; on Will Corry's script, 9; writes and directs *Dusty and Sweets McGee*, 5

National Film Registry, 157, 158

New Hollywood films, 44–45, 149–50

*Nog*, 10, 14–15

Oates, Jennifer, 69, 84, 92

Oates, Warren: on crew, 69; dies of heart attack, 123; drug and alcohol abuse, 92; on insistence on getting entire script, 83; on learning technical car talk, 82; on Monte Hellman, 91–92; on professionalism and nonactors, 83; as selling point for Tanen Unit, 51; takes role of GTO, 37; travels in motor home, 75

Oldham, Will, 167, 168–69

Peterson, Eileen, 12, 37–38, 89, 159

Phillips, Mackenzie, 125

Pinkard, Craig: on behavior of Hellmans and Laurie Bird, 87; on Boswell, 98–99; on Dennis Wilson, 90; on Jim Thornsberry, 90; on judge in Boswell, 98; on townspeople in film, 78; on Warren Oates, 69

"Portrait of Sarah, A," 164–66

Pow Wow Inn, 84–85

race for pink slips, 138

Record, Chuck, 64, 69, 90, 99, 100

*Red Desert*, 134–35

Reichardt, Kelly, 160–62

*Ride in the Whirlwind*, 5, 7, 30, 36, 130, 132

"Riding on a Railroad," 104

road movies, 16–17

*Road to Nowhere*, 129–31, 134, 156

Robinson, "Big Willie," 20, 62, 139

Roos, Fred, 32–34, 36–38

Route 66, 64–65, 67, 79, 84

Ruth, Richard: drag racing with Michael Laughlin and Monte Hellman, 25; on drive-in audiences and film's ending, 118; on '55 Chevy, 22–23, 127, 159; on filmmakers' knowledge of cars, 25; on first gas station scene, 65–67; on Hollywood car customizers, 22; on mechanics of hot rodding, 19–20; on objection to covering Chevys with primer, 24–25

Salvadori, Filippo, 166–68

Sandor, Gregory: on Armenian films, 30–31; on cinematography, 68; on gas station

scene, 94; and look of film, 94; and
IATSE, 30–32; as mentor to John Bailey,
30; on recognition for film, 31, 60
"Satisfaction," 153, 154
Scarecrow Video, 142–49; petition, 142,
147–48, 151
Scott, George C., 151
Selznick, Daniel: on Black Tower and
Universal City, 47; on budget for film,
54; and dispute over music in film, 111;
on *Easy Rider*'s success, 45; and George
Lucas, 125–26; and *The Last Movie*,
49–50; and Lew Wasserman, 112, 114, 126;
on Michael Laughlin, 52–53, 100, 101; on
Monte Hellman, 51, 101; on Ned Tanen,
47–48, 52; on poster, 115; on screening
first cut of film, 109; on storylines in
film, 109–10, 120; on Tanen Unit, 48–49;
on Universal, 113, 117
*Shoot the Piano Player*, 135
*Shooting, The*, 5, 7, 30, 37, 129–33
*Silent Night, Deadly Night III: Better Watch
Out!*, 129–33, 156
*Slacker*, 26, 121
Spielberg, Steven, 8
*Stanley's Girlfriend*, 129–31, 133
Stanton, Harry Dean, 36, 37, 94–95
Steiner, Mark, 143–47, 148–49
Storaro, Vittorio, 144–45
Stradling, Robert, 86
*Strange Behavior*, 8, 123
Stulberg, Gordon, 8, 42
*Sullivan's Travels*, 17
Swor, Ken, 72

*Taking Off*, 50
Tanen, Ned: on directors, 48–49; and
Michael Laughlin, 52; and Monte
Hellman, 51
Tanen Unit, 47–52, 126
Tarantino, Quentin, 144
Tavernier, Bertrand, 143
Taylor, James, 51; awarded Presidential
Medal of Freedom, 124; driving '55
Chevy, 63, 65; on drug use, 92; early
career, 35; on experience of filming, 103;
and fame, 99, 111; on "Fire and Rain," 99;
on first number 1 album, 124; and Harry
Dean Stanton's guitar, 95; on Hellmans'
efforts to help amateur actors, 77; with
Joni Mitchell, 84–85; manner on set, 70;
on Monte Hellman, 76, 87, 91; in opening
scenes, 63; and "Riding on a Railroad,"
104; on riding with Warren Oates,
75–76; on role in film, 36; on script and
dialogue coaching, 89; on snake dance,
76; on song for film, 110; on writing "Hey
Mister, That's Me up on the Jukebox," 100
Techniscope, 32
*They Might Be Giants*, 151
Thornsberry, Jim: and Boswell residents,
98–99; on confronting Dennis Wilson,
90; on divide between above the line/
below the line participants, 69; on Gary
Kurtz, 81–82; on Monte Hellman, 70;
praise for Jaclyn Hellman, 86
*Thumb Tripping*, 59, 64, 69
Tiemann, Scott, 20–21, 26, 139–40
*Trapped Ashes*, 128
*Two-Lane Blacktop* (film): ad with James
Taylor rejected, 113; becomes classic, 120;
bombs at box office, 117; and Boswell
residents, 98; budget, 54–56; car guys,
appeal of, 135–41; casting of, 33–41; and
Cinema Center Films, 42; clearing rights
to songs in, 107–8; contract between
Universal Studios and Michael Laughlin
Enterprises, 54; discomfort over Monte
Hellman's affair with Laurie Bird, 87;
drug use during production, 92–93; editing, 105–6; *Esquire* magazine on, 107–8,
116; filming of opening scenes, 62–63;
final cut, 111; final shot of film, 106–7;
gas station scene (Tucumcari), 93–94;
Gregory Sandor as cinematographer
for, 31; as Hellman's masterpiece, 128; Jay
Wheatley as mechanic for cars, 29; lack
of soundtrack, 36; location scouting for,
41–42; marketing campaign, 112; mixed
reviews, 115–17; musical tributes to,

164–68; Ned Tanen on set, 100; performance overseas, 117; on performances, 91; poster for, 114–15; as road movie, 17; scenes cut, 106; similarities to *Nog* and *Waiting for Godot*, 14; themes, 129; uncommercial qualities, 118–20; video release of, 149–56; Will Corry's original script for, 4, 5, 9

*Two-Lane Blacktop* (script): Chevy as specified by Will Corry, 25; comparison to finished film, 13–14; comparison of versions, 10–11; Daniel Selznick and Ned Tanen approval, 51; and *Esquire* magazine, 108–9; Will Corry original, 4, 5, 9, 10–11

Tyler, William, 164–66

Universal Studios: and ad campaign and theater bookings, 117; and counterculture filmmaking, 47; disappointment in film, 109–13; on marketing campaign, 112–14, 122; on movies in late 1960s and early 1970s, 44; reservations about film, 53–54; on rock star actors in film, 110–11; and Tanen Unit, 47; video release of film, 147–48

Vail, Fred, 39, 40–41
*Vanishing Point*, 17–18

Walker, Beverly: on above the line/below the line divide, 69; on Dennis Wilson, 89; on *Esquire*'s endorsement of film, 116; on Gary and Meredith Kurtz, 75; on Laurie Bird, 37, 72, 88; on Monte Hellman, 51, 71, 88; on movie's box office, 118; on photos of Laurie Bird skinny-dipping, 88; on Pow Wow Inn, 84; on press visiting shoot, 100; on rock star actors' music in film, 111; on film script in *Esquire*, 108–9; on untrained actors, 119–20

*Waiting for Godot*, 8, 14–15
Wasserman, Lew, 46–47, 112–13, 114, 117–18, 126
Weissman, Murray, 113

Welles, Orson, 45–46
Wenders, Wim, 146
Wheatley, Buck, 28–30, 92–93, 97, 103
Wheatley, Jay, 28–30, 63–64, 69, 102, 127
Williams, Cindy, 107
Wilson, Dennis; audition for film, 40–41; beats wife, 90; cast as the Mechanic, 33; and Charles Manson, 39–40; contract, 56; dies by drowning, 123; drug and alcohol abuse, 65–66, 92; early career, 38–39; flubbing lines, 65–66, 90; womanizing, 89
Wolff, Frank, 7
Wurlitzer, Rudy: appearance in film, 80; and audience's confusion, 112, 118; on his first experience acting, 12; on Laurie Bird as the Girl, 12; on rewriting film script, 10; underground reputation, 109; and Will Corry's script, 9, 10

*You Can Never Go Fast Enough*, 167–68

*Zabriskie Point*, 58, 70, 108, 119

www.ingramcontent.com/pod-product-compliance
Lightning Source LLC
Chambersburg PA
CBHW030623230426
43661CB00053B/2113